Christina Dunhill was born in London in 1947. She was a civil servant, a dancer and a secretary before becoming an editor. She worked for six years at Methuen before taking up freelance work for a number of different publishers: in particular, Methuen, The Women's Press (whose Livewire series for young women she helped to set up and commissions for) and Sheba.

THE BOYS IN BLUE
Women's Challenge to the Police

Edited by Christina Dunhill

VIRAGO

Dedication

Throughout my work on this book I have met, spoken with or heard of women whose bravery, in the course of brushes with the police, judiciary and sometimes the prison system, has taken my breath away. Some of them are contributors. Their stand, which benefits us all, has not been taken without extreme personal cost. This book is dedicated to them and others like them.

Published by VIRAGO PRESS Limited 1989
20–23 Mandela Street, Camden Town, London NW1 0HQ

This collection and introduction copyright © Christina Dunhill 1989

Copyright © in each contribution held by the author 1989

British Library Cataloguing in Publication Data

British Library Cataloguing in Publication Data

The Boys in blue : women's challenge to the police.
  1. Great Britain. Women. Attitudes of police
  I. Dunhill, Christina
  363.2′0941

ISBN 0-86068-967-0

Typeset by Florencetype Ltd, Kewstoke, Avon
Printed in Great Britain by Cox & Wyman Ltd, Reading, Berks.

Contents

Part 3

Stepping Up Control:
Police, Politics and the Law

Acknowledgements

This book could not have been produced without the help and support of a number of people. First I should like to thank all the contributors for the work they have put into it and for their skill and patience during the editorial process.

I am grateful to the GLC Women and Policing Network whose conference, organized in November 1985, first persuaded me that this book needed to be produced, and for their help in meeting me and giving me copies of the conference papers; and to Marie Staunton, then Legal Officer of the NCCL, for her many useful suggestions at the outset of this project. I should like to thank Teresa Thornhill for advice and for reading and making suggestions about many of the articles; Cathie Lloyd for information and suggestions; Chris Tchaikovsky for suggestions as to further contacts; Surinder Sandhu at GACARA and Carol Burgher, then at NMP, for their time and information; Rochelle Phillips and Maxine Sullivan, who did the research on which 'Working Relations' is based; the two ex-Specials I spoke to for their time and frankness; Lorraine Gonzalez for help and information and Martin Walker for information and suggestions. I am heavily indebted to the lamented Police Monitoring Unit at the LSPU for their workshops, publications and for letting me use their library and cuttings files and particularly – again in this connection – to Cathie Lloyd; also to Ann Singleton for her kindness and help.

I should like to thank Mary, Harriet, Pushpa and Marg for various help, and all my friends who have borne with me during the two and a half years this book has been in preparation. In particular, I want to thank Caroline for her ideas, patience, love, and for letting me her house to work in when I needed another four walls.

Introduction

Christina Dunhill

Are the police protecting women and pursuing our complaints with the rigour we would demand? What are the implications for us of a police force which is still overwhelmingly male and white? What happens to those of us who find ourselves on the receiving end of police powers? What is the significance of recent developments in policing industrial disputes, inner city violence and political demonstrations, particularly by Black people? And of the expanded police powers to arrest and detain, and to control demonstrations and pickets in recent legislation? What goes on in the name of upholding the peace in the six counties of Northern Ireland? Who are the police and on whose behalf are they acting? What has been the effect on policing of twenty years of feminist mobilization and action around crimes against women?

This book looks at contemporary policing from the point of view of women who have requested police action, and of those who have had action taken against them. It also looks at the history of policing and of recent developments from the point of view of women working in the law or in police monitoring. It presents a plurality of perspectives from individual women and women's organizations.

Throughout the articles, exception is made for sympathetic or positive police action, where appropriate. But the focus of this book is on the very real abuses of police power towards us and the shortcomings in the way the police deal with crimes against us, within the context of a vigilant and encroaching right wing ideology. The book is also a forum for discussion of women's issues and politics as they come up against the cutting edge of the state.

Safety in the Home

Violence against women by their husbands or boyfriends in their own homes is reality that too frequently lies behind patriarchy's happy-ever-after. It points up the irony in traditional cautions to remain in the home in times of trouble. It is an uncomfortable truth that many people would rather forget, brought to public attention by the work of Women's Aid groups in particular.

Violence against women is against the law. There is no exemption from the offences of assault, actual bodily harm, grievous bodily harm, manslaughter or murder where they are committed by a man against a woman he is, or has been, living with. But the enforcement of the law in respect of these crimes as they are inflicted on women in domestic situations appears to be discriminatory. In addition there is an exemption in effect, because the law does not protect a married woman from rape by her husband, who may use threats of violence to this end.

For many years, police dismissed domestic disputes. 'She could be hanging upside down from the ceiling and it'd still be a domestic,' said the local police to a woman fifteen years ago in excuse for not responding to her call on behalf of her sister who was being beaten up by her husband. How much has changed?

The report on domestic violence published by the London Police Monitoring and Research Group puts the number of women calling the police for assistance in domestic disputes in London at about 1,000 a week. In 1984 there were 15,619 injunctions granted in England and Wales and 5,800 applications for exclusion orders. But these figures represent only a small proportion of the total number of women affected, even in London. The true extent of violence against women in the home is unknown. Police call-outs are not recorded. But nearly every woman has either been affected herself, or has friends or relations who have.

Home Office homicide statistics for England and Wales for 1972–82 establish that the largest single category of murders (20 per cent) are committed against a spouse or cohabitant, and 80 per cent of the victims are women. Over half the women murdered in the UK are killed by men with whom they have a current or former relationship.

The policing of domestic violence is given priority within the first part of this book because it is an area where women most commonly need the intervention of policemen for their protection, and where traditional police inaction has sometimes resulted in a woman's death. Far too often, in spite of professed police policies to the contrary, women still do not get protection, because policemen are reluctant to intervene in what they see as a private domestic matter.

There are a number of contributions: from Women's Aid, Southall Black Sisters, from Kalsoom Sarwar on behalf of a London Asian women's group, and the Gurdip Kaur Defence Campaign (Gurdip Kaur was murdered in her home in front of her young son). Here, as in other areas, Black women experience particular difficulties in achieving police co-operation. These, and the dilemmas of Black women working with the police against men with whom they are united in the struggle against racism, including police racism, are also considered.

Taking the Blame

A survey by *Woman's Own* in 1986, found that one in four women had been victims of violence from a husband or boyfriend and one in six had been raped – one in ten by a family member. Violence against women and rape occurs within a popular context of blaming the woman herself, that is often echoed throughout the criminal justice system. Men who murder, maim or mutilate their wives are frequently given derisory sentences by judges who have accepted defence evidence that she 'deserved' it in some way – she 'drove him to it' by 'nagging' perhaps, by refusing sex or by having a lesbian relationship.

As Surinder Bains says in 'Crimes Against Women', a chapter which discusses the Manchester Police Monitoring Unit's survey into violence against women, it is women who are challenged and blamed for domestic violence and rape, accused, for example, of not keeping the house clean, of not looking after themselves, of staying out late, of wearing provocative clothing. Women quoted in the article by Women's Aid were told by police, 'Don't answer him back so much, it only makes him angry' or, 'Maybe if you cleaned the house up a bit and tried to make something of yourself, it wouldn't happen so often.' Police tend to collude, often unconsciously, with the violent man; they feel they should not intervene too forcefully. This behaviour reflects completely inappropriate ideas about the sanctity and privacy of the family. When they do take action, it is often similarly inappropriate, aimed at calming down and reconciliation. As Women's Aid report, women who have once called out the police for a domestic assault resolve never to do so again. Women who make repeated calls are treated as nuisances or even as persistent *offenders* by police who threaten to lock them up. Small wonder that Southall Black Sisters felt unable to co-operate with a local police initiative on domestic violence which would have involved them in handing over their files to the police.

The blaming of women and girls who have been raped for the crime itself has been widely documented. In spite of the 1976 Sexual Offences Act, which was designed to protect women from interrogation into their sexual history, judges frequently allow special applications from the defence for this subject to be raised. Whether or not a woman put up a fight is also frequently seen as a matter for cross-examination and women find themselves blamed either way – for having fought and brought upon themselves injuries which might have been avoided, or for colluding with the rapist by not struggling. The experience of the 'trial' at the police station, where the cross-examination starts – with police bringing rather too much zeal to their purported task of seeing whether a raped woman would stand up as a witness in court – has been widely exposed and quoted as a major reason for women not reporting.

Recent years have seen police initiatives on rape and domestic violence in response to consistent criticism from women. The 1987 Metropolitan Force Order on domestic violence is discussed by Women's Aid and Southall Black Sisters. Recent police promises of care and sympathetic treatment towards rape victims may be, as the police have claimed, partially responsible for the recent rise in reported rapes. However, Sara Scott and Alison Dickens take a critical look at the new initiatives from police and professionals and suggest that they may have more to do with containment and a current popular ideological emphasis on women's helplessness, than fundamentally altering a system which discredits and blames women who are raped. Home Office guidelines to the police still insist that a woman who complains of rape should not be believed.

In 1986 Susan Edwards published research she undertook on domestic violence for the Polytechnic of Central London which indicated that some policemen beat their wives. Policemen's comments and behaviour reported by writers here do suggest that they feel it is at least in order for other men to do so. Moreover this kind of blaming is consistent with conservative thinking in which, for example, Black people are blamed for racism, the poor are blamed for poverty and labour councils for inner city conditions that they are working to alleviate.

A girl who was repeatedly sexually abused by her father and other men, whose story is told in chapter 8, seems to have been seen by the local police as a liar and troublemaker. They seemed to accept her father's portrayal of his daughter as a slut, and subjected her, a young girl under so much stress she was making attempts on her life, to vicious cross questioning. Furthermore they were unable to prepare enough evidence against her father for the case to be heard in court, and he remains unprosecuted. The London Incest Survivors' Group reported in their paper to the Women and Policing Conference 1985 that in their experience the police are likely to support the abuser, particularly if he has made the first approach to them (for example if the girl has run away from home). Girls who have run away are unlikely to report their abuse to the police, for fear of being returned home. Another factor they noted was the girl's age; if she had reached puberty she was less likely to be believed.

Throughout the categories of rape, sexual assault, domestic violence and child abuse, Black women and girls are likely to be even more severely affected, as a result of racism, by disbelief, blaming and dismissal which is directed at them not only as women but as Black people who are stereotyped as trouble makers and criminals and Black women who are sexually stereotyped.

These conveniently dismissive notions seem also to lie behind police response to racist attacks, complaints about the inadequacy of which from Black people have been mounting for years. Again, despite public policies of positive action from urban forces such as the Metropolitan and the Greater Manchester Police, monitoring projects report that response to actual incidents has not improved. Almost a third of the Black women who responded to the Manchester survey on women and violence had experienced racist attack (see chapter 5). Racist attacks themselves are becoming increasingly violent, numerous and widespread as documented by a Runnymede Trust report in 1986, by the Newham Monitoring Project and Greenwich Action Committee against Racist Attacks (whose annual reports form the basis of chapter 6) and the Institute of Race Relations report, *Policing Black People*, 1987. Women are the most frequent victims of racist attacks for a variety of reasons including their gender itself, greater likelihood of being isolated within the home, and their greater vulnerability inasmuch as they are attacked by white women, girls and boys, as well as men.

Complaints about police treatment include slowness of response, reluctance to accept racism as a motive (in chapter 6 an incident in which a gang of white youths set upon a middle-aged Black woman was defined as an *inter-racial* incident), refusal to take the complaint seriously, dismissing the assailants and, on occasion, arresting the victim while the attackers are let free. Lack of response, letting assailants go free, and trivializing the situation are the common features which police response to racist attacks shares with their response to domestic violence. Police have refused to prosecute in clear cases of actual or grievous bodily harm, dismissing them as common assaults and recommending the complainant to take out a private prosecution. As chapter 6 recounts, this is what happened to Mrs S who was thrown down three flights of stairs by white neighbours and kicked and punched as she sought to protect her baby. She was covered in bruises and her attackers were known to her but the police refused to prosecute.

Sometimes the message seems frighteningly clear: your problems are your own – a message apparently reinforced by the targeting of Black individuals as criminals on the streets and of housing estates with large Black populations for particular attention under the Multi-Agency Approach to policing. This can only indicate to Black people that they and the police are on separate sides, and that, far from expecting protection from the police, they have every reason to anticipate aggression.

Racist attackers are likely to be receiving the same message from the police as men who beat up their girlfriends or wives, that they can get away with it. And is it any wonder when, whatever the public relations demands of community policing, the political demands of successive governments since the sixties, and the Thatcher administration in particular, have been formulated around containment and control of Black people, and successive immigration policies have fanned the flames of racial hatred? And when consequent sensational press coverage of immigration has frequently been followed by a rise in racist attacks?

It is notoriously difficult for women to persuade the police to take preventative action on an individual case. The police will say it is not within their power – that, first, an offence must have been committed. Or they will say that they do not have the 'manpower'. This does not stop them from acting on information only in cases they consider important, for example to apprehend and even shoot men carrying out a major robbery. But it leaves women who fear repeated acts of domestic or racist violence wide open to them. Women like Krishna Sharma, Balwant Kaur and Gurdip Kaur (see chapters 2 and 4) have died because the police would not give them protection when they knew their lives were in danger. Whatever police public relations policies state, it is clear that crimes against women are not the force's real priority.

Up Against It

A point of crossover between parts 1 and 2 of this book is the development of sexism and racism on the part of the police from the point where they are dismissive of proper action to the point where they become permissive of improper action. Part 2 deals with women who, because they are political activists, or they belong to communities which are criminalized, or because they are lesbians, or they are working as prostitutes, or for a number of other reasons, find themselves on the receiving end of police activities. It also deals with women who have attracted police attention for no reason other than the clothes they wore. It also provides a forum for reconsidering significant recent history from a women's perspective.

The initial chapter looks at the police themselves, at their own view of 'the job', and at their working relationships and culture. The Policy Studies Institute researchers who studied the Metropolitan Police described a working culture in which sexism and racism were central. The researchers still maintained that racist jokes between colleagues did not affect their actual dealings with Black people, although one or two of their own examples of incidents appear to belie this. Their research did not concentrate on incidents involving women in the same way. This is the province of this book. The encounters between women and the police described in both parts 1 and 2 do reveal a kind of prurient contempt on the part of the police consistent with what the PSI Report describes as the element of ritualized machismo in station gossip 'in which they played in their imagination the role of a man triumphing over a woman'. They also demonstrate all too clearly the correspondence between both racist and sexist private jokes and actual practice.

Not all the police are 'prejudiced' but research has shown that racism and sexism are attitudes shared by many officers, not just the one or two 'bad apples' Sir Kenneth Newman was fond of alluding to. In spite of its nominal inclusion of anti-racist training, police training as a whole appears to initiate and reinforce racism and the job perpetuates it into a culture.

What is the role of policewomen within this culture? Women still constitute only an average of 10 per cent of all officers across the forces, and are under pressures from their male colleagues and superiors – from sexual harassment to obstruction in their careers. The 'chivalry' they receive from male officers tends to have the effect of 'protecting' them from 'the action' and promotion. They are under pressure (and the Black WPCs who are part of the tiny minority of Black officers will have more pressure exerted on them) to conform and perform within the dominant male ideology. Some women officers talk of a less confrontational approach than their male colleagues in their dealings with the public. This approach, they say, often brings quicker and better results in a difficult situation. However, their career prospects will depend on making a certain number of arrests.

Some of the writers in this book (see chapters 8, 11, 17 and 20) make a point of mentioning that women officers can be just as aggressive as the men; in some cases, worse. It may be that some women officers are particularly hard on women, blaming them for breaking a well-behaved, law-abiding stereotype, which it is not only their job to enforce but to conform to themselves. In all events, while women and girls ought to be able to insist on seeing a WPC when reporting sexual crime, it would be naive to assume that women officers will 'naturally' be more supportive. Because of the unofficial quota system as regards recruiting women, and because of the constraints women in the police are under culturally and operationally, I think it is fair to refer to the police as a male enclave.

How then does this male enclave police women? We should, perhaps, not be surprised to find that the women writing in part 2 report levels of abuse from police officers which hinge around sexism and racism and which are quite frequently severe. Chapter 15, 'The Inappropriate Women', confines itself to the experience of white women who have attracted police attention because of their appearance and disregard for 'feminine' conduct. We see a young punk woman picked up in the street, pushed against a car and strong-armed to 'teach her a lesson'. We see a drug user hit so hard she was thrown across a room when she refused to give her name and address at the police station. We read of a middle-aged alcoholic who died of a cerebral haemmorhage after being admitted to hospital covered in bruises and with a blood clot on her brain after a period in police detention. These women were all either visibly non conforming, 'stroppy' or lacking in self-control.

The police want their authority accepted and some officers will not hesitate to take advantage of, or to 'punish' women with whom they come into contact. Women working as prostitutes have been told they would be let off prosecution if they agreed to sex with an arresting officer (see chapter 17). A woman suffering from a severe medical condition and consequent mental instability was held on the floor of a police van by two officers, one of whom kept his foot on her face, all the way to the psychiatric hospital. It was she herself who had called in the police after her husband had become violent (see chapter 18).

To judge from the high incidence of police verbal and physical abuse of women cited in this section, the police want to 'put us in our place'.* Women who have been subjected to this abuse cannot forget the experience. We are all, at some level, accustomed to the hatred we engender in men. When the

---

* Here and throughout the book, I have taken the decision to quote express verbal abuse where the authors have used it and where it seemed appropriate; it seems to me that only through repetition of specific insults can the full implications of the many ways the police abuse women at the level of sexuality and race be grasped.

police display this hatred, it can be quite terrifying because of the consolidation they represent of male and state power. We are 'punished' as women through verbal abuse, physical coercion and violence. Yet the police have no licence to 'punish' us; their powers are to arrest, detain and question us and bring us before the courts if appropriate.

In chapter 12, on policing lesbians, we read of two women who were bodily thrown out of the police station where they had gone to report being pursued by a gang of youths. As the doors of the station were locked behind them they were told that what they deserved was a 'fucking good meat injection'. When one of them kicked the police van in anger and frustration, they were both locked up and charged. Those officers were making sure the women understood what the officers felt about their relation to the law – they were seen as the targets, not the recipients, of policing.

One of the most common forms of sexual harassment practised on women under arrest at police stations is strip-searching. Although this is carried out by women officers, usually out of sight of male officers, women are frequently aware of the presence of male officers nearby (outside the screens) and it is frequently linked in the mind of the arrested woman with a decision taken by male officers, nominally the station commanding officer. Publicity about strip-searching is relatively recent, but it has been going on for several years, and in connection with quite routine offences.

Where women fall under direct suspicion, harassment and intimidation is focused around sexuality in a clear strategy of using women's sexual vulnerability and vulnerability as mothers (they may not have been allowed to make any provision for their children or not given any information about them or threatened that they will be taken into care) to 'break' them. Chapter 11 goes into the details of sexual mockery, assault and abuse used by the RUC. A similar strategy is also used against Irish women held for alleged 'terrorist' offences in Britain who are routinely subject to sexual abuse: comments about their bodies, threats of rape and frequent strip searching. In chapter 19 we read of how Annie Maguire was made to stand spreadeagled against a wall while menstrual blood flowed down her legs. Denial of sanitary protection seems to be a not uncommon tactic to distress women held in police custody. Greenham women also report it.

In chapter 13 we read of how Greenham women have had their breasts tugged and squeezed as they were dragged away from non violent actions and have been verbally abused at the two poles of male sexual anger toward women – as 'slags' and as lesbians. Both are labels which seem to facilitate police abuse, removing a woman from the mantle of their supposed chivalry which she has forfeited by taking herself outside male owner-ship. In effect, she has not 'policed' herself by living within the male domestic domain, and may therefore be punished.

We turn now to communities who are harassed by the police and the effect on women within them. The police seem to regard Black women and girls as in particular need of regulation. In chapter 20 we read of a young Black girl who, having already been in trouble with the police after an incident at her school, was then harassed by local officers in effect for walking down the street. She was arrested after struggling with one officer who was manhandling her friend and taken to the station where she was strip-searched, beaten up and charged with assaulting a police officer.

Black women are likely to find themselves questioned by the police if they come into routine contact with them. A traffic violation is likely to lead to an immigration enquiry (see chapter 21). Black people experience themselves as policed. They cannot but be aware of police racism and the state and social racism it reflects. Black people's uprisings have tended to spring directly from police activities. In chapter 10 we see how it was the policing of a demonstration outside the local police station, following the death of Mrs Jarrett during a police search of her house and the subsequent refusal of the police to suspend any officer, even temporarily, which led to the Broadwater Farm uprising.

Following the uprising, it was Black women who bore the brunt of the raids on homes on the Broadwater Farm estate. The police invasion of Black homes was central to the uprising, precipitated as it was by a raid in which a Black woman died, and in the aftermath of which the police avenged themselves with dawn raids throughout the estate. In chapter 10, we read about the ordeal of the women of Broadwater Farm who, as mothers, girlfriends and sisters, and in many cases together with their young children, suffered racist and sexist abuse and underwent considerable stress and terror as a result of the police investigation. Saturation policing of a community like Broadwater Farm affects everybody who lives there but women as carers and mothers are particularly deeply affected.

A community may be punished through the women who are at the hub of it. Irish women in the nationalist community in the six counties shoulder a good deal of the burden of the constant and often brutal policing operation there (see chapter 11). They are subject to interrogation and searches from street patrols of soldiers and the RUC and terrifying house raids in which their households and possessions may be torn apart in front of them, while they and their children may be placed under 'house arrest'. If their menfolk are arrested and held in custody for many months awaiting trial, they have to keep their families going single-handed and families of detained men are often harassed by the RUC.

The policing of particular communities is one of the contexts in which the police are demanding, and winning, the augmented powers which are the focus of part 3.

Stepping Up Control

The government has given the police expanded powers to fulfil their role of maintaining social control. Part 3 considers these and also looks at the criminal justice system as a whole and at the issue of police accountability in the context of a brief history of policing. It considers the rights of redress we have in the form of complaints made to the police, and legal action, and also the possibility of action we can take ourselves in the wake of the demise of formal council-funded police monitoring units to record and publicize police action and abuse of powers.

Recent years have seen an accumulation of confrontations between the police and certain key communities. In 1979 police attacked demonstrators against the National Front in southall and Blair Peach was killed. Anti-fascist demonstrations by the Asian community have continued to be aggressively policed. In some of the other major confrontations of recent history – for example the Broadwater Farm uprising, demonstrations in Northern Ireland, the miners' dispute of 1984/5, demonstrations at Greenham Common (discussed by writers in part 2) and the student demonstration at Westminster charged by mounted police in November 1988 – we have seen the police moving into a primary suppressive rather than a reactive role in the area of 'public order'.

Chapter 23 looks at the revised public order legislation in the Public Order Act, 1986, and the new technology the police have at their command, demonstrating the government's obsession with control of the streets. Military tactics such as snatch squads and wedge formations have been imported from British Army experience in Northern Ireland. So have the random stop and searches and roadblocks used by police in the miners' dispute. After the uprising at Broadwater Farm in Tottenham, which the police took as a bitter defeat, involving, as it did, the killing of a policeman, Sir Kenneth Newman warned the British public that the British police would use plastic bullets in a future serious 'public order' situation. (The devastating effects of these weapons are discussed in chapter 11.) Now territorial support group vans (used by the riot-trained police squads) carry riot gas and plastic bullets as a matter of course.

In its fixation on keeping democratic and collective action well under control, the government has reined in demonstrations and pickets with legal restrictions, leaving them totally vulnerable to police directions and the right to protest significantly limited. For example, demonstrations since the Public Order Act came into force have tended to have the teeth taken out of them by being rerouted away from main roads and shopping centres to deserted back streets.

Linked to the public order policing of particular events is the continuous targeting and surveillance of communities, individuals and organizations thought likely to pose a threat. Again, the ethos and the technology have been influenced by the conflict in Northern Ireland. The range and scope of surveillance activities undertaken by MI5, Special Branch and even local officers are discussed by Nadine Finch in chapter 25. Intelligence gathering is facilitated by the powerful Police National Computer into which most forces can link. Community policing initiatives such as Neighbourhood Watch and the Multi-Agency Approach (under which local statutory bodies meet together with the police and exchange information) may also provide the police with low level information which can become retrieval data (see chapter 25).

The augmentation of police powers of arrest, detention and questioning in the Police and Criminal Evidence Act is another step toward social control, altering the balance of civil rights in favour of the arresting officer and, in turn, the prosecution. These are not only powers which have been bestowed by an indebted government on its agents. They are powers the police have argued themselves into. Commissioner McNee argued to the Royal Commission on Criminal Procedure that his officers were so constricted by the law that they were constantly having to break it in order to do their job. The law was therefore amended to embrace police conduct which was previously unlawful. The provisions of the Act are discussed in chapter 24, and, in particular, how prolonged detention, the threat or actuality of strip-searching and the withholding of access to children, combined with the intimidating macho atmosphere of a police station, will put pressure on women to incriminate themselves.

The Criminal Justice Act (see chapter 27), for whose provisions the police also campaigned, has swung the balance of trials in favour of the prosecution, removing the right of jury trial for certain offences, abolishing the right of the defence to peremptory challenge and limiting the ability of the defence to cross-examine prosecution witnesses.

The police are not just the tools of the state; they have acted as its willing partners and as a power base in their own right, and are now a vocal political lobby, moving outside the idea of consensus or public service, to the assertion that policing is a specialized function whose needs and limits its own senior officers are best equipped to determine. When they cannot work within the law, they have worked outside it with relative impunity, as we have seen with the Police and Criminal Evidence Act and as in the Public Order Act which legitimized the roadblocks they had used so widely already. During recent disputes the police have become the law, rather than its agents, punishing and removing people whom the courts then failed to convict.

Throughout the entries in part 2 of this book, for example, from the women of Broadwater Farm and the Greenham/Cruisewatch women, we see a similar process of particular tactics designed to remove, humiliate, and sometimes to incapacitate. We see the process of retaliatory charges made when women are pressing complaints. Abuses of power, so common as to be detailed through every chapter, demonstrate behaviour which has no basis in law but every grounding in the confident misuse of authority.

The options available to women seeking some form of restitution for the way they have been treated by the police are considered in chapter 29. The police complaints system has always seemed less than satisfactory because, although the investigating officers are from another force, in effect the police are still investigating themselves, and the new Police Complaints Authority does not seem to have made much progress here. Throughout the book, women remark on the police complaints procedure which seems to treat them with contempt. Greenham women say that they are treated dismissively and obstructively, even though they only complain about the most serious incidents. Women's Aid say that women who complain have found themselves charged with wasting police time. The bodies dealing with racist attacks report victims attracting police harassment if they complain about the police response. The Gurdip Kaur Campaign were themselves investigated when they complained about the conduct of the police investigation into the murder.

A more optimistic note is struck by the experience of women suing the police and major awards have been made by the courts to women who have brought suits against the police for malpractice. For example, a Black woman who was severely physically and verbally abused when the police arrested her (quite improperly) was awarded £26,000 damages in the High Court in February 1986. Previously, the Police Complaints Board had accepted a police recommendation that no disciplinary proceedings should be brought against the officers who had insulted her (see chapter 29).

It is important that we use the courts in this way, not only to seek redress for incidents we have suffered but to preserve their independence from the designs of police and government. The government is anxious to curb the power of the courts, and, in particular, of judicial reviews which have declared some of its ministers' decisions unlawful, and which are the only avenue open, for example, to people protesting deportation (see chapter 22) to contest their high-handed decisions.

It is also anxious to see the end of police monitoring which has done so much to keep policing issues in the public eye. The abolition of the GLC and the rate capping of local councils has ensured that police monitoring units have been disbanded. The London Strategic Policies Unit police monitoring unit which did day-to-day monitoring, kept an exhaustive press library, published a regular bulletin, *Policing London*, commissioned major reports such as the one on domestic violence referred to in section 1, and held conferences, was wound up at the end of March 1988. The Manchester City Council police monitoring unit was wound up at the end of January 1988. Lespop, the lesbians and policing organization, lost its funding in mid 1988, in a year when it became more needed than ever. Some councils will keep on policing groups but they will be concentrating on issues like community safety and soft-pedalling on policing and the state. The National Council for Civil Liberties will continue its important work as a focus for independent observation of police behaviour. Particularly important now will be the work of ad hoc monitoring groups springing up around individual issues. Sheffield Policewatch, whose account of systematic observation of the miners' strike and the fight for media publicity for their alternative view forms chapter 28 of this book, is an excellent example. This chapter is of interest not only for its first-hand information but for its account of the setting up and working practices of the group itself.

Policing, with a basis like that of the new economy in information technology, seems to be moving more and more away from the protection of the individual and particularly of the individual woman, toward social control. Multi-Agency policing depends on the co-operation of local bodies and it seems likely that at some stage non co-operation such as Southall Black Sisters' (see chapter 2) will be made unlawful or financially penalized.

In the light of all this we should, perhaps, not be too surprised by the shortcomings of the police in dealing with those crimes which particularly affect women and girls: domestic violence, rape, sexual abuse and racist attacks. These crimes are perhaps not a threat to the smooth running of government and commerce. They happen in individual homes or as isolated incidents which don't usually cause a breach of the peace. They happen to women and women are second class citizens. A cynic might even add that fear of these crimes is itself an aspect of the social control of women.

Further, victims of these crimes are still blamed, not only in the popular imagination and the media but by the police and through the courts. Women suspects and offenders, on the other hand, as we see in part 2, frequently seem to be 'punished' by both police and courts *as* women, particularly when their actions have caused them to break with acceptable feminine behaviour.

The bottom line of the new conservative 'Victorianism' (as with the old) is victimization of the poor. 'Traditional' women offenders who have turned to petty theft or prostitution to supplement inadequate incomes, still make up over half of all women in prison. Policing those who have been pauperized by economic policies is an aspect of social control which has always been with us. Most of these women, and the numbers are, of course, growing all the time, are in prison because they could not pay fines. Whilst there, they are separated from their children who are taken into care or fostered.

This book is an introduction to the issues raised by the policing of women and women's politics within the overall politics of policing itself. It is published in the wake of the demise of the major police monitoring bodies without whose contributions and co-operation it could not have been produced. It is published in the context of the systematic stripping of local authority autonomy and power by central government, which will ensure that plans for greater local accountability of the police remain on the drawing board. It is up to women and women's groups to continue debate and action around these urgent issues that affect us all.

Part 1

Protection or Aggression?:
Police Response to Women in Danger

1. Women's Aid

Policing Male Violence in the Home

Gill Hague, Nicola Harwin, Karen McMinn,
Jane Rubens, Margaret Taylor

One of the most significant challenges to the police as far as women are concerned, is to protect them from repeated physical assault by men with whom they are living. Women need a swift response when they call out the police in an emergency and they need them to take effective action against the violent man. This article, and the three which follow it, will assess how the police have responded to this challenge, both in words and action.

We will start by relating the experience of one woman who stayed in a Scottish Women's Aid refuge.

Jean's Story

Jean's husband began hitting her and verbally abusing her soon after they were married. When she took a part-time job, it got worse. She tried to get him to agree to end the relationship and move out; they went out one evening to discuss a separation. At the end of the evening, Jean refused her husband's offer of a lift home. He followed her in his car and attacked her, dragging her onto some waste ground, putting his hands round her throat and then pushing his hand into her mouth, forcing her to choke on her tongue. She managed to get free and hailed a police car which just happened to be passing. The police took her home and called the doctor (whose report mentioned severe facial bruising, laceration, swelling, inflamed mouth, thumbprints on neck and scratches). The police did not charge Jean's husband with assault. They took no further action.

He moved back in, refusing to accept that the relationship was over. Jean was terrified of him, but she began divorce proceedings and applied for custody of her two little girls. She also took steps to obtain an exclusion order (a court order banning her husband from the premises). She would have preferred to move herself but because the tenancy was in her name, the council would not give her and her children another tenancy.

On the day that these actions were to be decided in court, her husband took the girls and disappeared. They were gone for six weeks, during which time he rang at intervals to threaten Jean and the children. Then he returned the girls to Jean's mother's house and went back himself to Jean's flat. Jean moved into the Women's Aid refuge. She had by this time been granted custody and an exclusion order but this had to be served on her husband by Sheriff's Officers, whom he managed to avoid for two weeks.

The day after the order was served, Jean returned to her flat with the police to make sure her husband had gone away. He was still there. Although the police had the power to arrest him, they did not, but simply told him to go away.

During the early hours of the next morning he returned, broke into the flat and threatened Jean with a loaded crossbow. She could only persuade him to leave by agreeing to give him access to the children a few days later, although she was terrified he would snatch them again. He told her he would kill her if she told the police about the incident. She did not. Women's Aid complained informally on her behalf. The police visited the flat and Jean denied the incident because she knew her husband was watching the flat. The police told Women's Aid they couldn't do anything.

Four sleepless nights later, Jean thought she heard her husband breaking in again. In a panic, she broke a window and jumped out. As she sat on the ground dazed, a man came from a flat opposite and helped her to his flat. Her husband was there. He refused to allow them to call an ambulance but after Jean's cut hand had filled a basin with blood he sent her to hospital with his friend.

At the hospital Jean worried about her children, whom she had left in the care of the wife of the man in the flat opposite, where her husband was also still staying. She called the police who kept watch on the flat because she was afraid that her husband would abduct the children again. Early in the morning the police went to the flat and took husband and children to the station. They searched the flat and found the crossbow and bolts.

Jean made a full statement as to what had happened and her husband confessed to most of it. He was charged with five counts of assault, including the near strangling which had occurred two months before, and with possessing an offensive weapon. Next day he was remanded in custody. Two months later, he pleaded guilty to all the charges in return for a reduction in the seriousness of the assault charges. In court the Procurator Fiscal did not reveal that the crossbow had been loaded when Jean was threatened with it. After the prosecution had described the offences, her husband's defence lawyer alleged that Jean had provoked his violence by having numerous affairs and staying out all night. There was no opportunity to rebut these totally untrue statements. The Sheriff accepted that there had been a degree of provocation and sentenced Jean's husband to nine months' imprisonment, backdated to his arrest. With remission, that meant four months' imprisonment from the date of the trial.

Throughout this time, against all odds, Jean had kept her job and the council had put her name on a list for rehousing nearer her work. But as the time of her husband's release from prison approached, she was still waiting. Moreover, her divorce had gone through; this meant her exclusion order with its power of arrest was no longer in force. She began to feel more and more afraid. Two weeks before her ex-husband's expected release from prison, she gave up her council tenancy and her job and left the area.

The above story clearly shows the extent to which a man can exercise power over a woman (and children) through violence, and the limited effect of the police and the judicial system in protecting her from the dangers which the situation presents. We told Jean's story in some detail so as to make explicit the full implications of domestic violence for a woman's life. We turn now to analyse the generality of women's experience in relation to calling on the police in cases of domestic violence.[1]

Without doubt, the police are the agency which women most often contact for help when they are facing assault in the home and other forms of domestic violence. Yet it is well recorded by women themselves, by Women's Aid groups and refuges, and by academic researchers, that such appeals are very often unsuccessful from the abused woman's point of view. After years of pressure from Women's Aid groups, and despite a growing public awareness of domestic violence issues, it still seems that the police quite simply do not take violence against women in the home seriously. The following quotes from testimonies offered by women who have suffered abuse and from Women's Aid workers in England and Wales speak for themselves.

On being threatened with a cut-throat razor, a friend and I called the police. It took five officers to remove him from the premises. They took him two hundred yards away, talked to him and let him go. On leaving the house, the sergeant involved left the razor with us. When we suggested that, if they did nothing else, could they not charge him with carrying an offensive weapon, we were told no, they could not do this.

J. called out the police seven times over a thirty-six hour period. Each time, she left home to make the phone call. Each time, the police returned her to her home, and, after talking to her husband, left her and her two children there to face further violence. At no time did they inform her of the existence of the refuge.

K. attempted to press charges against her husband after she had been badly beaten up and had been in hospital for twenty-four hours. In the presence of a Women's Aid worker, K. was told by the police that they thought she might have beaten *herself* up to get at her husband, and they refused to co-operate with her. Among her injuries was a severe eye laceration, and a suspected broken cheekbone.

Domestic violence is a very serious problem both in terms of the number of attacks and the severity of the violence inflicted on the women attacked. In London alone, research on Metropolitan police responses to domestic violence has indicated that over 1,000 women a week call the police for assistance.[2] Crime surveys suggest that incidents of domestic violence for the capital may number as many as three-quarters of a million over a year.[3] One half of women murdered in the UK are killed by men with whom they have a current or former relationship.

The police, however, have traditionally placed domestic incidents at the bottom of their list of priorities.[4] Because criminal convictions in domestic cases are rare, the work is not useful to police officers in terms of promotion. They may regard the work as a waste of time, calling more for a mediating social work approach than for traditional law enforcement. This is partly because women who have been assaulted by their husbands or male partners are often caught up in a web of financial, psychological and emotional connections with them, and may find it hard to press criminal charges, or to stick with an initial decision to do so as the case looms nearer. The police are very often convinced that women will not press charges in the first place. They tend also to become frustrated and sometimes irritated when a woman does press charges but later withdraws them after a case has been prepared. For a complicated mixture of such reasons, a very large percentage of domestic violence cases are 'no-crimed',[5] disappear from police records and criminal statistics, and are not pursued. Even worse, Scottish Women's Aid report that some women who have complained about the manner in which the police treated them have found themselves charged with 'wasting police time'.

On another level, it seems that the police tend to collude, often unconsciously, with the violent man, and to feel that they should not intervene too forcefully in private domestic disputes. In this, of course, they accurately reflect traditional ideas about the 'sanctity' and privacy of the family, the dominance of the man within it, and his right to exercise power over his wife or partner. Women who contact Women's Aid cite many instances where police response meets neither their needs as victims of assault, nor their expectations as innocent members of a community whom the police are supposed to serve. Comments like these from police officers are reported: 'You would have to be black and blue from head to toe, with broken bones as well, before we would do anything for you'; [to a husband] 'Give her another child, that will keep her happy for a year or two'; 'Maybe if you cleaned the house up a bit and tried to make something of yourself, it wouldn't happen so often'; 'Don't answer him back so much, it only makes him angry'.

In extreme cases, a police officer's sympathy for, and possible identification with the male partner can result in an almost unbelievable disregard for the woman's safety. One woman gives the following account of an incident where the police were called out after a very violent attack on herself and her son. Before the attack, she had hidden her husband's gun. She said that while waiting for the officers to arrive:

> My husband re-appeared at the window carrying a breeze block, and threatened to break in. I was terrified. It seemed an age before we heard the engine of the police car. Only one policeman got out. He talked at length to my husband at the farm gate and they came in together. He asked where the gun was. My son and I had taken it to pieces a few weeks before and hidden it on the advice of friends. I had been living in a state of terror for weeks.

Instead of assisting in the situation at hand, the police officer supported the husband in accusing the woman of wrongful possession of the gun.

> He then asked for the gun and my son got it for him and put it together. The policeman then asked who was the licence holder of the gun. My husband was, of course, and the policeman put the gun into his hands as he sat there.

She went on to say that the officer repeatedly tried to dissuade her from leaving her home, apparently influenced by her husband's position as a local schoolteacher. Later, when she did leave, he refused to give her a lift, even though she had many miles to walk to the nearest doctor who could attend to her visibly ill son. The boy ended up in hospital for three days with a suspected fractured skull. It appears that in this instance the police officer did have suspicions that the husband was in need of psychiatric help, but was predisposed to believe him since he was a plausible and authoritative man of high status in the country area concerned. The officer did absolutely nothing to assist the woman and boy who had both been violently attacked, and who were the ones to call him out for help.

One of the most common complaints about the police response to domestic violence is that the officers concerned persist in attempts at reconciliation without properly investigating the risk to the woman. For example, Ms P. suffered violence from her boyfriend. On one occasion she ran to the local phone box to phone the police. Their response was to collect her boyfriend from her house and to bring him to the phone box for a reconciliation.

Many women feel that they are simply not listened to by the police, whose sympathy seems almost automatically to lie with the man. Repeated incidents tend to be treated *less* rather than more seriously, as their nuisance value to the police increases. One woman reports:

> They refused to take me seriously. When I phoned the police they arrived and ejected my husband, but then handed him my keys and told him to let himself in the next day. They were laughing among themselves.

Commonly, officers appear to believe that if a man was 'provoked' by a woman, his violence is understandable. Provocation, however, is *never* a justification for violence. No woman ever 'asks for it'.

Under English and Welsh civil law, a woman who has suffered domestic violence may apply for an injunction to prevent the man from attacking her and/or from entering the home.[6] The police should have a copy of the document so that they can act upon it. In practice, however, the police frequently do not know whether injunctions are in force, and, in any case, are usually loathe to intervene where an injunction exists without a power of arrest attached. In most areas of the country, it is a difficult task for a woman to get a power of arrest attached to an injunction. Violence has to have been severe for a judge to consider such a request, and the experience of facing the violent partner in a frightening courtroom to fight for this power to be attached to an injunction is usually a deeply traumatic one. Furthermore, once a woman has managed to get her 'power of arrest' the police are quite likely to choose not to enforce it.[7]

In Northern Ireland and in Scotland, exclusion and protection orders, and interdicts under the relevant legislation (the Domestic Proceedings Order 1980 and the Family Protection (Scotland) Act 1981 respectively) carry an automatic power of arrest. But this power is discretionary and the police often use their discretion not to act (as in Jean's story). As one Women's Aid worker in Northern Ireland put it:

> Legal sanctions against the practice of wife-assault have now existed for a considerable period. Whilst it would be naive to assume that the existence of such legislation would prohibit wife-abuse, it is reasonable to expect that some changes would be apparent. It is evident to us that whatever sanctions exist, they have been singularly ineffective in either providing protection to the victims of the assault or in deterring further assaults.

Northern Ireland Women's Aid Federation (NIWAF) carried out an independent survey to document and examine police response to domestic violence. They had hoped to interview police officers as well as women, but were unable to obtain the co-operation of the RUC. They had a response from sixty-seven women. The results clearly indicated that despite 'official' recognition of the problem and the availability of legal protection, the suffering of large numbers of women and children in the home was still, to a great extent, being ignored. Of the women interviewed, 62 per cent were dissatisfied with how the police dealt with their cases. The majority of women perceived the police as holding negative attitudes in dealing with the problem. A staggering 95 per cent of all women interviewed said there were times when they had needed police help but had not contacted the police. Over 50 per cent reported that this was because they had no confidence in the police. Only 3 per cent of the interviewees unconditionally agreed that they would advise a victim of domestic violence to contact the police.

Particular factors may exacerbate an already difficult situation *vis-à-vis* the police for women who suffer domestic violence. In the Northern Ireland survey, women were asked about the effect of the 'troubles' on their own situation and on police response to domestic violence. A total of 31 per cent felt that the troubles had affected them in some way. There were three main areas identified. Firstly, access to the police: in areas where there was local hostility to the police, difficulties might arise where a woman requested police assistance. Secondly, effectiveness of police action: in areas where attacks on the police had taken place, the police had a policy of investigating the request to ensure it was a genuine one. This could take anything between one and two hours. In these cases, there was no possibility of an emergency response for women in danger from their partners. Thirdly, collusion between the police and violent men: a few women were particularly at risk because their partners were either in the security forces, or in one of the paramilitary organizations and so had firearms in the house. One woman reported that the police were reluctant to intervene on her behalf because they were sympathetic to her husband in the security forces. It is therefore evident that living in Northern Ireland can add an extra dimension to the problems affecting abused women generally, and the particular circumstances affecting the police in Northern Ireland may be one of the reasons that domestic violence is not always given the priority it demands.

Hostility and abuse from the police are also problems for other women. Black women have to deal with the racism of the police at the same time as coping with the emergency for which they are requesting help. Police racism can be compounded if the assaulted woman does not speak English. In addition, black women's groups have pointed out how the police may use a supposed response to violence against women in order to increase surveillance of the black community. These disturbing aspects of police racism are further discussed in chapters 2, 3 and 4.

Women's Aid and other organizations run refuges throughout the country for women who have suffered domestic violence. Police protection is generally better once a woman has arrived at a refuge; some police forces are even helpful at this stage. Most refuges have attempted to develop good relations with their local police station, and the police often arrive more promptly when called out, and investigate cases more thoroughly, as a result. However, in some refuges it has been noted that the police respond far more quickly to calls from refuge workers than from women residents, which is a matter of some concern. Every refuge, of course, can describe incidents where the police have not taken situations seriously enough, as well as incidents where they have. It is a distressing fact that even in refuges with confidential addresses and secret locations, women are still badly injured by violent partners who break in. Balwant Kaur was murdered by her husband in a refuge in front of her children in 1985. Caroline Myland was shot dead while under police protection in hospital in 1986. There have been other such tragic and preventable murders.

Through Women's Aid, women have been arguing for a better police response to domestic assaults on women for many years. The development of women's refuges and Women's Aid out of the women's liberation movement in the early 1970s led to increased pressure and publicity on the issue. In 1975 the Select Committee on Violence in Marriage drew attention to the need for the police to respond more effectively. This was followed in 1976 by the Domestic Violence and Matrimonial Proceedings Act, and in 1978 by the Domestic Proceedings and Magistrates Courts Act. It was not, however, until the 1985 report of the Women's National Commission on Violence against Women that the need for police training and improved police procedures became more widely acknowledged.[8] These concerns were reinforced by the report of Dr Susan Edwards, 'The Police Response to Domestic Violence in London'.[9]

In recent years, Welsh Women's Aid and some English Women's Aid groups have made an input into police training, though as this work is largely unfunded and undervalued, training is not nearly as extensive as it should be. While police training can contribute to a change in attitudes and procedures, experience shows that unless constant pressure is maintained by Women's Aid groups, old habits die hard.

In 1986, the Home Office issued a circular reminding police of their powers under the 1984 Police and Criminal Evidence Act. However, a report in the same year from a London Metropolitan Police Working Party on Domestic Violence (which was 'sat on' by the Home Office) made more extensive suggestions on training, referrals to refuges, and advice and information for women. This was followed up by a very good report by the London Strategic Policy Unit whose recommendations have been endorsed, broadly speaking, by Women's Aid and other women's organizations. Some of the vital recommendations in this report include:

1. The recording of all incidents in a statistically retrievable form.
2. An instant response to all urgent calls from women (including repeat calls).
3. Positive intervention by police, instead of inaction or conciliation.
4. Separate police interviews for women, away from the man. Provision of information about Women's Aid and other agencies.
5. Police provision of transport to a refuge or other safe place.
6. Police arrest and charging of the man rather than inaction. Recording of appropriate offences as ABH or GBH rather than common assault. The use of Police and Criminal Evidence Act 1984 if appropriate.
7. Police should not discourage a woman from pressing charges but should recognize that she may be afraid to do so. They should be prepared to proceed without her testimony, but not against her wishes.
8. Police must be aware of the intimidating effect of mental and

emotional violence (which should also be grounds in court for 'powers of arrest').

9. Injunctions must be kept on file and easily accessible.
10. Where an injunction with 'power of arrest' is in force, police must arrest for breach on the basis of the woman's report. It should not be necessary for an officer to witness the breach.
11. Full training should be available on dealing with domestic violence, and should include challenging racist and sexist attitudes, and information on Women's Aid and other agencies.

These recommendations are to be welcomed and pressure now needs to be exerted to get them put into practice throughout the country.

Of recent police initiatives, it is difficult to assess whether the Force Order issued to the London Metropolitan Police in June 1987 will have a significant impact on police response.[10] The Order amounts to an instruction to all police officers to take domestic violence seriously. It reminds officers to bring prosecutions under the new provisions in the Police and Criminal Evidence Act 1984, compelling victims to give evidence.[11] It insists that all incidents of domestic violence are to be formally recorded, and not 'no-crimed'. It also refers to increased training, to making WPCs available where possible, to separate interviewing of the woman and the violent man, and to better liaison with agencies such as Women's Aid. Reports from Tottenham and Brixton refuges, areas in which women officers have special supervisory responsibility for domestic violence, suggest that, in the short term at least, there has been better liaison between the police and Women's Aid and more referrals. However, a Force Order is only a memo to officers and has no guarantee of implementation. In addition, no monitoring has been set up under the Order and Women's Aid has no funding to enable them to undertake this themselves. Without such monitoring, a true picture is unlikely to emerge. Input from Women's Aid in training programmes is to our mind extremely important, but whether or not Women's Aid are able to set up training initiatives depends on the officer responsible for training in a particular force. This training is very rarely funded. If it is set up on the initiative of a sympathetic training officer, it may well be forfeited if that officer is replaced by another. In any event, the training often applies only to junior officers and although they are the ones dealing with domestic violence call-outs, without the involvement of senior officers, the training lacks authority. In the future, we must turn our attention to trying to liaise with senior officers as well, so that our input commands authoritative attention. But most groups do not have time to do this work, having barely the resources to run the refuges essential to women in emergency.

Moreover, the Metropolitan Force Order has no implications for the rest of England and Wales. In the majority of police forces the basic problem remains the lack of recording by the police of domestic incidents and therefore the impossibility of adequate monitoring, not only of the extent and severity of domestic violence itself but of police responses to it. A complete overhaul of police recording, retrieval and monitoring systems is essential if we are to be able to review progress made and see a way forward. There is also an urgent need for liaison with the Home Office at a national level. Their reluctance to liaise with or indeed fund Women's Aid nationally indicates that domestic violence is seen only as a social problem, rather than a criminal matter.

Currently there is also concern about the impact and implementation of the 1984 Police and Criminal Evidence Act. In particular the measure which makes women 'compellable witnesses' has had a mixed response from Women's Aid. While police prosecution would clearly label domestic violence as a criminal offence, in the absence of adequate safeguards at present it can substantially increase the risk of violence to a woman who is compelled as a witness.

In the end, whatever the contribution of the Act, the crucial point for us is that police officers must treat assault in the home as a serious crime, and *listen* to the woman's point of view. In order for the police to do this, the courts must also take domestic violence seriously. Domestic violence legislation must be reviewed and extended, and there must be adequate funding for enough refuges to provide twenty-four hour help, shelter and advice throughout the country to assist all women and their children in need. The role of the police in combating domestic violence is and will remain absolutely crucial.

Notes

1. Throughout this article, it is assumed that women will be dealing with a policeman or policemen, partly because this is statistically by far the greatest probability (policewomen still constitute only 10.3 per cent as a national average of all police forces) and partly because it is likely that at least one, if there are two officers sent, or the officer if there is only one, will be a man. This is because the officer or officers will be expected to deal with a violent man.

2. S. Edwards. *The Police Response to Domestic Violence in London*, Polytechnic of Central London, London, 1986.

3. London Strategic Policy Unit. *Police Response to Domestic Violence*, Police Monitoring & Research Group Briefing Paper, 1, p. 1, London 1986.

4. ibid, p. 29. Also see *Police and People in London*, vol. 4, Policy Studies Institute Report, London, 1983, p. 64.

5. London Strategic Policy Unit, op. cit., p. 12.

6. Domestic Violence and Matrimonial Proceedings Act, 1976. See also Domestic Proceedings and Magistrates' Courts Act, 1978.

7. Under the Domestic Violence and Matrimonial Proceedings Act, 1976, any woman, married or unmarried, can apply for an injunction in the county court against a violent partner. This is an order requiring the partner not to molest, threaten or harass her. It can require the man to be excluded from, or the woman to be let back into, the home. A married woman also has the option of applying for an injunction in the magistrates' court. In both cases, the injunction may have a power of arrest attached but this is at the discretion of the judge or magistrates and it will be attached only if there is *evidence* of actual bodily harm in the past and also of a future *imminent* risk of violence. Many solicitors do not argue for a power of arrest to be attached to an injunction, and women do not know that they should persuade their solicitor to do so, if appropriate.

8. Women's National Commission Report 1985. See recommendations on police training and procedures and recommendations to the judiciary, Ch. 4.

9. S. Edwards, op. cit.

10. Guidelines to all Metropolitan offices dealing with domestic violence were announced on Wednesday 24 June 1987 and followed recommendations made by the Metropolitan Working Party into Domestic Violence, which had been set up two years previously. The Working Party consisted of representatives from social services, women's organizations, and other 'relevant organizations'.

11. 'In any proceedings the wife or husband of the accused shall . . . be compellable to give evidence on behalf of the accused'. Section 80, Part VIII, The Police and Criminal Evidence Act 1984.

Bibliography

Select Committee on Violence in Marriage, HMSO, 1975
Home Office Circular 69, 1986
Welsh Women's Aid – 'Dialogue for Change' – Police Conference Report, 1986
Metropolitan Police Working Party on Domestic Violence 1976
J. Pahe, *Private Violence, Public Policy*, Routledge & Kegan Paul, London, 1985

2. Southall Black Sisters

Two Struggles: Challenging Male Violence and the Police

In June 1987, the Metropolitan Police issued a 'Force Order' relating to domestic violence to all police stations in the London area, which directed officers' attention to new provisions in the Police and Criminal Evidence Act 1984 (see pages 35, 287). It also recommended close liaison between the police and groups in order to deal with domestic violence jointly.

Southall Black Sisters do not believe that the Order's emphasis on prosecution and its recommendations for liaison with local groups are serious attempts to address the problem of how the police should respond to domestic violence. Women have always criticized the police for not acting on powers that they already have and for not providing an effective emergency response to violence in the home, regardless of whether prosecution takes place in the final instance or not. Without such an emergency response women remain at risk from violence and in danger of their lives. The Force Order guidelines do not address this issue. Instead, they emphasize the need for the police to 'liaise' closely with local groups. This is known in police language as the 'Multi-Agency Approach' and was one of the key recommendations of the Metropolitan Police Internal Working Party Report on domestic violence. Exactly what the Multi-Agency Approach is, what it means and why it should be adopted at this particular moment are all questions central to any discussion of current policing, including police response to domestic violence.

For black people, the police in this country have always

represented the most overtly repressive face of a racist state. The uprisings in London's Southall and in virtually all other inner cities in the last twenty years have been urgent and spontaneous expressions of the despair, anger and frustration of many blacks in the face of growing homelessness, unemployment, immigration controls and racial attacks on the streets. The state's response to the uprisings and growing unrest has been to strengthen the police force by giving it new powers through legislation and increased resources as a way of diffusing protest and resistance.

In recent years, the state and the police have redefined their priorities and objectives, so that the very attempts of black people to organize themselves have become criminal offences (for example, with the prosecution of the Newham Seven and the Newham Eight – youths who sought to defend themselves against racist gangs). Nor is this onslaught restricted to the black community. Increasingly, sections of the white community have come under attack. The Thatcher government's campaigns in respect of the inner cities do not stem from a concern for urban decay, poverty and deprivation but from a need to control the unrest that arises from these conditions. They ignore the real issues at stake: unemployment, homelessness, health and education. The police, for their part, have ensured that their policies and objectives are in line with the government's aims. They are intensifying a process begun in the late seventies which sees targeting, surveillance and control in the inner cities as the main policing priority.

Ironically, for black women, in the face of harassment, intimidation and violence from our communities, the police have continued to be the only agency to whom we are forced to turn for immediate help. The majority of women have no faith or confidence in the police, but because of a lack of any alternative, women have had no choice but to make demands for protection and safety from them. For black women, challenging an issue like domestic violence within our own communities and challenging the racism of the police at the same time is often fraught with contradictions. On the one hand, we are involved in campaigns against police brutality, deaths in police custody and immigration fishing raids. On the other, we are faced with daily beatings, rape and sexual harassment. We are forced to make demands of the police to protect our lives from the very same men along whose side we fight in anti-racist struggles. The struggle against racism cannot be waged at the expense of the struggles within a male-dominated and patriarchal community whose traditions and customs confine the woman to the home and deny her the right to determine who she wants to live with and how. Many of us feel that to make this struggle secondary to the struggle against racism means at best to ignore women's experiences and at worst to passively collude with those patriarchal practices. Instead, our view is that somehow both struggles have to be waged simultaneously without losing sight of the consequences each can have on the other. Our demands must take both struggles into account.

Asian women have challenged the idea that the 'honour' of their families rests on their behaviour and their silence. Women like Krishna Sharma and Balwant Kaur dared to 'break the silence' by asserting their right to live independently, free from violence. Both women were killed by their husbands, precisely because they posed a threat to their husband's authority, and by implication to the male-dominated community. The deaths of both Krishna Sharma and Balwant Kaur were preventable, if only the police had bothered to act on their pleas for help hours before they were murdered.

Kirshna Sharma died in Southall in May 1984, after suffering violence from her husband for years. Finally, unable to bear it any longer, she called the police for help. The officer who turned up at her door said he could find no evidence that Krishna Sharma's husband hit her, although he had admitted to slapping her sometimes. He advised her that she would have to bring a private prosecution against her husband. Within a matter of hours Krishna Sharma was found hanged, with her clothes torn and with several bruises on her body. Yet later an inquest into her death returned a verdict of suicide.

Balwant Kaur, a young Asian woman and mother of three, was murdered in Brent Asian Women's Refuge on 22 October 1985. Having already lived through eight years of abuse and violence at the hands of her husband, she had finally managed to escape to the refuge in July 1985. Previously, whilst at her marital home, the police had been called but had failed to provide protection. Balwant Kaur's husband, Bhagwant Singh Panesar, unable to bear the fact that he was no longer able to 'possess' her, tracked her down to the refuge. On the night of 18 October he came to the refuge with two hired accomplices. He had told the two men that he intended to burgle the refuge, but when they learned of his real intention to kill his wife, they abandoned him. Those same two accomplices returned to the refuge the following day and warned Balwant about her husband's intentions to kill her. The refuge immediately informed the local police and asked for protection in the form of a twenty-four-hour patrol. The police sent an officer who spoke to the residents of the refuge and then went away. No further action was taken. Several days later, Balwant was stabbed to death by her husband in the presence of her three young daughters. Not only had the police failed to respond to the threats made on Balwant's life, but soon after the murder they divulged the whereabouts of the refuge to the media, who broadcast the address all over London and thus endangered the lives of all the other women in the refuge. The total disregard for the safety of women and children and of the refuge shown by the police meant that the refuge had to be evacuated within twenty-four hours of the murder.

The deaths of both Krishna Sharma and Balwant Kaur show with frightening clarity that the police choose to direct their resources at priorities other than violence against women, and that as a result the lives of many women are at risk. We believe that the problem here is one of the ethos of 'success' in police operations. The police measure their success in terms of rates of prosecution and conviction, and not in terms of the safety and protection they can provide. The problem is also one of police priorities. Whilst police officers are readily deployed to control protests against loss of civil liberties, poverty and deprivation, countless women who live in fear for their lives at home are ignored.

More than a year after the issuing of the Force Order, it seems to us that the police have failed to implement their own guidelines. In our experience, it has been left to individual officers to interpret the Order in the way they choose to do so. Moreover, the majority of officers seem not to know of the Order's existence and still refuse to acknowledge that domestic violence is a serious crime.

However, what we have found, certainly in Ealing, is that the local police force as a whole is following the Order's recommendation of a 'Multi-Agency Approach' to domestic violence. This approach is presented in terms of close co-operation between the police and local statutory and voluntary agencies, but in reality, it has less to do with providing an immediate emergency response to domestic violence than to building up a profile of each community. The terms of reference for such 'co-operation' are set by the police. In the process of 'working together', agencies such as social services, schools and the DHSS move away from the original ethic of social welfare, and are transformed into a role where they are there to aid the police. The consequences for black people as for all other disadvantaged sections of the community are all too clear.

In Southall we have experienced directly how the Multi-Agency Approach to domestic violence is taking shape. In February and March 1987, we attended meetings called by the Southall police in order to discuss their response to domestic violence. During the course of these two meetings the police were very clear and frank. Their proposal was to set up a 'domestic violence panel', composed of social workers, probation services, psychiatric nurses, volunteers from the local victim support schemes, and of course the local women's groups. This panel would meet regularly in order to hold case conferences. The terms of reference for the panel were set by the police. All the different agencies were asked to provide information on 'problem families' and as part of this, we were to pass on our domestic violence cases to the police.

The police gave no indication of what they intended to do with the information.

Needless to say we decided to play no part in this scheme. Its terms of reference clearly reflected the police attitude and policies on domestic violence. Domestic violence was redefined as characteristic behaviour of 'problem families', who would then become the subject of police attention. These families might be stigmatized solely on the basis of the whims, prejudices and assumptions of individual officers. We were at pains to point out that domestic violence can occur in any family, regardless of race, religion and class, at any time. It is not confined to 'problem families' however that that expression may be defined. The role of the police is not to take away women's initiative in this respect. It is rather to respond swiftly and effectively when women call, whatever their family circumstances.

Throughout our meetings the police maintained that domestic violence was a 'family' problem and so argued that it was not possible to intervene to enforce the law. They were worried about the negative image that men might have of the police force if they did act! In an area like Southall, with its predominantly Asian population, this reluctance was also backed by racist assumptions. Factors such as arranged marriages and a different culture were cited as reasons for lack of intervention on the part of the police. They also argued that older Asian women are supposed to have a higher tolerance level and therefore be less in need of immediate help. One wonders whether such assumptions were responsible for their inaction when confronted with cries of help from Krishna Sharma and Balwant Kaur.

The approach to domestic violence adopted by the police in Southall, as elsewhere, ties in neatly with police rhetoric of community policing and consultative meetings. Working panels on problem areas such as racial harassment and domestic violence create the illusion of police concern and a readiness to 'involve the community', and at the same time allow the police to shift the focus away from their own responsibilities. Ultimately, the police's approach is a distraction which shifts the emphasis away from demands for police accountability in dealing with these issues.

In the light of the experience of black people in such areas as Southall, Brixton, Notting Hill, Handsworth, Toxteth, St Paul's and Tottenham, black people cannot place any trust in such schemes as the Multi-Agency Approach. These and other schemes only confirm to us that the police will use increasingly sophisticated tactics to control black people.

Experience has shown that the police are not on the side of women and blacks. It is therefore no accident that the police have chosen to prioritize domestic violence by targeting 'problem families'. The Multi-Agency Approach remains a propaganda exercise aimed at a section of the community, that is women, who for years have suffered violence and even death as a result of police inaction. At the same time the Multi-Agency Approach serves to extend the net of corporate policing.

The deaths of Krishna Sharma and Balwant Kaur have raised important questions for those of us who know that we have to continue making demands of the police in the absence of any alternative. However, we must recognize that the police force itself is becoming increasingly sophisticated in its operations and in setting its own priorities. It has taken upon itself the task of social control, and it has been campaigning vigorously for the powers and resources to carry out that task. It is our responsibility in the light of our own experiences to fight for the powers and resources of the police force to be redirected to meet our needs.

3. Working with Asian Women and the Police

Kalsoom Sarwar

Having been involved in Women's Aid refuges over the years, and being currently employed at an Asian Women's Centre in South London, I have worked closely with women who have been beaten up by their husbands or boyfriends at home. I have come to the conclusion that the law does little to secure the safety of women suffering from domestic violence, whether the women are white, Afro-Caribbean or Asian. The assumption that domestic violence occurs only or particularly within certain communities or at certain levels of society has to be dismissed immediately. Domestic violence has no social barriers. Moreover, one should not assume that injuries resulting from it are minor.

However, although domestic violence appears to be universal, the responses to it, from statutory bodies like the police, the housing departments and the courts, differ enormously. Victims of domestic violence from the 'ethnic' communities already suffer a lack of supportive provisions, in terms of re-housing and the supplementary benefit system. The attitude of the law enforcing agency, the police, can amount to an additional hurdle for them in combating domestic violence.

In a number of cases, clients at the Centre where I work opt for reconciliation. However, they still require some form of counselling and therefore continue to visit the Centre, albeit secretly. Other clients have found it necessary to take legal action against violent men. In this case, we may refer a woman to an Asian women's refuge. Whilst there, she will be able to make decisions about her future in a safe environment with practical and moral support at hand. However, there are practical problems in referring to a refuge. There are very few refuges which cater specifically for Asian women; many of these are under-funded and situated in buildings which are too small or run-down. At present, the Asian women's refuge in our borough has space for only three women and their children; thus demand far outweighs the resources available.

In cases where no refuge space is available, the next option is to approach the local Homeless Persons Unit (HPU) but problems have recently arisen there too. In July 1986, an elderly woman who had suffered from domestic violence throughout her married life approached us following a particularly violent assault by her husband. She was sure that she would never be reconciled with him but was unwilling to be referred to a refuge unless it was an Asian women's refuge, and even then she would have been hesitant to accept a place because of the stigma attached to refuges. We therefore referred her to the local HPU who responded very sympathetically, and came up with an offer within three weeks. However, in the same situation today, it is doubtful whether the HPU would be able to offer even emergency temporary accommodation as the housing problem in the borough has risen to such proportions. Thus a woman in the same situation will have to rely on friends or relatives willing to offer support. Recently, a young woman staying with relatives whilst waiting for refuge space was found by her husband and viciously beaten. In another case, we referred a client to an HPU in a nearby borough but were informed that if the woman could not speak English, the unit would not be prepared to help; nor would they take it upon themselves to provide an interpreter.

This is the background, then, in which we have to look at police intervention in cases of domestic violence. Frequently, refuges need to call upon the police. For example, it is necessary to request a police escort where a woman needs to collect her belongings from the marital home. When I first began working at the Centre, such a request entailed at least a two-hour wait at the police station until an officer was available. Thus, it was a very time-consuming task. On one occasion, I had spent a number of weeks trying to arrange for a client to take some time off work during the day since she wished to go to her house when her husband was least likely to be indoors. Finally, we met one afternoon and went straight to the police station to request an escort. Much probing followed, implying that surely we could manage on our own! I was adamant that neither my client nor I was prepared to take such a risk. We were informed that we would have to wait until an officer was available. After waiting for just over two hours, my client began to feel that it was too late, as her husband would be due home. Two hours of waiting and worrying had led her to believe that a confrontation with him, even with a police officer present, would be too traumatic. She decided not to go; so the time and energy spent had all been in vain.

This and similar experiences have taught workers at the Centre now to approach a sympathetic local solicitor before going to the police station. The effect of a solicitor's phone call is far weightier than that of a couple of Asian women who turn up at the station. This method has proved successful in reducing time and anxiety since we now receive the attention of the police immediately after the solicitor's phone call.

In another case, where a husband had chased his wife and snatched their child from her, our solicitor telephoned the police to request a police escort to the matrimonial home where we believed him to have taken the child. On our arrival at the police station, my client and I were questioned by an officer who appeared to assume that we were both hard of hearing. Questions were posed very slowly and loudly. He seemed to think that neither of us would be able to understand him otherwise. I hasten to add that my client speaks English very well in a cockney accent and I possess quite a strong Northern accent. During our wait, I noticed that he spoke quite normally to the other people who approached him. The fact that a child's life was at stake appeared to matter little to him. Eventually, a police escort was provided reluctantly.

When we arrived at my client's home, I noticed that the officer directed his attention solely to her husband. My client was relieved to find her child safe but was crying uncontrollably, whilst her husband turned on the charm; he seemed cool and rational, articulate and impressive. No kind of assurance was offered to the woman, whilst the husband received a sympathetic ear from our escort. Evidently, he had convinced the officer that he would not harm a fly. The same client phoned me two weeks later; she was screaming and crying out for help. Her husband was beating her again; he even grabbed the phone from her to hurl abuse at me.

The provision of interpreters may also be a problem for Asian women who suffer domestic violence. In one instance, a woman had informed me that her husband and brother-in-law had walked out of her home threatening to return to kill her. On that afternoon, I was dealing with two other similarly urgent cases and I rang the police to request that they look into the matter. I suggested that, if a home visit took place, they might require an interpreter. The policewoman told me that an interpreter was out of the question and added rudely that if she sent her colleague to visit my client: 'he will be very angry when he finds out that she can barely speak English'. Needless to say, I found her attitude offensive, patronizing and totally uncooperative.

Asian women who have recently arrived in this country do not even have the limited recourse to rehousing and police protection described above, because of the immigration laws. Women who arrive in the UK as 'dependants' do so on condition that they will have no recourse to state funds. Leave to remain here 'indefinitely' may be granted after a year, provided there has been no change in circumstances, that is, provided a woman is still living with her husband and the relationship is stable. The consequences for women who have recently arrived from the Indian subcontinent and are suffering from domestic violence are harrowing. If they approach the social services, the DHSS or the housing authorities, they risk jeopardizing their chances of remaining in the UK. The fact that they have had 'recourse to public funds' may become known to the Home Office, as may the fact that their marriage is in difficulties. If they approach the police, their immigration status may soon be identified by investigating officers and the effect will be similar. The vulnerable position of Asian women in these circumstances can easily be, and unfortunately is, often taken advantage of by violent husbands.

The police need to re-examine the enforcement of the law regarding domestic violence, to recognize it as a criminal act and respond accordingly. Where Asian women are involved, police co-operation is vital so that Asian women can benefit from what should be a public service. The provision of inter-preters, where required, is essential. Changing police attitudes towards Asian women will be a lengthier and more difficult task. It may prove to be a long and slow process but the issue of police racism must be confronted if Asian women are to have any faith in the service that the police should provide for all of us.

4. The Gurdip Kaur Campaign

Fighting for Justice

On 11 May 1986, Gurdip Kaur Sandhu was brutally beaten by her brother-in-law, Harbax Singh, in the presence of her husband, Gurbax Singh. At the inquest on 28 August of that year, her death in hospital was ascribed by a Home Office pathologist to 'heart and lung failure from a fractured larynx', injuries consistent with her having suffered continuous blows to the throat.

Gurdip Kaur was born in Africa in 1952, and came to Britain from India when she was a teenager. At sixteen she married Gurbax Singh Sandhu and moved to Reading. From then on she was subjected to persistent physical violence and mental cruelty from her husband, and had to suffer frequent beatings and humiliation in front of her children and family. In 1984 Gurbax Singh was given a three-year prison sentence for a drugs offence. He was released in December 1985, having served half that time. Four months later, Gurdip Kaur managed to obtain an emergency court injunction which gave the police power of arrest against her husband, and they separated. For the next few weeks she tried to live an independent life with her children, free from violence, despite the lack of support from the Asian community, with their constant reminders of *izzat* (her 'family honour'). Her separation and planned divorce was said to bring disgrace on her husband and their joint families, and there were many pressures to return to him and attempt a reconciliation.

On 11 May 1986, Gurdip Kaur agreed to allow her husband

to come to the house to pick up some clothing. He arrived about 8 p.m., closely followed by his brother, Harbax Singh Sandhu. Both men had been drinking. Gurdip Kaur was alone in the house, apart from the youngest of her three sons, twelve-year-old Ravinder. After a few minutes she went into the kitchen to put her tea cup in the sink. Harbax Singh, her brother-in-law, followed her in, grabbed hold of her, bashed her head against the kitchen unit and punched her repeatedly in the throat. When Ravinder saw what was happening he rushed in and tried to drag his uncle away, but found himself collared in a half-nelson by his father, Gurbax Singh, who thrust him out of the room. Ravinder picked himself up and ran to call the police, but finding the front door locked, came back through the house. He saw his mother lying on the floor, looking 'as if she were asleep', and his uncle pushing a glass to her mouth. After hearing the kitchen drawer open, he saw his father, clutching a large knife, blade downwards, like a dagger in his fist. Gurbax Singh aimed the knife at Gurdip Kaur, saying he was going to kill her, but was stopped by his brother. Gurdip Kaur was then bundled into a borrowed van and driven away by Harbax Singh to the house of a friend of his. After he'd left, the friend called the police. Harbax Singh then dumped Gurdip Kaur in the hospital casualty department and went back to his friend's house, where he was arrested. Gurdip Kaur was put on a life-support machine. Five days later, it was switched off and she died.

The information above was heard in Winchester Crown Court in January 1987, when Harbax Singh Sandhu was tried for the murder of Gurdip Kaur. The medical evidence showed that Gurdip Kaur had died as a result of a fractured larynx; the prosecution alleged that this had been caused by Harbax Singh when he punched her in the throat, and that therefore he had murdered her. The prosecution's case was largely based on the testimony of Gurdip Kaur's youngest son Ravinder, who presented a clear and unshakeable account of the events of the night of 11 May. The defence contested that a punch could not have caused the fatal fracture, but that the damage had been inflicted by Gurdip Kaur's husband, Gurbax Singh, who had stamped on his wife's throat while she was on the ground. In his summing up, the judge told the jury that if they were not satisfied that the punches from Harbax Singh had caused the fracture then the verdict should be 'not guilty'. However, if the punches had caused the fracture then he was responsible for her death. If this was the case and he had intended to kill her, or to do her really serious bodily harm, then he would be guilty of murder, but if that had not been his intention then he should be found guilty of manslaughter.

The jury was out for nearly four hours at the end of the three-day trial, coming back twice for clarification of the law. They returned with a verdict of 'not guilty of murder, but guilty of manslaughter'. The court then heard that Harbax Singh had already served time in prison. In 1981 he had received a three-year prison sentence (of which he served two years) for twice attempting to employ men to kill his own wife. This news appeared to shock and distress the jury.

Harbax Singh Sandhu had not only tried to have his own wife murdered, he had also subjected her to a level of violence that sent her to hospital twice. After his term in prison, he had abducted their son, and escaped to India. His wife had finally managed to win back the child through the Indian courts, but she and her son were then hounded by Harbax Singh and forced into hiding.

The British laws of evidence made it impossible to present this information in court during the trial. Legally, it would be said to have no bearing on the case in hand which involved his brother's wife's death. However, Harbax Singh had also persistently threatened the lives of Gurdip Kaur and her family. Over the telephone he had frequently told Gurdip Kaur that she was going to die. The police were well aware of this fact; on several occasions they had listened to these calls, but nothing about the threats was mentioned in court, not even as a prosecution question to the defendant.

The prosecution has complete discretion as to what information it wishes to present in court. Had the jury known of these phone calls, even as hearsay evidence, perhaps the verdict would have been different. Harbax Singh was not the only man threatening Gurdip Kaur and her family. After her death, when Harbax Singh was in custody, the phone calls continued. The family were blamed for the charges against Harbax Singh, blamed for the existence of the Gurdip Kaur Campaign, and told that they would die. On the last day of the Crown Court trial, Ravinder was told over the phone that he would not live another day. Some of these threats are known to have come from his father's family. Gurbax Singh had stopped his son from trying to save his mother; he had brandished a knife on the night she died; he had played no part in getting his fatally injured wife to hospital; he had not even rung for an ambulance. The defence counsel alleged that he had killed Gurdip Kaur. But Gurbax Singh Sandhu made no appearance at the trial of his twin brother, not even as a witness to the events of the night of 11 May.

Gurbax Singh was arrested after the attack on his wife. But he has never been called upon publicly to account for his actions at the time of the assault – all charges against him were dropped on the advice of the Chief Prosecuting Solicitor for the Thames Valley Police, and the reasons for this are not known to us.

When a number of local women became aware of these facts, they came together to start the Gurdip Kaur Campaign, a group mainly comprising Black women, most of whom were Asian. The campaign demanded justice for Gurdip Kaur: that Gurbax Singh be tried for his involvement, and that the public be made aware of this horrific example of male violence against women. It was felt that if the state would not bring Gurbax Singh to justice then the campaign would, even if this meant instigating a private prosecution. Information about the case was circulated through leaflets, mailings and articles in the women's media. The campaign soon received the support of individuals and organizations from all over the country. There were many letters and donations, and hundreds of women signed the petition demanding justice for Gurdip Kaur. Women also joined pickets outside the magistrates' court in Reading where Harbax Singh had his remand hearings. There was a demonstration at Winchester, where Harbax Singh had been tried for murder.

The campaign also attracted the interest of the police, who soon started to investigate the group. The organization which acted as the contact address for the campaign, and members of the local alternative newspaper that had carried information about the case of Gurdip Kaur, were visited by police officers from outside the Reading area. They said that they were following up a complaint received by the Director of Public Prosecutions from the family of Gurbax and Harbax Singh, and that they wanted the names and addresses of the members of the campaign so that they could talk to them about any planned demonstrations during the trial. It was suggested they write to the campaign to arrange a meeting, but no correspondence was forthcoming. The police officers also wanted to know where the campaign's leaflets had been printed, what machine had been used and how the campaign was being funded. They advised that they would continue their investigations should the campaign continue its demonstrations.

The family of Gurdip Kaur were also visited and questioned about the campaign by these police officers. During the committal hearing at Reading Magistrates' Court reference was made to the campaign as a factor in deciding where the Crown Court trial should take place, with an assurance made that the police were aware of the involvement of several local activists. The trial therefore took place nearly fifty miles away from Reading in Winchester, 'due to the strength of local feeling' – presumably an attempt to shake off the 'local' demonstrators. At Winchester, the judge warned the court that demonstrators could be imprisoned for carrying placards. The protesting women outside the court were moved, but continued the action with an impromptu march around the town.

The campaign has always been very cautious about promoting itself. The whereabouts of meetings and the names of members were kept very quiet. This was originally due to wariness of Gurbax Singh and his family, who were still threatening Gurdip Kaur's relatives. However, caution then became a habit due to harassment from the police. The campaign could understand a fear that its activities might prejudice the trial, (and it was careful not to do so), but the police could have written to the group had that been the problem. We would have thought that in some ways we were on the same side, wanting to see a criminal brought to justice, and those under threat safeguarded. How ironic therefore that a perfectly legal campaign organization should be pushed into hiding by the police themselves.

Gurdip Kaur and her family might certainly have expected a more sympathetic reaction from the police, who had been aware for some time of the violence suffered by them, having had to remove Gurbax Singh for the night on more than one occasion. However, when asked for help, they could only suggest that Gurdip Kaur move house. They offered her no assistance with getting an injunction. This she finally obtained with the help of Social Services. The police had listened to telephone death threats from Harbax Singh and his brother, but when asked for protection could only suggest a change of telephone number. They said they could not do anything until something definite happened and that such a situation was only to be expected within the Asian community.

After the death of Gurdip Kaur the family were treated very insensitively. Ravinder, who was only twelve, underwent intensive questioning for several hours at a time, and other members of the family were heavily interrogated about their activities in attempting to bring Gurbax and Harbax Singh to justice. After Gurbax was released the police warned the family that if they threatened him in any way, they would be the ones in trouble.

At the time of writing the campaign still exists. Harbax Singh is in prison, Gurbax Singh is free and Gurdip Kaur is dead. There was some media interest after the trial, but many of the national papers, television and radio did not consider the case significant, or sufficiently newsworthy, despite the highlighting of the issue of domestic violence at the time. A private prosecution now seems impossible for many reasons. Apart from the expense, and other inherent difficulties, such as the need to collect statements and persuade witnesses to give evidence, the court case of his brother makes it appear that Gurbax Singh has committed no crime. Although a court has heard evidence that he was involved in the events for which his brother has been imprisoned, that he tried to stop his son from protecting her, that he made no attempt to call the police or an ambulance, that he played no part in getting his wife to hospital, there is no such charge as 'accomplice to manslaughter'. A jury has decided that the death of Gurdip Kaur was an accident.

The campaign appears to have no option but to keep pressurizing the Department of Public Prosecutions to reopen the case, although the letters of many women and men, including sympathetic MPs have so far resulted only in rare and disappointing replies, which generally say that there is not enough evidence for a conviction.

The police failed Gurdip Kaur for seventeen years. She had visibly suffered violence at the hands of her brutal husband, had often been seen with cuts and bruises, or had been publicly degraded by him. She and her family had made the police aware of this, and of the threats to her life, and yet the police failed to take action to protect her, or even to take this information seriously. This once again demonstrates the lack of interest shown by police everywhere in crimes that can be termed 'domestic', their inability to recognize the danger confronting so many women, and their reluctance to face the issues involved. The police still seem to have the attitude that violence in families is not their concern; in such a case they seem even more inclined to regard male violence as an inherent part of family life, to be dealt with by the community to which the woman appears to belong.

The judicial system failed Gurdip Kaur by denying her the means to protect herself. Later, it did not effectively punish those responsible for her death. The court failed to present to the public all the available information about her case, or to give anyone the opportunity to speak for a woman no longer able to speak for herself. The court also encouraged racist assumptions, such as the argument that Sikh men will be more affected by alcohol – a statement which no doubt added to the 'mitigating circumstances' in the minds of the jury, and which once again allowed alcohol to become an excuse for men killing women.

The Asian community failed Gurdip Kaur – failed to allow her to live her life without violence. An Asian woman in Britain is prevented from challenging her husband, brother or father, not only by the state's external controls on her, but by the community's internal controls. For her to leave a violent situation is to leave the family completely, away from the disapproving Asian community in a society which is both racist and sexist. Those women who take such action are often accused of staining the family honour or *izzat* of their husbands and relations. For members of the Asian community to have allowed Gurdip Kaur to live free of violence would have meant recognizing the existence of such violence within the home and within the community. They would have had to challenge it as oppressive, rather than accepting it, as many do, as a vehicle by which men exert their authority and power over women.

These basic facts of male violence are, however, universal in all societies and cultures. Women all over the world are subjected to male violence in all spheres of life – a violence which induces fear, and as a result, subjugation. Everywhere we see the covert sanctioning of this oppression, and thus the implicit condoning of male violence against women. The police, the courts, our communities and society as a whole allow women such as Gurdip Kaur to suffer violence and die, through the unthinking and unspoken belief that domestic violence is a natural part of family life, indeed expected as an instrument of the patriarchy that upholds the status quo.

The Gurdip Kaur Campaign brought together Black women and white women from all over the country to demand justice for Gurdip Kaur and for the thousands of women who every day suffer violence at the hands of men. All of us who have grieved for Gurdip Kaur must ensure that she is not forgotten, using her memory to strengthen our struggles for change.

We will not mourn her death in silence.

5. Crimes against Women

The Manchester Survey

Surinder Bains

Myths about crimes against women abound. There is a commonly held belief that we put ourselves in danger by the clothes we wear, by where we go and how we behave. If we are assaulted by our husbands or boyfriends we are often thought to have asked for it by reasons ranging from 'nagging', to spending money on ourselves, to not keeping the house looking nice and clean. If we are raped we are said to have deserved it for being out at night, for walking down a deserted street, for wearing provocative clothing or for 'leading the man on'.

As women we know that these are myths. We know that all types of men, of all races and classes, rape women, that all kinds of women whatever their race or class are raped. We know that policemen and doctors and other so-called professionals beat their wives and girlfriends, that these crimes are not just committed by 'perverts' or men who are 'sick'. We know and have always known that women are victims of crimes in their own homes, whether these homes are pristine showhouses reflecting their owners' wealth, or ordinary council houses.

Women's lives are controlled, to varying extents, by violence and the fear of sexual crimes. We go out and we clench a set of keys in our fists. We carry pepper. We try to keep to well-lit streets. We don't look at strangers. We don't talk to strangers. We get taxis; if we don't, we walk in a purposeful, determined fashion. Even if we do not suffer crimes of violence, all of us live with the fear of them. But that fear makes us angry and that anger helps us to demand change. The Manchester survey on women and violence carried out by the Manchester City Council Police Monitoring Unit[1] to which we had 1,841 replies adds the voices of women in Manchester to those of Women's Aid, of Rape Crisis, of Incest Survivors Groups and of women up and down the country who have replied to other surveys about violence against women.

The Official Response

The Home Office recently produced a booklet entitled 'Violent Crime – Police Advice to Women on How to Reduce the Risks'[2]. The booklet begins with the statement that, 'The chances of becoming a victim of serious crime are very low', and gives advice on fitting good locks, having telephone extensions, getting taxis, avoiding isolated bus stops and so on. The booklet assumes that women have the financial resources to undertake these measures, and offers little practical help or advice for women who cannot afford locks, taxis and telephone extensions, who live in dimly-lit estates or who have to get buses from isolated bus stops. The British Crime Survey[3] states that women's fear of rape may result from 'exaggerated estimates of its likelihood' (Hough and Mayhew 1985). In implying that women's fear is irrational or excessive, and certainly unjustified, it totally negates and trivializes women's experiences. But women's fears *are* justified. Seventy per cent of women responding to our survey reported having experienced violence against themselves. Yet this alarming figure does not take account of the number of times each woman may have experienced a particular type of crime.

A survey conducted by *Woman* magazine in 1987,[4] which drew 7,000 replies, found that one in six women had been raped, and one in ten raped by a family member. One in four women had been victims of violence from their husband or boyfriend. The Manchester survey in the same year found that one in twelve women had been raped, one in seven had been sexually assaulted, one in six had been assaulted, and one in three had experienced indecent exposure. Nearly one in four had suffered indecent suggestions. Nearly one in three black women had experienced racial attack.

Women often trivialize their experiences because they are socialized to accept certain types of treatment as a way of life, as the norm, as something they cannot do anything about. Many women are subject to sexual harassment and intimidation every day of their lives but feel unable to challenge it or deal with it. Women who work in situations where they have frequently to suffer being touched, pinched and so on may not actually identify these incidents as sexual assault, despite finding them threatening, offensive and frightening. Complaining about this kind of behaviour in a male-dominated environment often leads to women being ridiculed because 'it's only harmless fun'; 'you can't take a joke', 'you must be frigid or a prude', are the common responses.

There are many incidents in which women suffer from male violence and never identify it as something they should or can report. One woman who replied to the Manchester survey lived in a refuge for battered women yet did not indicate that she had experienced any crime of violence. Other women may find themselves in violent relationships and not report the incidents because they feel they are to blame, not the assailant. Often, this also leads to women hiding the abuse from everyone including friends and family, pretending it has not happened, because they feel at fault. Admitting that it happens is to feel that they have failed in some way.

Women raped by husbands or boyfriends may not identify these incidents as rape. Studies have found that often women will say they have not experienced rape, but if they are then questioned specifically about their experiences of violence within their marriage they will give accounts of rape within marriage. The law does not recognize rape in marriage as a crime but even in cases where the offence is recognized, women seem more likely to try to forget it has ever happened than to tell anyone about it.

Women see their experiences ignored in all areas of society and learn to do the same thing themselves. As Ruth Hall states:

It is common then for women to absorb within themselves the pain of violent, degrading and undermining assaults. Women's ability to survive and not only to survive but carry on working, caring for children, responding to others' needs – says a great deal about human resilience. The tragedy is that this courage is often used against us, to say that we have not really been harmed.[5]

This attitude was confirmed by one respondent to the Manchester survey who had been raped. She said that she didn't tell anyone because, 'I didn't want the humiliation of recounting what had happened.'

Reporting Sexual Assault to Police

Three-quarters of women responding to the Manchester survey did not report rape or sexual assault to the police. The national survey conducted by *Woman's Own* the year before, to which 25,000 women replied, found that three-quarters of raped women did not report to the police.[6] A woman raped by a taxi driver who responded to our survey said: 'I did not go to the police because I felt so ashamed and I thought they wouldn't believe me. I can't explain why, but I felt it was my fault even though I did not encourage him in any way whatsoever.' A woman raped whilst unconscious wrote: 'I did not report it to the police because rape is sexual intercourse by force, against a person's will. I was blacked out, poisoned by excess alcohol. I hadn't a chance of saying no.'

It seems that women do not expect the police to believe them, certainly in the cases where the assailant is known to them, if they are out late, or if there are other reasons why they feel the police will blame them. Even if there is strong evidence of the offence, women tend to feel that it is they who will be blamed. Even if the police do believe rape victims and do not blame them, there is little chance of the rapist being brought to justice. Therefore reporting the rapist will only leave a victim open to possible retaliation.

The experiences of women who do report rape to the police seem to justify the reluctance of others to do so. In some instances, the police appear to be sensitive and sympathetic to the woman. One respondent said, 'The police were very understanding and reassuring.' Yet in many cases, the police response is inappropriate, insensitive and unsatisfactory. Many respondents reported a lack of understanding and sympathy, and a worrying disregard for their wellbeing. Here are some of their comments: 'When I was sexually assaulted they had me there for hours and broke me down to tears'; 'One PC on duty took a joking attitude, looking me up and down'; 'I was in the police station for fourteen hours. There were no toilet facilities; nobody told me what was happening. In the morning, I was driven home by a policeman who was totally obnoxious, suggesting I was "asking for it." '

In many cases, the police blame the woman for putting herself at risk. Women are disbelieved; the police often side with the man and refuse to take any action against him. In calling the police for protection, women are often left in an even more vulnerable situation because of the police response. Yet if women defend themselves from violent men, they run the very real risk of being arrested and charged themselves. A woman responding to the Manchester survey said she was charged because, 'I put a bottle over a man's head in a pub because he put his hand up my skirt.'

Many women responding to the Manchester survey reported indecent exposure from men (32 per cent). Obscene and threatening phone calls were reported by another 35 per cent. Only 10 per cent of these women had reported the incidents to the police and only one woman said that the offender had been caught. These offences are often treated as a joke, yet they can be extremely frightening, particularly for girls and young women. This must be clearly understood both by the police, who should seek to prosecute all known flashers, and by the judiciary who should deal with them in a manner which reflects the often terrifying effect of their behaviour on women.

The Experience of Black Women

For black women all of these fears and experiences are compounded by the additional fear and reality of racism culminating in violent attacks. The Manchester survey found that nearly one in three black women had experienced racial attacks. Such attacks force individuals or families to live in constant fear, subject to humiliation, severe distress and physical danger. These families, in many cases headed by single women, are often too afraid to allow their children to play outside. Even a trip to the local shops can be a harrowing ordeal. Racial attacks are often accompanied by abusive phone calls, bricks through windows, paint daubed on walls and damage to cars. Akhtar Hussain, Community Relations Adviser of Manchester City Council's Housing Department, made the following statement in referring to racial attacks in Manchester, 'I've seen things since I took up this job that I never thought would be possible for one human being to do to another.'

Most women who reported racial attacks in the survey did not report the incidents to the police. They said that they didn't think the police would do anything. Half said they didn't think the police could do anything. Nearly half said they thought they'd be disbelieved, and the same number said they could not stand the thought of all the police's questions.

In January 1982, the Greater Manchester Police (GMP) established a system which was intended to 'afford the best possible protection for the whole community, especially those belonging to ethnic minority groups who believe they are at special risk'. The scheme involved the monitoring of incidents by filtering all reports to the Assistant Chief Constable who had a direct remit to ensure that they were investigated. More than four years later, the Manchester survey found that of the sixteen women who said they had reported racist attacks to the police, over half were dissatisfied with the police response. Five were satisfied and two gave no answer. Only one woman who reported an incident to the police said that the offender was caught. Of those who indicated that the police response was unsatisfactory the main reason given was that the police said there was nothing they could do, that they were disbelieving and unsympathetic, that they did not take the women's cases seriously and that there was no follow-up by the police.

The Chief Constable's Report (1986) stated the objective of

promoting 'good relationships between police and the general public, with special reference to problems of racial discrimination, harassment and attacks'. In practice, the police response to racial attacks takes the form of particular recording practices specifically to deal with such incidents. This is a public relations exercise which seeks to assure black communities of the priority being afforded to racial attacks. The development of a 'Multi-Agency Approach' has been criticized as offering little in the way of evidence that the police are doing anything more than they did before to arrest and prosecute offenders. The policing of racial violence does not require any special response. It requires only diligent application of existing standard police procedures, and an understanding of racism, including institutional racism and its existence at all levels of the police service.

There has never been a study which focuses specifically on crimes against black women. The work which has been done on black people's experience of policing has tended to concentrate on the experience of black men. Whilst this is important, the particular form of double oppression faced by all black women needs to be recognized. It is vital that a study should be carried out by, or in consultation with, black women, which focuses on their experience of policing in relation to racial attacks and crimes of sexual violence, and that its recommendations should be acted upon by the police.

Conclusions

It seems that, despite racism and sexism in the police force, in some instances the police response is sensitive, sympathetic and appropriate. Why is this not always the case? Why is there so much variation in the ways in which different officers deal with incidents? That so many women are dissatisfied with the police response is a matter of grave concern; their accounts raise questions about whether the police really regard rape and other crimes of sexual assault and violence as serious, about whether police training is appropriate and relevant, and about how high a priority the training gives to crimes against women.

The Greater Manchester Police states its policy of dealing with crimes of violence against women sensitively. According to a statement made in November 1986:

> The greatest care is exercised by Greater Manchester Police in the investigation of offences of this order. The recommendations contained in the report by the Women's Commission have been Force policy here in the GMP for some considerable time.[7] Every effort is made to deal with victims of crimes of this nature with the greatest degree of sensitivity.

However, police practice is to allow the individual officers a considerable amount of discretion as to how they respond at the scene of an incident. This discretion can make a mockery of police policy statements. The result is that some officers behave in a way that leads women, like this respondent to the survey, to complain: 'The reason I told you all that was to show you what men are allowed to do to women and get away with it. Basically, we haven't got the law on our side. The law is men and a lot of them seem to look down on us.'

There seems little point in the police having policies unless they are enforced through training, supervision and monitoring. Junior officers, who are most likely to deal with the incidents concerned must be made accountable to senior officers, and senior officers to stated police policies. Most importantly, the police must be made accountable to the women who seek protection from racism. Structures must be developed to enable the police to be made properly accountable to women, to enable women to have a say in policing; policies developed in this way must be monitored to ensure that they are effective at the operational level.

The report of the Manchester survey findings calls for steps to be taken to ensure that racism in police ranks is stamped out as a matter of urgency. We had a number of reports of police racism in response to the survey. It must be said that the number of black women respondents overall was disappointingly low but this is quite evidently not because they have no complaints. We are aware that many black people feel so alienated by their experiences of policing in Manchester that they have become cynical about any initiatives to do with it. Only if the police begin to demonstrate an *active* commitment to their policy of anti-racism will there be any hope of changing these perceptions.

Black people will not be taken in by PR statements from the police about anti-racism if they bear no relation to police practice. Changes in police practice will only take place when police acknowledge their own racism, including the institutionalized racism within the force, and when we have a police force which is truly accountable to black people – and not merely superficially, through the process of consulting with 'community leaders' as at present. Local authorities also have their role to play in ensuring women's safety. The survey report makes recommendations to various council departments. But the real onus is on the police to take positive action to protect women from violence both inside and outside their homes. The report calls on the GMP to adopt the measures in the Force Order issued to the Metropolitan Police (see chapters 1 and 2) which prioritizes crimes against women and is based on the premise that violence in the home is as much a crime as violence on the streets. The report also calls on the GMP to recruit more women officers and for more policewomen to be readily available to deal with crimes against women.

None of our demands is new; women have been making these demands for years. Women remain as much at risk as ever, yet our access to the criminal justice system continues to be severely limited by bad police practices. For black women, who have the additional risk of racist attacks, access is further curtailed by police racism. And even when we do gain access, the criminal justice system fails to protect us. Men who commit crimes against women continue to do so because their actions go uncontested. Women have a right to be protected, and our demands for protection must be met.

Notes

1. 'Manchester's Crime Survey of Women for Women: Women and Violence Survey Report', Manchester City Council Police

Monitoring Unit, October 1987. Available from: Information Centre and Bookshop, Town Hall, Manchester, M60 2LA.

2. 'Violent Crime – Police Advice to Women on How to Reduce the Risks', Central Office of Information, HMSO, 1987.

3. Hough and Mayhew, 'The British Crime Survey: First Report Study 76', HMSO, London, 1985.

4. *Woman* magazine's general survey on women's lives in the eighties, 14 November 1987.

5. Ruth E. Hall, *A London Inquiry into Rape and Sexual Assault*, Falling Wall Press, Bristol, 1985.

6. *Woman's Own* survey on rape, 23 August 1986.

7. Women's National Commission, 'Violence Against Women', Cabinet Office, London, 1985.

6. Women, Racist Attacks and the Response from Anti-Racist Groups*

Christina Dunhill

Racist harassment and attacks are not declining; in fact they are on the increase. The problems range from verbal abuse, spitting, banging on doors and windows, racist graffiti, to stone-throwing, gang assaults, arson, stabbings and murder. Violent attacks are increasing; weapons like knives, hammers and ammonia are being used. Arson attacks on people's homes, halal meat shops and places of worship have occurred across the whole of East and South-East London. Families live in fear, boarding up letterboxes and windows against incendiaries or bombs. Some parts of East London, for example E.16, have become no-go areas for Black people, who are afraid to walk the streets, even in daylight.[1] The problem of attacks in and around schools, pubs and social centres is also growing.

Many Black families suffer from continuous harassment and provocation, spanning a lifetime. This may be verbal abuse, serious physical assault on the street or violent attacks on their homes. The knowledge of the horrific reality of knife and arson attacks is the context in which everyday harassment such as verbal abuse or spitting are experienced.

According to the police's own figures, racist attacks in Newham were up by 60 per cent in 1986 from the same period in 1985. There was also an increase in the viciousness and

* This article is very largely based on information supplied by the Newham Monitoring Project and the Greenwich Action Committee Against Racist Attacks, to both of whom I am very grateful.

physical brutality of attacks.[2] Newham Monitoring Project fear there will be deaths if police do not take serious action to apprehend the perpetrators of these attacks. As yet, the Project has not been able to document a single case of racially motivated arson which the police have been able to solve.

Black women are the most vulnerable victims of racist attack. Nearly a third of the Black women who responded to the Manchester women and violence survey had been racially attacked (see chapter 5). This was a staggering figure. Single women living either alone or with children and women who are at home alone all day are particularly vulnerable. Just under two-thirds of racist attacks dealt with by the Greenwich Action Committee against Racist Attacks during 1984 to 1986 involved attacks on women.[3] Women complain of daily harassment from white men and youths who hang around outside their homes or bang continuously on the door. They become not only afraid to go out but frightened to stay in. Mrs A, an African woman who was beaten up by six schoolgirls, became forced to make sure that she left her maisonette at the same time as her husband in the mornings and stayed with friends and relatives all day until 4.30 when her teenage children would be back from school.[4] It is often thought that racist attacks on women are of a minor nature but there is not much difference in the actual types of attacks faced by Black women and Black men. The difference is that Black women and girls are more likely to face the brunt of attacks and are attacked by white women, girls and boys, as well as by men.[5] It is also thought that only Asian women suffer these attacks, but as the incidents mentioned throughout this essay will show, this is a fallacy.

Police Response

The lack of police response to racist attacks has been documented since the fifties and stands in its own right as an indictment of police racism. Black people see it in the context of their experience of police investigations of crimes where they themselves are suspected, which is that no stone is left unturned in police investigation.[6] In recent years, police forces have claimed to be doing more to tackle racist violence. But the Greenwich Action Committee Against Racist Attacks (GACARA) and Newham Monitoring Project (NMP) report a consistent failure by police to take racist attacks seriously; it is difficult to avoid the interpretation that this is because they view them through a lens of their own racism. Time and again, victims of racist attacks report that the Metropolitan Police take a long time to arrive, do not take attacks seriously, fail to take statements (or even notes), do not seem to go out of their way to find or prosecute attackers, do not interview or chase up witnesses, do not make follow-up calls, and deny the racist motive of the attack.

Mrs V and her family suffered constant harassment from neighbours and groups of white youths around their estate. Mrs V was punched by a white woman neighbour, pushed to the ground and had a lighted cigarette thrown at her. Her daughter witnessed the attack. Rubbish was continually dumped in her garden. Her daughter was hit on the head in the street and her son was punched when he went to answer the front door.

All these incidents were reported to the police who always took a long time to arrive and played down the incidents, calling them minor neighbourly disputes. On one occasion, a police officer, told that the attacks were racist, replied, 'I'm not having any of that – it's not racist.' This was in spite of the fact that 'Pakis Out!' had been scrawled on the front door. In the case of the initial assault, the police tried their best to get Mrs V to take out a private prosecution even though the attack had been witnessed and she had clear signs of injury.[7]

Racists realize they can escape justice by presenting their action as part of a neighbour dispute. The police are resistant to accepting racism as a motive for attacks and this resistance is reflected throughout the judicial system. Mrs H struck her Black neighbour, Mrs M, and then took out a summons against her. Mrs M (who spoke no English) had actually called the police, but they took her to the magistrates' court where she believed they were acting on her behalf, but it transpired they were responding to Mrs H and taking out the summons. Mrs H's case was thrown out by the magistrates in a few minutes but her action was sufficient to deter the council from proceeding with action against the H family (in respect of whom they had received over thirty complaints) and this in turn influenced the Newham courts, who would not consider the actions of the white family as racist harassment.[8]

Nasreen Saddique and her family also suffered persistent harassment when they moved to a new house in E.15. Nasreen reports:

> Soon after we moved in, in 1982, there were kicks at the door and when we looked out there were about forty or fifty white youths outside, shouting 'Pakis!' and 'We don't want you here!', that kind of thing. My father went to the police station because we didn't have a phone then. The police came and just told the youths to go away. They went off then, but of course they just kept coming back. We had stones thrown at our house and windows broken. One stone just missed my mother's bed. The police just didn't want to know. We had minicab drivers from the business next door pissing under our door. The police say, 'We'll deal with it', but the most they do is go and talk to the people involved. And it just goes on.
>
> These people were trying so hard to get us to move away again, and sometimes it seemed as if the police were on their side. Once my brother was working on his car outside the house and a group of white youths came up and started swearing at him. We called the police and when they came, one of the youths punched my brother right in front of them. The police just took no notice. My brother gave up then.
>
> My mother is quite infirm, she suffers very badly from asthma and the continual fear and worry we were living under was aggravating her condition. On one occasion, she went to the local off-licence and some white youths spat at her. This was the only time that the police took action, and we thought they were taking some notice at last, but the result was that not only the white youths but my mother too were all bound over by the magistrates to keep the peace for a year. This was because she had been carrying milk bottles at the time and the police and the magistrates defined it as an 'inter-racial' incident.[9]

Failure to Prosecute: Excuses

Complaints of police failing to initiate a prosecution, calling a racist attack a 'common assault' rather than categorizing it as 'actual bodily harm' is made frequently. 'Common assault' is defined in the legal textbook, Archbold, as 'an act which intentionally – or possibly recklessly – causes another to apprehend immediate and unlawful violence'. 'Actual bodily harm' is defined as meaning 'some actual bodily injury'. In practice, because of the burden of proof, common assault is usually taken by the police and courts to be an incident (for example, spitting, a slap or punch) which leaves no visible marks on the body. Actual bodily harm is a blow leaving a mark of injury, no matter how slight.

The police are obliged to prosecute for actual bodily harm, which is a criminal offence. They may, but are not obliged to, prosecute for common assault.[10] Monitoring projects report that the police appear to have an unofficial policy of classifying racist assaults as common assaults, even where there is clear evidence of physical injury, and that they then refuse to prosecute.

Mrs S was attacked by three white women whilst walking to her third floor flat, carrying her baby. She was thrown down three flights of stairs, desperately trying to hold on to her baby who eventually crashed into a wall at the end of the landing. She was kicked and punched as she sought to protect her baby.

Although Mrs S was covered in bruises and her attackers were known to her, the police refused to prosecute, saying it was only a common assault. They tried to force her into taking out a private prosecution. They were patronizing and authoritarian, telling her that she should go to court, without saying why. When Mrs S asked, she was told that it would be 'for her own good'. They seemed to think that because she was an Asian woman, they could get away with it. When Mrs S stood up for herself, saying that she could not afford a private prosecution and that it was for them to initiate proceedings, they became impatient and aggressive.[11]

Another excuse for not prosecuting is that there were 'no

witnesses'. If an attack was witnessed by members of a family or friends who are also Black, the police have been known to say there were no *independent* witnesses, the racist implications of which are clear.[12]

For example, two families living on an estate were terrorized by a large gang of white youths. Rubbish and burning material was pushed through their letterbox; scaffolding pipes and bricks were thrown through their windows and there were numerous physical assaults on both families. Although the case was taken up by the Community Involvement Officer, the police insisted that they could not prosecute as there were no independent witnesses, even though an Asian shopkeeper on the estate could testify to many of the incidents.[13]

The effect of these two misrepresentations used by the police against Black people must be to exclude them from the protection of the criminal justice system. Black women may be left bearing the heaviest burden of this denial, in that they and their homes are so frequently attacked.

Through Blue Eyes: Police Racism

Over their years of monitoring racist attacks and advising those at whom they have been directed, NMP have been forced to conclude that, 'Whatever the nature of the attack and the extent of injury to the victim – even death – the police response is always the same: the presence of Black people is seen to be the root cause of the violence directed against them.' The following encounters, with their terrifying implications as to police allegiances, would seem to bear this out. An African refugee family suffered continual harassment from their neighbours culminating in one neighbour sending a written death threat and holding a gun up at a nine-year-old. The policeman who interviewed the family was hostile and returned from interviewing the neighbour saying that he couldn't see anything wrong in the letter and that the aggressor had been 'born in this country'.[14] In another case, an Afro-Caribbean woman was at home with friends when two white neighbours burst in with pitchforks and started smashing furniture. When the police arrived, they arrested one of the Black people for possession of an offensive weapon – he had picked up a small stick. Neither of the white attackers was arrested.[15]

Mrs W and her mother were sitting on a bus when white passengers got on and demanded they give up their seats. Mrs W and her mother were spat on and abused and Mrs W's hair was pulled. The bus driver stopped the bus and called the police. When they got on, they arrested Mrs W and took her to Woolwich police station and charged her with using offensive language. No attempt was made to arrest the racists.[16]

When Mrs G, who suffered attack after attack after she and her family moved to Canning Town, reported an incident to the police, she was told that 'things like that happen in Canning Town'. After the front door of her home was kicked down in 1982, Mrs G suffered a nervous breakdown.[17]

In June 1986, the home of the R family in E.6 was petrol-bombed. Neighbours heard two explosions and, seeing the house ablaze, called the emergency services. Pieces of milk bottle were removed from the wreckage, yet police officers asked neighbours if there had been any 'inter-racial' trouble in the road. The next day they suggested to one resident that the attack had been the result of an 'arranged marriage'. This was the fourth attack in the same road but the police still refused to take positive action to identify and arrest the attackers.[18]

Frighteningly, these instances also demonstrate the seeming inability of many police officers to recognize Black women and men as the victims rather than the perpetrators of crime. It is difficult to avoid the impression that police stereotype Black people as offenders, when the victims of racial assault are arrested and the perpetrators of these crimes walk free. The police response to Black women complainants may be compounded not only, as illustrated above, by racist sexual stereotyping but by sexual and physical abuse. Black women are aware of what happened to Mrs Groce and to Mrs Jarrett in their own homes and this, coupled with the apparent futility of making complaints, makes many women too frightened and too pessimistic to call in the police, even when harassment reaches an extreme level.

Even worse, monitoring organizations report an increasing number of serious assaults on Black individuals by police officers themselves, including a brutal attack on a sixteen-year-old girl who was being held in a police station. This girl was picked on by a police officer in the street and taken after a struggle, to the police station. When she asked, 'what for?', she was told, 'we'll think of something'. She was called a 'black bitch' and 'black whore', and at the station she was tripped up and sat on. Her hair was pulled and her head was banged, and one officer tried to put his hand up her skirt. When she left the police station, she could hardly walk, and was found on examination by a doctor to have serious internal injuries. She was later charged, in a characteristically pre-emptive manner, with assaulting a police officer and using threatening behaviour.[19]

The Harris Crime Survey, commissioned by Newham Council and carried out in the summer of 1986, revealed that only 5 per cent of racist attacks were reported to the police and that three-quarters of Black residents felt that it was they who were on the receiving end of police discrimination.[20]

When Black women decide whether to call in the police, they have to weigh up the urgency of their need to protect themselves against their awareness of police hostility to Black people, and the forms which it takes against Black women in particular. They will be aware of the way Black women are criminalized in their homes as are Black men on the streets, of Multi-Agency Policing as surveillance of the Black community, of racist immigration questioning, of drug raids on social centres and homes and the targeting of Black estates, of the aggressive confrontational policing of Black demonstrations. They will have in mind the possibility of being strip-searched in a police station. They will remember the number of deaths of Black men in police custody.

The Kelly Hayre Case

On 7 November 1985, Kalbinder Kaur Hayre (Kelly to her friends), a young Asian girl walking home from Dartford College with two girlfriends, was killed when a transit van with five white youths inside was driven onto the pavement and crushed her against a wall. She immediately lost consciousness and, two weeks later, her family had to decide to turn off her life-support machine. The youths had run away, leaving Kelly trapped, and passers-by had had to use ropes to free her. Eventually the youths were arrested.

The van's driver was not charged. The police told the family that he had been 'dealt with' for drinking offences. However, at the time of the incident, the police had stated that there was no evidence that he had been drinking when he was breathalyzed. Later, the police informed the family that the driver had been acquitted of drinking offences arising out of the incident. One of the front seat passengers was charged with manslaughter. The driver had told the police that this passenger had seized the wheel and forced the van in the direction of the girls after saying, 'Let's give them a fright.' In court he denied this. At the start of the trial, the judge directed the jury not to consider the question of 'race' in the proceedings. This passenger was not found guilty.

For the Hayre family and Kelly's friends, the verdict came as yet another devastating blow.

Recent Events: Promises and Provocation

The Metropolitan Commissioner, Peter Imbert, has said that he will make racist attacks a policing priority. So did Kenneth Newman before him. In 1985, NMP found that police took action in only 7 per cent of the cases they dealt with, a figure which made such statements and the assurance given by senior officers at various local police stations, look weak, to say the least.

Recently there have been professed changes in police policies in dealing with racist attacks. A Metropolitan police mandate of July 1987 instructs officers to prosecute automatically in the case of any 'racial incident' in which an assault has occurred, instead of telling the victims to take civil action. But the Attorney General's guidelines for the prosecution of racist attacks still require a standard of proof which is artificially high.

The police have set up Racial Harassment Units in Newham and Ealing, and specific procedures have been set up under them to record racist attacks. Between February and April 1987 the police mounted pioneer racial harassment campaign schemes in Newham and Ealing to encourage people to report attacks. They distributed 100,000 leaflets in Asian languages and, during this period, the number of attacks reported to them increased almost 100 per cent; yet the percentage of people prosecuted did not increase.[21]

The police are still reluctant to provide support for a particular family under incessant threat, or to patrol an area where attacks are occurring regularly. NMP have asked for this sort of intervention fifty times and the police have responded on only six occasions. Their excuse is lack of resources. This might seem more acceptable if it were not a response occurring within the context of significant police expenditure on operations which harass Black people on the street and in clubs, pubs, and even in private homes.

In spite of the repeal of the 'sus' laws, young Black people are still targeted for questioning and searching on the street, and massive police raids are mounted on Black venues on the pretext of looking for cannabis. For example, up to 150 officers, some armed, were deployed in a raid on Bentley's nightclub in Newham in 1986. This was criticized as sensationalist overkill tactics by the Chair of Newham Police Committee Support Unit, who concluded:

> Given the relative poverty of the haul (i.e. a few knives, a hammer or two and cannabis) it appears this raid was more of a morale and public relations booster for the local police rather than a serious exercise in policing.

This raid occurred near an estate where the police had failed to provide basic protection for Asian families who were victims of racist attacks.

At 11.15 p.m. on 5 June 1988 fifty police surrounded a house in Plaistow where some Black people were holding a christening party, insisting all guests leave. One young man who explained that he was staying because it was his girlfriend's flat was grabbed in a stranglehold and arrested. Three other young men were arrested when they objected. All four were dragged to the lift and racially abused; their heads were bashed against the walls and they were forced to lie on the floor of the police vans they were taken away in. They all now face charges of assault and obstruction.

Can the police really justify spending thousands of pounds on such raids in this context? There is also the factor of the media attention the police acquire as a result of such activities. In the same way, police characteristically release their own interpretations of racist attacks to the media. It is such actions which make NMP view police community policing initiatives and their attempt to co-opt the community into a consultative forum as hypocritical.[22]

Racist harassment and attacks are increasing. If responsive policing does not change, more and more Black women and girls will be harassed, abused and assaulted on the streets and in their homes, partly because the effect of police attitudes is that racists get away with it.

Notes

1. Newham Monitoring Project, Annual Report, 1985.
2. Newham Monitoring Project, Bulletin, 1986.
3. Greenwich Action Committee against Racist Attacks, Annual Report, 1987.
4. ibid.
5. ibid.
6. Newham Monitoring Project, Annual Report, 1987.
7. Greenwich Action Committee against Racist Attacks, Annual Report, 1987.
8. Newham Monitoring Project, Annual Report, 1987.

9. Interview with Nasreen Saddique, 21 July 1987.

10. Greenwich Action Committee Against Racist Attacks, Annual Report, 1987.

11. ibid.

12. ibid.

13. ibid.

14. ibid.

15. ibid.

16. ibid.

17. *Spare Rib*, January 1988. Liz Fekete's article was based on *Policing against Black People*. Institute of Race Relations, London, 1987.

18. Newham Monitoring Project, Annual Report, 1985.

19. Newham Monitoring Project, Bulletin, 1986.

20. Newham Monitoring Project, Annual Report, 1987.

21. Newham Monitoring Project, Annual Report, 1987.

22. ibid.

Newham Monitoring Project publications are available from: Newham Monitoring Project, 382 Katherine Road, Forest Gate, London E7 8NW

Greenwich Action Committee against Racist Attacks publications are available from: GACARA, First Floor, 78 Sandy Hill Road, Woolwich, London SE18 7AZ

7. Police and the Professionalization of Rape

Sara Scott and Alison Dickens

'Every woman has the right to be safe. We ought to be able to go wherever we want and do whatever we choose.'

This is not a quote from the feminist press, but the opening line of a video on women's safety introduced in 1987 by the Metropolitan Police.[1] Feminist rhetoric has filtered through to places where it has never been heard before, and the police are making statements promising widespread improvements in their treatment of women reporting rape.

So why aren't we celebrating? Firstly, because we suspect the proposed changes are more of a public relations exercise than symptomatic of real progress. And secondly, in a Tory era of 'post-feminism', it seems unlikely that our ideas could be having a major impact in such a traditionally misogynist quarter.

The police are not creators of ideology and it is therefore essential to examine their initiatives within a wider context. The scale and importance of the problem of rape is gaining widespread acceptance. However, the increasing interest of the government, media, medical profession and police is not directed to the perpetrators of the crime or to the causes of rape – the aspects most crucial in a feminist analysis – but rather to the 'victim' and the impact of rape on her life. Having acknowledged the long-term effects that rape can have, the authorities jointly insist on the necessity of 'expert' intervention, which undermines the feminist insistence that women regain control over their own lives and which ignores years of work by Rape Crisis Centres. Against this background, their establishment's interpretation of caring looks like just another form of social control.

We Asked For It

Early in 1982 an episode of the BBC series 'Police' showed a live police interrogation of a woman reporting a rape. The origins of the current wave of police concern about the treatment of rape cases by police officers can probably be located in the public outcry which followed this display of 'unmitigated toughness' and 'low-key brutality' as it was described by the *Guardian* (19 January 1982). The programme clearly demonstrated to the public what women already feared: that if they reported rape, they would not be believed.

In immediate response, various police forces issued public statements. They were sometimes as tellingly contradictory as these two statements in a speech by James Anderton, Chief Constable of the Greater Manchester Police: 'I want to assure the authority and the public that the Greater Manchester Police has always been very sensitive to the problems of women *involved* in this awful crime' (our italics). He added, 'It is quite extraordinary the extent to which complaints are made which prove to be wholly unfounded'.[2] By early 1983 the Home Office had updated its guidelines on police treatment of women reporting rape. They recommended that investigating officers exercise tact and understanding in an atmosphere of care and concern. They also recommended that women should be informed of relevant local services and kept up to date about subsequent legal proceedings. In spite of emphasizing the pre-eminence of ungendered compassion, the guidelines acknowledged that *some* women might prefer to be interviewed or examined by another woman. However, given that these guidelines upheld the popular belief that women make false allegations of rape, they look more like a male response to the problem of hysterical women – from whom, moreover, the police are obliged to get factual information (in the form of statements) – than a genuine re-evaluation of police practice.

The police have always been obsessed with the problem of false allegation, a problem which arises as much from a patriarchal view of women as lying, devious and vengeful toward men, as from the exigencies of the criminal justice system. The vast majority of reported rapes in Britain still never surmount this first obstacle of police suspicion.

Softly, Softly Task Force

> The emphasis is on the needs of the victim and the new measures are designed to make her feel as comfortable as possible in what is always a distressing situation. (Metropolitan Police Press Release)

An obsession with 'sensitivity' and nice surroundings seems to inform much of the new policy strategy. For example, West Midlands nominated eleven hospitals to designate special areas for the treatment of rape victims, while the Met proposed setting up 'rape suites' throughout the region:

> The police examination suites have a comfortable sitting room, a medical examination room and a bathroom, where you can have a bath or shower after the medical examination. Replacement clothing is available, also personal toiletries such as combs, toothbrushes, shampoo, talcum powder, flannels and bath towels. (Metropolitan Police, publicity leaflet)

> Each one is decorated in pastel colours and designed to provide a mood of relaxation. (*Guardian*, 25 January 1985)

Other initiatives include the use of Victim Support Scheme volunteers to provide aftercare for women, and 'enhanced [police] training to guarantee a sympathetic approach' from the senior officers investigating rape and the women police constables designated to take initial statements.[3]

Women police officers have traditionally fulfilled what are designated 'caring' roles within the police force, and this has recently been exploited to the full. Thames Valley, noting the 'embarrassment involved in [a woman] giving intimate details to a man'[4] set up an all-female rape squad; the Met strategically deployed 121 WPCs 'chosen for their compassion, sympathy, tolerance and empathy' throughout the district.[5] The deployment of WPCs or women police surgeons to rape cases does not necessarily mean that the police have taken on feminist points of view. It is in fact perfectly consistent with a patriarchal view of women. The problem is not that the new police initiatives bear *no* relation to what feminists have been arguing for since the early seventies. We have repeatedly pointed to the attitudes of contempt and lack of concern which women have been shown by police, and the lack of facilities at police stations. We have exposed the obligation faced by many women wishing to pursue a complaint at an understaffed station to be questioned by a male police officer and/or examined by a male police doctor.

We therefore welcome the provision of showers and comfortable chairs and the greater involvement of women police officers. However, these practical improvements do not address the main problem, which centres around the unwillingness of the police to believe women reporting rape.

Pressure on the police to do something to improve the reportage rate for rape and sexual assault continues through the 1980s. In 1985, Police Authorities were claiming that the sensitive approach was already encouraging more women to report.[6] However, as Scotland Yard admitted, they were unable to say whether 'the figures reflected an increase in the number of women coming forward, or simply a greater readiness by investigating officers to record each complaint as a rape.'[7] The *Woman's Own* survey published in 1986 found that the vast majority of women who are raped still do not report to the police. They found that 76 per cent of women who are raped do not report to the police and only 45 per cent of those who do report once would do so a second time.

By 1986 the Home Office Guidelines directed that a clear distinction be made between the recording of *unsubstantiated* and *false* complaints, thus acknowledging the difference between lack of evidence, a woman's unwillingness to pursue a rape complaint, and the making of a false accusation. Previously all complaints not pursued were recorded as 'no crime' i.e. no distinction was made between a 'false allegation' (a lie) and an allegation which a woman chose to drop for any reason, or which was dropped because there was insufficient evidence to take the man to court. Consequently, police officers tended to believe that there were a lot more false allegations (seen as a waste of police time) than there actually were. Making this distinction in recording practices is important firstly because it affects the way police view rape complaints in general; and secondly, because we can now get statistics proving that only a tiny minority of unpursued cases are in fact false allegations.

Feminists have always argued that the unwillingness of the police to believe rape complainants is central to the problem. It is a point the police have been slow to accept, but in a recent book by policeman Ian Blair, it is argued that ridding themselves of the idea that women lie about rape is in the police's own interests.[8] As work in the United States has shown, such a change in attitude improves the quality of evidence and ultimately increases the number of convictions.[9] If there were a police initiative which might represent the possibility of genuine change, this would be it.

We feel the change in recording practice resulted from bad press and public pressure about the low reporting rate for rape, and not from a fundamental change in police attitudes. Moreover, the change can be used by the police as a way of 'cooking the books' to show that their new initiatives are making more women report. In fact, it could well be that the *same* number of women are reporting but that some cases which would previously have been consigned to the 'no crime' file now appear as unsubstantiated rape reports.

We suggest that the changes in police policy and practice amount to a public relations exercise which has concealed the police's failure to make the fundamental changes in attitude that would undermine the institutionalized sexism and racism within the police force. Besides, the Guidelines carry no guarantee of implementation and there has been no indication that action might be taken against police officers not following them.

Medicalization

In the late nineteenth century medical experts and the gutter press 'helped to create and maintain a belief in the lying, imagining, hysterical and malicious rape complainant',[10] and this stereotype endured. In the 1960s, when the emphasis on female chastity was declining, the effects of rape on a woman were taken even less seriously. Rape became unwanted sex, a cost of sexual liberation on a level with abortion or divorce, and one which women were expected to 'get over' in much the same way.

From the beginning of the modern Women's Liberation Movement in the early seventies, feminists have fought for rape to be regarded as a serious crime and for recognition of its meaning and impact on all women. It was feminists who first exploded the myth that most rapes are committed by strangers in dark alleys. We argued, as we still argue, that the idea of a society in which most men protected women from a few sex-starved maniacs was a lie. We understood that all men benefit from women's fear of rape. We pointed out that women whose perceptions of previously loved and trusted men (and of men in general) changed dramatically as a result of rape were not going mad, as they so often feared, but were simply beginning to see through one of patriarchy's most fundamental deceptions. For the most part, we have been ignored.

When the medical profession began to concentrate on rape, their analysis, focusing on the woman as 'victim', became paramount. For we were not the only people to recognize the common patterns in women's responses to rape. By the mid seventies, psychologists and psychiatrists in the United States had begun to take an interest in rape and had given these responses a name: Rape Trauma Syndrome. They noted the feeling of disbelief that so many women experience, their withdrawal from and distrust of men, and their difficulty in returning to 'normal' heterosexual relationships. They began to claim that their expertise was essential in enabling women to deal with the after-effects of rape. We described the same 'symptoms', but while we stated that the change in a woman's perceptions of the world was a realistic response, and saw our role as enabling her to make sense of her new understandings, therapists claimed that the change was a result of trauma and that they could 'cure' her.

Over the last few years, there has been an unprecedented growth in professional interest in identifying, classifying and treating both victims and perpetrators of rape and child sexual abuse. Although it has largely been admitted that rapists cannot be identified by the distance between their eyes or the dirtiness of their mackintoshes, psychologists, unlike feminists, still claim to be able to identify features which both set them apart from normal men and allow for the possibility of individual cure. However, the real focus of interest has been on the trauma of girls and women who have experienced assault, and its treatment.

The Sexual Assault Referral Centre (SARC) which opened at St Mary's Hospital, Manchester in 1987 (much heralded as the first of its kind in the country) is a joint initiative between Greater Manchester Police and South Manchester Area Health Authority. The following quotes show something of the competing purposes those involved wish the Centre to serve:

> We hope the centre will dispel unwarranted scepticism about Police procedure. (Robin Thornton, GMP Press Officer)

> [The counsellors at the centre] will attempt to persuade the women to formally report the matters to the police. (Minutes of visit to SARC by Manchester Community Health Council Community Care Review Group)

> Will the police be involved? Only if you want them to be. You will be put under no pressure to report the incident to the police. (SARC publicity leaflet, 1987)

The centre offers the ubiquitous 'pleasant surroundings': showers, full-time nurse counsellors, women police surgeons on call who offer pregnancy and VD follow-up as well as the 'morning after pill' and WPCs to take initial statements and psychiatric referral:

> If you have been assaulted or raped either recently or in the past, the Centre's trained counsellors will help you overcome any trauma you may have experienced as a result of the attack. The counsellors will continue to help you for as long as necessary to help you recover from the assault and become a survivor rather than a victim. (SARC publicity leaflet, 1987)

As these initial statements from police and Centre show, feminist words and phrases have been incorporated in the publicity, but without the politics which underpin them.

Feminist counselling is increasingly being dismissed by references to the need for 'trained professionals'. It has even been said that it is a sad reflection on our society that something so important could have been left in our hands for so long:

> Professional bodies have done hardly anything to help the victims of violent crime, especially victims of sexual assault and it has been left to self-help groups to do the little that has been done.
> Organizations such as Rape Crisis Centres have been set up because the professions have failed the public in this respect.[11]

The significance of reporting rape to a hospital rather than a police station lies in its contribution to the emerging reconstruction of rape as a medical rather than a political problem. But the powerless, feminized victim is not an image we wish to see become any more prevalent.

The various medical responses to the problems of women who have been raped are intent on getting women back to 'normal'. At a time when the 'natural order' of marriage and the family are being reasserted by the Right, the popularity of these medical responses to rape is not surprising. And it allows us to see the new police initiatives, which are sometimes presented as conscientious responses to feminist criticisms, within the context of a thorough reworking of ideology around rape.

Right-Wing Views of Rape

It looks as if the subject of rape no longer belongs exclusively to feminists. We have shown that it occupies a significant place in the power relations between men and women. Others, recognizing the truth of our observation, but rejecting our revolutionary conclusions have begun to pay serious attention to a subject that was once shrouded in silence. The new interest of right-wing ideologists in the subject of rape emanates from two related sources: the first and most straightforward, is the overall emphasis on law and order and the right of the majority of law-abiding citizens to be protected from 'criminal elements'. Outdated notions of the protection of the weaker sex and a 'manly' desire for the punishment of violators of women have helped to popularize the government's concentration on law and order. The second source is anti-feminism and the subjugation of women within traditional sex roles. The New Right has a profoundly anti-feminist stance. In their enthusiasm for the 'traditional' family and rigid sex roles, they make much of abuses against women. The sanctity of the family demands that rape is a serious crime because sex is a serious business, or ought to be.

The Right's ideology of 'separate spheres' (implicit in traditional family roles) may well mean stiffer sentences for rapists, and a new and chivalrous attention to women as victims. However, the result is not an end to rape but the reinforcement of women's helplessness and the stabilization of the family within a law-and-order society, in which the police have a prime role.

Placing the new police initiatives within the context of the medicalization of rape allows us to see that services for women who have been raped are now a contested area in which professionals are competing for control, a process which invariably results in the marginalization of feminist understandings. At best we become bumbling do-gooders, at worst fanatical brainwashers. Either way we are seen as in danger of doing more harm than good. The existence in Manchester of a 'respectable' alternative to feminist services threatens the very existence of funded rape crisis work.

The Media and the New Charities

The media has a well established role in the creation and dissemination of myths about rape, and its most recent priority has been to display the devastating after-effects of rape and child abuse on people's lives.

Problems adopted by the media are usually individualized and sensationalized, and in the cases of rape and child abuse, this treatment accords with the depoliticized version of the problem beloved of the different 'experts' now claiming it as their own. The portrayal of individual tragedies undermines even quite radical conclusions. The *Woman's Own* survey on rape 'that every woman should read and no man can ignore', found that most women knew their attackers and that women failed to report rape primarily through fear of disbelief, but their presentation of the problem continues to dramatize and individualize its effect on women:

> For the last 47 years she might just as well have been dead. Ever since that moment her life has been wrecked. She has been filled with panic each time the door bell rings or the wind rattles the windows of her tiny one-bedroomed flat. There have been no smiles or laughs in those 47 years, just the constant fear that it could happen again.[12]

The media has always adopted and discarded issues with alarming regularity. What has changed in recent years is that its dabblings in subjects such as Aids, drugs and child sexual abuse have been reinforced by state campaigns and direct charitable interventions. Both charity itself and the issues with which it is concerned, have been given a trendy new image.

The new charitable initiatives are using a vocabulary of words and images of vulnerability and helplessness which run entirely counter to the feminist emphasis on women's strength and survival. In the case of Esther Rantzen's 'Childwatch' and 'Childline', the media has taken upon itself not only to expose a problem but also to provide a solution. Predictably, there has been no acknowledgment of the role of the women's movement in first raising public consciousness about child sexual abuse or in providing counselling and support services. In the professional and media rush to answer public concern, feminism is written out; only the experts count. The media's faith in doctors and therapists who will verify the seriousness of the problem, while offering neat and tidy personal solutions and absolving men of responsibility is no accident.

Where Now?

Some of the aspects of police practice which have been most heavily criticized by feminists over the last fifteen years appear to be changing. At the same time, our analysis of rape is under direct attack. In many parts of the country, police forces are collaborating with Home Office funded Victim Support Schemes to train rape counsellors and thereby provide an alternative to Rape Crisis Lines (RCLs). At the same time, the medical profession is claiming that only within its ranks can the skills be found to deal with anything as serious as Rape Trauma. For many RCLs, these changes could lead directly to cuts in funding.

In relation to rape, we think it is unlikely that there will be a backlash equivalent to that which took place in the Cleveland controversy around child sexual abuse. As far as child abuse was concerned, the reaction of Stuart Bell MP and others was that of defending the 'ordinary' man and his family against professional intrusion. However non-feminist Esther Rantzen's approach, the simple acknowledgement of the scale of the problem made it impossible for society to avoid some uncomfortable conclusions about the role of 'ordinary' men in family life. The new attention to rape does not necessitate a similar re-evaluation. The public has always known about rape. That rape is more common than previously believed can be accepted without challenging the myth of rapists as sick individuals. 'Ordinary' men stay clean.

The previously dominant definition of rape as an issue of crime and punishment left the field free for feminists to define the response of women who had been raped; because no one else was interested. With the reconstruction of rape in medical terms, and the growing concentration on the 'victim' by police and media, our territory is being usurped. If we wish to maintain any place in the debate we must start fighting on the new front this change represents – naturally keeping an ever-distrustful eye on police practice.

Notes

1. 'Positive Steps', video on women's safety, Metropolitan Police, 1987.

2. *Rochdale Observer*, 10 February 1982.

3. Thelma Wagstaff, Chair of Metropolitan Police Working Party on force procedure on rape, 'The Job' (Metropolitan Police internal paper), 25 January 1985.

4. D.C.I. Brian Warren, *Daily Mail*, 2 June 1982.

5. *Police Review*, July 1985.

6. *Woman's Own* rape survey, 23 August 1986.

7. *Guardian*, 31 July 1985.

8. Ian Blair, *Investigating Rape, a New Approach*, 1985.

9. Harry J. O'Reilly, *Perspectives on Rape and Sexual Assault*, ed. June Hopkins, Harper & Row, London, 1984.

10. Susan Edwards, *Female Sexuality and the Law*, Robertson, Oxford, 1981.

11. Raine E. Roberts in *The New Police Surgeon*, ed. W.D.S. McLay, Northampton Association of Police Surgeons, 1983.

12. *Woman's Own* rape survey, 23 August 1986.

8. Helen's Story*

Child Sexual Abuse and the Law

Christina Dunhill

Helen has been abused and terrorized by her father since she was three. He not only raped her himself but sold her to other men for sexual purposes. He was, and probably still is, one of the central figures in a vice ring of child abusers operating at home, on the streets and in a rented house. Helen's childhood and early teenage years were a nightmare of physical and psychological violence caused by the man who should have loved and protected her as his daughter, the man she loved as a father. Not only sex, but sadistic rituals were involved. However, Helen's father is seen as a respectable family man and a pillar of the community; to this day, he has never been to prison for what he has done.

Helen was already putting out distress signals at school. She had become distracted and inattentive. She was constantly fainting and appearing in school with cuts and bruises. Between the ages of eleven and thirteen she was in and out of the local hospital's casualty department ten times. Once she appeared with a cut across her throat after her father's friend had 'taught her a lesson' as to what he'd do if she ever told what was happening. Nobody questioned her at school or at the hospital. This was happening in the late seventies, not long ago, but before child abuse had the public profile it has developed more recently. She began to mutilate herself. When she was

---

* This story is based on an interview with a young survivor of sexual abuse and her friend who works as a psychotherapist. All identities have been disguised.

twelve, she cut herself seriously and her father seized the opportunity to take her to the police station (so that in his first contact with the police as regards his daughter, he would appear as a caring parent – as well as making sure she gave nothing away). Because she could not face the truth nor bring herself to betray her father Helen told the police she had been attacked by a gang of masked men. They let her go.

One Christmas Eve, she bought two packets of razorblades and went into a field and cut her arms and legs open: 'A man found me. Now I thank him for saving my life but then it wouldn't have mattered to me if I'd bled to death.' She was taken to hospital, where a social worker visited her and told her they wouldn't let her home till she told them what was wrong. Helen told them her uncle was abusing her at home. She was unable to say anything about her father. She was taken into a children's home. Her father visited her that evening and pleaded with her to say nothing about him.

Two policewomen came to see her the next day. Helen was extremely distressed and could not stop crying throughout the interview. One of them, WPC A, was kind and supportive; the other, WPC B, was aggressive and hostile. Obviously, the police had the earlier incident on record and suspected Helen of being an unreliable witness, a liar. Helen was desperate to protect herself but extremely disturbed and terrified of what would happen if she gave her father away. He had said he would kill her, if she told, and she had no reason to disbelieve him. She didn't dare tell the truth; she couldn't even face this herself. Instead she told them about her uncle and she told them some 'stories'.

It is common for girls who have been severely abused to do this. Attitudes to the truth are therefore crucial in child abuse cases. A child must be believed when she reports abuse; when she tells a wild story, the signs should be 'read', not dismissed as conventional lying. Obviously, this is an area of extreme sensitivity and conflict in police investigations.

On this occasion, WPC B moved threateningly close to Helen and frightened her with aggressive questioning. But WPC A was comforting. She 'believed' Helen. She had already been suspicious about Helen's father from his behaviour in the earlier episode and had told her colleagues about her suspicions, but they didn't believe her. Subsequently, she visited Helen in her off-duty hours and was then dismissed from the case for becoming too involved.

Helen's uncle was brought to trial and given an eighteen month sentence after he pleaded guilty. In mitigation, the court accepted that he was under strain because his wife had left him, taking their children with her.

It was not until Helen went home on a day visit that she was able to tell anyone anything about her father. He had come home in his lunch hour and abused her. She had told him that when she got back to the children's home she would tell. He gave her a bottle of pills. 'He knew if he gave me a bottle of tablets, I was going to take them.' She took them an hour later. She was found in time and taken to hospital where she told the nuns she didn't ever want to go home again. They told a social worker and Helen's father was arrested the next day.

From this time, Helen gave evidence to the police about her father and about the other men who had abused her. As a result six men were convicted of rape and indecent assault. All pleaded guilty. Helen's father was not among them. Instead, he was put on remand by the court and made to report to the police station every month for a year. At the end of this time the case against him was dismissed in court for lack of evidence.

At the same time as Helen was giving evidence in the cases of rape and sexual assault brought against her father and the other men, she had to go to court to give evidence against her father in a care hearing, so that two of her sisters could go into a children's home. Since the investigation had begun, they had been staying with an aunt. In open court, Helen's father's barrister called her a liar and a thief. She said that Helen was promiscuous and made up stories as a cover-up. Helen had no right of reply to these accusations. As in all rape and child abuse criminal cases, Helen was only a witness for the prosecution whose evidence the defence needed to undermine. The prosecution barrister was appointed by the social services and Helen had never met him before, so she had to listen to slurs on her character with no defence barrister acting for her to rebut them. On the other hand, her father was not required to listen in court to the detailed allegations made against him by his other daughters in camera. Helen was so angry that she called out to her father's barrister to get him into court to hear the allegations, and was rebuked by the judge. She told the judge to 'stuff his court up his arse' and ran out of the courtroom.

Although this hearing was successful, in that her sisters were given places in a children's home for three years, Helen left the courtroom feeling that, like the police station, it was a place where she would be further abused. All the authorities seemed to believe her father rather than her. She felt as if she had no one on her side and gave no more evidence to the police. She felt her estrangement from her family acutely in spite of everything that had happened. She concentrated on forming relationships at the children's home where four counsellors were working with her. She was not allowed calls from either of her parents.

When Helen was eighteen, she became ineligible to remain in the children's home. She was offered a flat but felt too much at risk to take up the offer and live on her own in her home town. She went to a conference on child abuse, where she met Mary, a consultant psychotherapist specializing in child abuse, with whom she became friendly. Helen now lives with Mary and her daughter at a considerable distance from her home town, having counselling from someone outside the family. Helen felt safe enough to visit home a year later for New Year. She arrived home on 2 January, at about 11.00 in the morning thinking that her father would be at work but he was at home. He raped her. Her mother and one of her sisters were still in bed; the other two sisters were out. When her father left for work, Helen told her mother, who just turned over in bed away from her. She 'couldn't' hear.

Later, her two sisters came home for lunch and the family (apart from the father) were together in the kitchen. There was a knock at the door and one of the sisters answered. She called out to Helen, 'You're wanted at the door'. There were two men there. They told her to go with them and drove her to a house where they raped and violated her. Helen realized that her father must have told them at work that she was home and sent them round. (Helen's father was always careful not to be the only one who abused her — so there would be no conclusive evidence.) When she got home, she was bleeding but nobody said anything. Her mother did not want to know; she had become dependent on drugs rather than face the reality of the situation. They had all entered a conspiracy from fear generated by her father; they were unable to 'see' what was happening. Half an hour later, her sisters took her to the bus stop and she went to spend the evening at an old people's home where she used to work. She could not bear to report to the local police again.

After she returned to her new home and told Mary what had happened, they reported the incident to the police. This time the police concerned were a policewomen's unit in Mary's local town and this was the beginning of a totally different experience of police evidence gathering and interviewing. The policewoman who interviewed Helen always deferred to Mary, to ask her permission to question her or proceed with a line of questioning. She let Helen break down without interruption and she made space for Mary to give her some support as the need arose because she was so severely distressed. Most importantly, she made Helen feel she was believed. She was completely objective; she was doing her job but she was sensitive to Helen and supportive of her at the same time. The next day, when Helen returned to the station to sign her statement on the way back from hospital, the policewoman gave her a bunch of flowers. 'These are for you after all you've been through,' she said.

But nothing had changed when the report was made back to Helen's local police station and they took up the investigation. Two local officers, both of whom she had every reason to distrust from before, WPC B and a male officer, PC D, travelled to where she now lived to interview her. They questioned her anew and at length on everything she had already made a statement about to the policewomen's unit, which the unit had passed on to them. They behaved as if they were suspicious and hostile and fired questions at her continuously. They professed disbelief in all her evidence because she couldn't name the two men or say where the house was. To cap it all, they said 'You don't look very happy. Wouldn't you be happier back home?'

Helen's father was arrested and detained twelve hours for questioning. The rest of the family were also interviewed and they all rallied round him. They had invented a completely different story (in line with her father's attempted portrayal of his daughter as a slut and a troublemaker). They said that Helen had wanted to go into town but they had stopped her in case she got into trouble, that nobody had called at the house and Helen hadn't left the house except when she went with her sisters to the bus stop. In common with many families of abusers, they had chosen private fear and suffering as preferable to public humiliation.

The local police demanded that Helen go back home for further questioning. When she held back because she was so frightened of them, as well as of returning to her home town, WPC B threatened her with arrest for holding back evidence. Helen became extremely distressed. Mary was away on business. Eventually, Helen agreed to go on the understanding that she could take somebody with her, be met by an old friend from the children's home at the train station and return the same evening.

Finally, after Mary returned, she and Helen were able to agree conditions with the local police for another harrowing round of interviewing. Mary would accompany Helen and be present at all times. WPC B would not be present at all and WPC A would meet them and be present at the interviews too. Helen and Mary caught the train, WPC A met them at the station and there was a warm reunion between Helen and the policewoman who had believed her from the beginning. However, as soon as they got to the police station, WPC A was whisked away and Helen and Mary never saw her again.

The interrogation began in Inspector E's office. He fired questions at Helen about the statement she had given to the policewomen's unit. The two other officers who had travelled to interview her joined them, WPC B and PC D. Although this meant that the local police had now broken their promise, Helen and Mary agreed to continue. They drove out with the police officers to try to find the house where Helen had been taken on 2 January – the house the abusers ring used. Helen was unable to identify it. There was a terrible atmosphere in the car. The officers all behaved as if they believed Helen was lying; not being able to find the house clinched it.

When they returned, Inspector E continued with the investigation alone. He subjected Helen to a barrage of questions, cutting her off from her answer to each question as soon as she had started it and asking another. It was an aggressive questioning technique designed to confuse. When Mary protested, he turned his attention on her, using another technique of professed exasperation, implying that he was a reasonable man whose patience and credulity had been stretched too far. Mary told him he was to treat her with respect or she would leave. He looked at her condescendingly: 'Tell me the truth, she's mentally deranged isn't she?' he said. Mary accused him of wanting to call Helen mad because he didn't want to believe what she was saying. He became angry and accused her of believing anything anybody said. 'This house,' he said, 'it doesn't exist, does it?' (Helen's account to the police had revolved around the house where she was taken by the two men who abused her. She maintained that this house was habitually used for child abuse by the ring of abusers.) Mary then became furious at his attitude, which made her feel totally frustrated and outraged. She also became seriously professionally concerned when she thought about the effect such questioning would have in the majority of child abuse cases, where a young girl would be questioned in a police station hours after the abuse had taken place – instead of six weeks later, as was the case with Helen, who had also already received support and counselling. Mary challenged him. 'How can you make out she's a liar when six men were convicted on her evidence? She wasn't a liar then, she's not a liar now. It's always the same with sexual abuse and rape. The victim's put on the defensive; it's up to her to prove it. And by the very nature of the crime, it's in private. But here you've got a situation where it isn't, there's a group of men involved. How did those two men know she was there?' Inspector E just said, 'What two men?', implying that the story was a fabrication.

So far as Helen and Mary know, the investigation has now been abandoned because Helen could not identify the house which would have enabled the local police to raid the ring. The ring of men presumably continues to abuse children and trade in child violation. Helen believes her father continues to abuse one of her sisters. Helen herself has been alienated once again from the local police who are the only agency who can initiate bringing her father and the other men involved to justice – a private prosecution being out of the question to victims who have no financial independence. She will have to weigh her self-preservation carefully against further co-operation with them.

Helen's experience with the policewomen's unit suggests that the police aim of collecting evidence need not be incompatible with care and support of the victim. Helen's experience shows that it is clearly not the case that all WPCs are good at dealing with child abuse cases. But it may be that the organization of a unit staffed entirely by women, and the fact that the policewomen involved have all chosen to work with women and children, has something to do with their more satisfactory approach.

But Helen's local police appeared to believe that it is only through hostile, aggressive and bewildering interrogation of the victim that they can arrive at the truth. This technique is entirely inappropriate for girls who have been sexually abused and are already physically and psychologically traumatized. They become casualties, while sexual abusers benefit. In Helen's own words, 'They just treat you as if you're the one who's done wrong. There's no way if you've been to them once, you'll ever want to go to them again.'

Part 2

Up Against It:
Women on the Receiving End of Police Powers

9. The Boys in Blue

Christina Dunhill

> To the outside observer, one of the outstanding characteristics of
> the police force is that it is like a club in which people are expected
> to share certain assumptions and expectations; to conform to
> certain patterns of behaviour and thought, but in return receive
> support from their comrades even when they are wrong.[1]

Before hearing from women about their experiences at police
hands in the following chapters, it seemed appropriate to look
at the police themselves and the research which has been done
on the police as an institution.

In 1983 the Policy Studies Institute (PSI) published a four-
volume report based on a study they had carried out on the
Metropolitan Police in operation at the request of Sir David
McNee, Commissioner. The report gave lengthy documentation of the pervasive ideology within a force composed overwhelmingly of white men (with only 10 per cent women and
1 per cent Black people). The police had given the researchers
full co-operation, and were embarrassed by the findings. The
report drew attention to racism and sexism which was not
occasional or accidental and which did not suggest, as police
spokespersons would have us believe, that there are only one or
two 'bad apples'. It pointed to institutionalized racism as a
fundamental part of the police ethic, their 'club' morality.

Although the PSI researchers did not look at police response
to crimes against women, their findings go a long way to
explaining criticisms of the police that women make. The
investigators found:

ideas about sex, drinking and violence linked together in a cult of masculinity which is thought to provide the key to the criminal world . . . a cult of masculinity which also has a strong influence on policemen's behaviour towards women, towards victims of sexual offences and towards sexual offenders.[2]

They described a culture which revolved around racism and sexism in its attitudes, subjects of conversation, approaches and modes of expression. Police officers talked of Black people 'running round in the jungle, plucking what they want from the trees . . . and killing someone for it if necessary'.[3] They saw Black people as belonging somewhere else and being, by definition, a problem within British society. The report's findings substantiated what Black people had been saying for years – that they are picked on by the police, both stopped and arrested disproportionately.[4]

Eight years after the Sex Discrimination Act, the Met, as other forces, was still resistant to the intentions of the Act. It employed only 10 per cent women, nearly all of whom were young women at constable level, and had every appearance of a male bastion. It had initiation ceremonies like tests of strength and drinking bouts for its male recruits and – in some cases this was cited as actual incident, in others as active myth – female recruits having their bottoms stamped by the station sergeant.

Violence, force and the exercise of authority were seen by the men as crucial to their work:

> the central meaning of the job for most police officers is the exercise of authority and force is for them the main symbol of authority and power, even if they actually impose their authority in other ways.[5]

Of course, facing and dealing with violence is only a tiny part of the work of the police but it is the aspect which most policemen seem to see as crucial and which seems to lead to confrontational attitudes such as those described in the following chapters.Where we do not see these confrontational attitudes, very conspicuously as regards their dealings with violent husbands in domestic violence, for example, the entrenched sexism described by the Report may have some bearing on the seeming difficulty for the police in identifying a 'villain' (police slang for criminal or lawbreaker), as opposed to an ordinary man.

Criticisms of macho policing are a commonplace of policewomen's reservations about the approach of their male colleagues. Superintendent Rachel James gave press interviews when she left the Met after 30 years, during which time she had been rejected for promotion to Chief Inspector twelve times during thirteen years, always by an all-male promotion board. She spoke of 'the sheer awfulness of the great macho image many of the men affect and how that swaggering maleness makes them bad policemen'. She accused macho policemen of inadvertently provoking fights and assaults and criticized their bringing of assault charges against members of the public as something to be ashamed of, suggesting that it meant they were not doing their job properly. She maintained that the non confrontational approach of policewomen was a far more effective way of handling difficult and often dangerous situations. She criticized police tactics at the Wapping dispute: 'It's completely unnecessary, all those horses and riot shields and helmets' and lamented the fact that integration of women officers meant their involvement in macho tactics in the front line of riot duty with the men.[6]

Violence is also a concept at the heart of group solidarity, which is extremely strong between officers, particularly among small groups working together. It serves to exclude women who are thought not to be up to facing it. Very high priority is given to going to the aid of a colleague under physical attack. Equally important is mutual protection if things go wrong. Officers stand by each other against force discipline which they see as an attack on the in-group. The crime squad sergeant who told the PSI investigators that if a mate committed a serious assault on a prisoner, 'I would get all of us together and I would literally script him out of it',[7] was a portent of what happened in the Holloway case.

This case was a telling example of what the cult of violence and the solidarity code can lead to. Four boys, two of whom were Black, were beaten up by police officers using fists, feet and truncheons after one of the boys had made a rude gesture at their van. It was not until four years later in July 1987 that five officers were gaoled as a result. Two and a half years of internal inquiry had failed to identify the officers. It was not until there was a public outcry after this was revealed that a confidential phone line led to an anonymous phone call identifying the individual police officers. During the court case, it was revealed that the officers involved had gone into a nearby park after the incident and concocted a cover-up story together. Eight members of the team protected the five and they kept to their story throughout the inquiry, although suspicion had fallen on two other van teams. One of the convicted officers revealed in court that, 'When we got back into the van, everyone treated it as a vast joke. There was talk of doing it again.' The Old Bailey judge said that the men had behaved 'like vicious hooligans and lied like common criminals'. Among the convicted men was their duty sergeant who was given three years for conspiracy to pervert the course of justice and for failing to protect the schoolboys. (See also chapter 29.)

Another factor influencing the way policemen behave was said to be the imitation of the 'villain'. In the CID in particular, a lot of time is spent drinking in the 'villains' pubs' – to gain information and acceptance from a whole world of criminals and informers.[8] But drinking also becomes part of the police's ethos; officers organize special outings to get seriously drunk. Drinking becomes part of working life, to help cope with the long hours of boredom and the occasional exciting event. The kind of 'villain' imitated, of course, is the 'good' villain (the bank robbers, the jewel thieves and so on), not petty offenders and certainly not 'inadequates'. The PSI reporters suggested that violence was also seen by police 'as a way of showing their credentials to villains who, they think, respect a show of force'.

The PSI researchers found that conversation in police stations reflected the priorities of violence and the exercise of authority, concentrating on stories of fighting, violence and feats of drinking, combined with titillating talk of sexual conquests:

> Bawdy talk is a kind of game . . . in which they play, in their imagination, the role of a man triumphing over a woman. This kind of talk is pervasive among groups of men in the Met, often lurid and extreme, and often continuing when women are present.[9]

It is even more of a problem in that these men are working side by side with women. Policewomen are thereby put in their place. Alongside the talk is the joky flirting behaviour police-women suffer from policemen.

Women in the Force

Policewomen are referred to by policemen as 'plonks'.[10] Going on street patrol with a WPC is called 'puppy walking'. They are turned into sex objects and flirted with. Two ex-Special constables (voluntary occasional police officers who help out with routine policing duties) I spoke to told me they found the atmosphere at the station very difficult; the regular policemen did not stop at appraising their faces and legs, but made remarks about their breasts as well. One of their colleagues had been forced to leave because of the sexual innuendo they made out of her name. One woman had worked in London, the other in Leeds. Both reported that the stations where they worked were rife with rumour-mongering about the women's reputations and about affairs between the men and the women. 'If you're personable,' said one, 'you have to be careful of your reputation.' She said that it was difficult to talk to policemen without their bringing in sexual innuendo. Many of the women were given nicknames. They both said that they thought they were treated worse than regular WPCs because they were Specials (and therefore working voluntarily; no Specials were well treated by regular officers) but that the regular police-women were treated in the same kind of way.

The male Specials were not nicknamed except for one Black Special. The ex-Special whose station this man was at was called a nigger lover for working with and befriending this man. Both women said they found the level of station 'infidelity' depressing; it tended to consist of older married men having affairs with younger unmarried WPCs. Both women had joined the Specials out of a sense of civic responsibility, of wanting to be of some practical use. Both felt disappointed by the police culture they found, not only because it sought to humiliate them (although they took pride in coping with it) but because they thought it sometimes led to provocative, aggressive and less effective policing.[11]

There have been several press interviews with ex-policewomen over the last few years, which back up what these ex-Specials said. For example:

> I thought I'd be treated with respect . . . God, that was naive.
> As soon as any policewoman gets a promotion or a decent posting, you know what the reaction of the men will be: 'Who's she been sleeping with?'[12]

> They think that women are only good for one thing. Every time you're partnered with a man in a car you get a seduction attempt. They treat you badly because you reject them. But if you agree to sex with them, it's the woman who's posted to another station if the secret comes out.[13]

Detective Chief Superintendent Thelma Wagstaff of the CID has said that women in the force are regarded as 'a bit of a joke'. Alison Halford, the Assistant Chief Constable of Merseyside, remarked:

> I think the most difficult thing was the rudeness of the instructor when I was being trained. 'Get your tits off the desk!' he'd say. The excuse would be that this was the kind of abuse I'd have to face on the job.[14]

There seem to be various oppositions underlying the dominant police ethos: white against black, respectable people against 'riff-raff', and so on. Women are certainly one of the principal 'out-groups' to the police's 'in-group'. Womanhood is one of the things that the male group is defined against, to maintain an ideology of toughness, bravery and authority. The police therefore face something of a dilemma in dealing with women within its own ranks. Before the Sex Discrimination Act 1976, the conflict had an easy resolution. Policewomen worked in a 'separate sphere', a specialist department dealing with women and children. But the Act changed all that, hitting the police like a thunderbolt. Male police officers protested that the Act could not apply to the police force. Chief police officers and the Police Federation were 'shoulder to shoulder' in their attempt to secure exemption from its provisions, because of the 'unfeminine' nature of police work.[15] The Federation confidently announced that 'the very nature of the duties of a police constable is contrary to all that is finest and best in women'.[16] However, parliament gave the police no exemption and the police were dragged, kicking and screaming, into the twentieth century.

The specialist departments were disbanded and women were nominally integrated. Numbers of WPCs rose. The Met had only 4 per cent of women officers in 1975 and 10 per cent by the time of the PSI investigation. That is how it has stayed. The PSI were told that it was unofficial force policy to keep to a quota of 10 per cent women officers[17] and at the time of writing (December 1987), women officers are still only 10 per cent of the Met force, and the national average is 10.3 per cent.

Despite the move towards integration, attitudes and working practices which discriminate against women are entrenched in the police force. Women are not accepted as full members of a working team or as colleagues on an equal basis. They are told they are a liability – for example, on car duty – since not only could they not support their partner in a crisis, but they would themselves need protection in the event of danger:

> I've been crewed with policemen before, when we had an incident car, and if it's a rough situation, they'll say, 'stay there', because they really do protect you . . . like their wives.[18]

Supposed vulnerability, constructed sexuality and ideas about childbearing are all brought into the battery of disqualifiers.

Women are criticized as a group for only staying five years on average before leaving the force to have children; but if they stay on, they are seen as 'unnatural'.[19]

Of the sixteen specialized sections in the two large county forces studied by Bryant, Dunkerley & Kelland of the sociology department at Plymouth Polytechnic, only five contained women. Sections commonly said to exclude women were scenes of crime, drugs squad, firearms, CID and dogs. All these are seen as glamorous and masculine:

> There are large tracts of informal no-go areas for women. They rarely enter the high-status specialist departments like Special Branch. They rarely qualify to drive fast cars.[20]

In 1985, Sandra Jones was commissioned by the Equal Opportunities Commission (EOC) to report on equality of opportunity in the police force. She based her research on a force covering a large urban and country area. She too, found that equality did not exist other than nominally in terms of training, work experience, and acceptance by male colleagues as an equal partner or group member. Superiors often did not regard WPCs as reliable choices for particular jobs, nor did they give them opportunities for promotion. She found policewomen 'hampered not only by the curtailing of their experience but also by the effect this curtailment can have on their own confidence and expectations'.[21]

There were 11,000 women in the police in England and Wales in 1985. Men outnumbered women 11:1. Sandra Jones found that 93 per cent of all the policewomen were only constables, as opposed to 73 per cent of the men. At the higher levels, only 3 per cent of all sergeants were women, 2 per cent of all inspectors, 1 per cent of all superintendents and, of the 852 top jobs from chief superintendents to chief constables, only twelve were held by women. Policewomen in senior positions were also often shunted, like their more junior sisters, away from the sharp end of the job.[22]

At the end of 1986, of 2,634 women officers in the Met, two were commanders, two chief superintendents, three superintendents, five chief inspectors, eighteen inspectors, 206 sergeants and 2,197 constables. There were only 201 women in the CID, of whom three were superintendents, four chief inspectors, four inspectors, 29 detective sergeants and the rest detective constables.[23]

Discrimination starts early in the police force and women often become disillusioned early on. Informal practice limits their work to the more mundane tasks – station duty (keeping women 'at home'), working the computers and typing (keeping them in service roles). Even where they are nominally performing the same roles as men, there is in fact a substantial difference in the quality of their assignments. Women patrol officers are the ones chosen to be kept back for routine station duties. Where they are given beat duty, the beats are the less busy and dangerous ones and they are usually paired with a male officer. Women are routinely deployed on traditional activities dealing with women victims and offenders, children and juveniles (see below). Supervisors are less likely to send women out to unpleasant incidents such as bad road accidents, removal of dead bodies, some domestic disputes and 'dirty' jobs like searching through rubbish tips.[24] Dirt, danger and difficulty tend to be colonized by the men and the women tend to be kept in the station as servicers and sex interest.

Women police officers are usually better qualified than their male peers because fewer women applicants are accepted and because women face greater difficulty in gaining promotion. They will need to be determined and resilient to make progress. The PSI researchers noted how few women were in the CID, for example (4 per cent of officers and 9 per cent of uniform officers), broadly because the 'cult of masculinity' was stronger in the CID than anywhere else. A CID sergeant told the interviewers that he thought he would have to get rid of the WPC in his squad because none of the men would work with her. The WPC said, 'I am the first WPC to be allowed into this crime squad and they're trying to make sure that I'll be the last. Eventually, I decided to go out on patrol by myself. I started bringing bodies in on my own.' Although she gained some respect from the men for doing this, the sergeant was still preparing to throw her off the squad.[25]

Policewomen have had to use the sex discrimination law to fight cases of direct discrimination. Their employers have tended to argue that this law did not apply to them. When the nature of policing in Northern Ireland changed in the mid 1970s and the role of the RUC in suppressing the republican struggle became predominant, the contribution of women in the RUC came under question. By the late 1970s, the women, all of whom had previously been working part-time in quasi-community service roles, were told they could not work full-time and their part-time hours were re-arranged to be both extremely limited and extremely inconvenient. Thirty former policewomen and one serving reservist brought a case and Sir John Hermon admitted in evidence that the RUC had delibera-tely set out to make life difficult for policewomen in order to encourage resignations. The case lasted for seven years, largely due to the RUC's line of defence which was that the Chief Constable's actions should be exempt from review in court on grounds of national security and public safety. A Belfast Industrial Tribunal awarded the women £250,000 compensa-tion and awarded costs believed to be in the region of £100,000 against the RUC.[26]

At the beginning of 1984 an industrial tribunal ruled that an internal ruling made by a Chief Superintendent in South West London contravened the Sex Discrimination Act. WPC de Launay was one of only two women working with seventy-eight men in the South West Area Traffic Division. There were two teams of forty, with one woman in each. She worked in a 'posted partnership' with a man, PC Attfield. (Posted partner-ships are working partnerships chosen by both parties and sanctioned by the duty sergeant.) Inevitably, the partners become friendly, spending most of their working time together and meeting in off-duty hours. PCs de Launay and Attfield fell foul of the station gossip network and within seven weeks of the start of the posted partnership, it was suspended by the duty sergeant who ruled that from then on, only partnerships of the same sex would be permitted, with a possible exception where both parties were married (WPC de Launay was not married). The duty sergeant took this action without any notice to PCs de Launay and Attfield, and without asking for their comments on the rumours, in the interests of 'station morale'. The Chief Superintendent gave the duty sergeant automatic backing. PCs de Launay and Attfield asked for support from the Police Federation but got none and were advised to drop the grievance. De Launay then took the case to the Equal Opportunities Commission. When she told the Chief Superintendent she was doing so, and handed him a question-naire, he told her she was behaving like a twelve-year-old and added, 'you know this job acts in strange ways and there are many indirect ways it deals with people who do this sort of thing'. Three months later he had put both de Launay and Attfield back on foot duty for 'rocking the boat'.

In court, the Chief Superintendent argued that the Sex Discrimination Act was not applicable, that the requirement was justifiable because it was imposed in the interests of discipline, welfare and morale. This was in spite of the fact that they accepted that de Launay and Attfield were not having an affair. In addition, he argued that it was not to de Launay's detriment because it was for him and the Commissioner to decide what was beneficial for traffic patrol officers. However, the Tribunal ruled that the requirement was discriminatory because in effect it prohibited de Launay from working in the team at all.[27]

As well as illustrating the high-handedness of superior officers, the predominance of the male gossip network and the difficulties women are up against working in divisions which are male bastions, this case illustrates the kind of internal discipline which, presumably, in other similar incidents, goes unchallenged. Decisions at the lowest level are apparently rubber-stamped as a matter of course throughout the hierarchy.

Nothing in the above discussion of women's role in the police should be taken to suggest that policewomen are immune from the criticisms levelled at the police throughout this book. Its purpose is to show the extent to which sexism operates within the police force itself (as other chapters show sexism in action) and how it is endemic in police culture.

Another question raised by the issue of sexism within the police force is whether whatever integration policewomen can win is likely to be to the advantage of the rest of us. We need to be able to insist on seeing a policewoman if we have come to report, for example, a crime of sexual violence, and should be able to do so whenever else we want or need to. At least her gender will not be threatening in itself. But in 1976, policewomen lost their specialist function of working with women and children and are still negotiating their role. Women had a particular area of expertise, a good deal of which, according to women interviewed by Bryant, Dunkerley and Kelland, has now been lost. Some policewomen argued for replacement specialist policewomen's units to be set up,[28] and this suggestion has been taken up by at least one force. Certainly, the most positive experience of policing reported within this book came from such a unit (see chapter 8). But most policewomen have no wish to return to specialization and want the opportunities now nominally open to them. The PSI found that it was mainly men (62 per cent) as opposed to women (22 per cent) who thought women should return to specialization.

Policewomen are working within a very taxing set of boundaries and expectations and are under pressure to knuckle down to feminization or to assert themselves within a male-defined profession. Supported by the EOC, policewomen have now entered the male bastion of riot duty, they were on the line at Wapping – where the police fed the media stories about their (minor) injuries, highlighting their vulnerability! – and no doubt we will be seeing more of them in future uprisings or major industrial action.

Women officers are likely to become increasingly involved in the confrontational and violent suppression of Black people's action, industrial action, anti-fascist action and women's action. Some WPCs appear, from the occasional example mentioned throughout this book, to be particularly antipathetic to women. Policewomen also have special opportunities to intimidate and humiliate us if we are arrested and strip-searched.

Police Racism

The PSI reported that racist talk was 'expected, accepted and even fashionable'.[29] It was never interrupted or criticized, except sometimes in private. It seemed to reinforce group solidarity against a clearly perceived external threat. Racism justified tactics of stopping people in the street. It was common for the police to insist to the PSI interviewers that it was reasonable to stop Black people in cars because nine times out of ten they'd have drugs. The report found that Afro-Caribbean people are much more likely to be stopped by the police than white people and that the police tend to equate crime with Black people. In fact, only 3 per cent of all stops lead to arrest and charge.[30]

The PSI found racialist theories to be widespread, linked to right-wing politics, colonial guilt and fear of retribution:

> Blacks are repaying whites for their bad treatment in the colonial days. They aren't just against the police but against all white people. The police are an obvious target because they represent white supremacy.[31]

It appears that racialist attitudes are not challenged at the outset in police training school. This was borne out both by a Black officer quoted in the PSI report who said he couldn't enjoy training school because of the racialism of both the other recruits and the instructors, and by the John Fernandes incident. Fernandes, a Black sociology lecturer at a local College of Further Education, was seconded by the Met to teach at Hendon Police College after the 1981 Brixton riot. This was shown to be another PR exercise for the police when it became clear that Fernandes was prevented from taking a genuine anti-racist line in his teaching. Fernandes was so appalled by the racism he and a colleague had encountered in cadets' essays (which was of a rock-bottom 'England is a white country and that is how it should stay' and 'Blacks in Britain are a pest' variety) that he complained and released them to the press, and was suspended.[32]

Women have also criticized attitudes at training school (see

Alison Halford above). The PSI criticized police training as a whole for not being tough-minded enough to make the recruits think properly about the subjects discussed: 'Sessions designed to challenge unthinking or reactionary views sometimes had the reverse effect because recruits holding those views would often be in a majority and the instructor's contribution was weak'.[33]

Black officers are barely visible in the force (only 1 per cent of all police). At the same time as publicly courting a higher Black intake, the police seem, predictably, to find it difficult to welcome those whom they see as an outside group within their own ranks. Both Asian and Afro-Caribbean police talked to the PSI investigators of the way racist talk continued in their company and how they were supposed not to make a fuss but to tolerate it with a sense of humour, in the same way that policewomen are supposed to tolerate sexism. A Black police-man talked of the time he'd been crossing the road in front of a white colleague who hadn't stopped his car until the last minute. 'I know,' he found himself saying, 'you couldn't see me because I didn't stand out against the tarmac.'[34] White police-men said they thought Black officers took racist jokes in good part and justified them, as training officers justified them, by saying that Black officers had to get used to racist abuse. In fact, all Black officers said they resented the racist talk and jokes in their relief very much. From the PSI report a separate perspective from Black women officers does not emerge, but it is probably safe to say that they experience a double level of abuse.

The PSI reporters did say that the majority of police, being white men, did not like taking orders from Black supervisory officers. This is likely to perpetuate the status quo. As the reporters concluded, 'The modest increase in the numbers of police officers belonging to ethnic minority groups that can be expected in the short term is unlikely to make a fundamental difference to the norms or behaviour of working groups of police officers.'[35]

Racism and the macho ethos culminate in confrontations such as in Southall in 1979, when the police turned on demonstrators protesting the National Front's electioneering meeting in the heart of the Asian Community:

> We went wanging down there, jumped out the van and just started fighting . . . It was a great day out, fighting the Pakis. It ought to be an annual fixture.[36]

A great many people were injured by the police that day and Blair Peach was killed. There was an internal inquiry into the Special Patrol Group (SPG) who were particularly implicated. It criticized the fact that members had unauthorized weapons in their lockers and made cosmetic changes. But the men involved protected each other; no one would confess to having seen anything. No policeman was ever disciplined or brought to court over the horrifying incidents which took place at Southall.

One of the themes of the PSI Report was that senior officers were out of touch with their rank and file, and unable to exercise a restraining influence on the excesses of younger officers. Sir Kenneth Newman reorganized station management throughout the Met in response. But an examination of the views and actions of some of the men at the very top has implications for whether they, or superior officers under them, are likely to exercise enough of the restraining influence we would require.

Some people have made their position very clear

'Some people have made their position very clear. Thank goodness, they have.' So said Mrs Thatcher of James Anderton, Chief Constable of Manchester, then President of ACPO, of his anti-gay bombast in late 1986.[37] Anderton says the things that other senior policemen dare not say. Some of us may have thought that Anderton would fall victim to his own rhetoric and be eased out as an embarrassment to government and police. But on the contrary. Fortunately, Anderton's zeal for enforcing the work of God as relayed to him by the Almighty is still limited by the law. Otherwise numerous women working as prostitutes and gay men in Manchester might find themselves languishing in police cells for long periods to remove them from the 'cesspool of their own making'. But unfortunately, Anderton's fundamentalism is not out of tune with the conservative right and we are now seeing measures carried through parliament which begin to relegitimate homophobia. These strike at the right of free expression for lesbians and gays. In December 1987, Anderton announced that homosexuality should be made a criminal offence. In the same week, clause 27 of the Local Government Bill was introduced which prohibited local authorities from 'promoting homosexuality' through teaching, publishing or funding clubs and organizations, and is now law.

Anderton and the government are pretty much of one mind. Both are anxious to restrict local accountability in the shape of local authority powers, and local police committees. Both do so by accusations of totalitarianism in the opposition:

> I sense and see in our midst an enemy more dangerous, insidious and ruthless than any faced since the Second World War. . . . I firmly believe there is a long-term political strategy to destroy the proven structures of the police and turn them into the exclusive agency of a one-party state.[38]

This was Anderton speaking on local police accountability after wrangles with the Manchester Police Committee about plastic bullets he had bought without consulting them. Anderton proposed 'non-political' Police Boards instead of Police Committees, appointed by the government. After an earlier Local Government Bill, the Police Committee was replaced in April 1986 by the Police Authority, which continues to debate the plastic bullets issue.

On 18 November 1987, the Court of Appeal backed Chief Constables in applying directly to the Home Office for plastic bullets and CS gas, bypassing their police authorities and thus destroying their only real power.[39]

Sir Kenneth Newman was Commissioner of the Metropolitan Police from 1983 to 1987. His appointment coincided with the publication of the Scarman Report criticizing the Met for its role in the Brixton riot in 1981 and the Policy Studies

Institute Report. In response, Newman initiated management reforms aimed at decentralizing power – local inspectors and superintendents were to regard themselves as managers. He also introduced the Multi-Agency Approach to policing (criticized by authors here) with the aim of publicly redefining the police as responsible to their communities. One reform suggested by the PSI that Newman did not see fit to act on was to increase the numbers of women officers in the police force.

Newman's peculiar talent was that he was an autocrat in sociologist's clothing. He boasted that he read *New Society*. But in his lectures we see how thinly his sociological diction disguised his thinking. He spoke of 'heterogeneity' and of society being a collection of competing interests, and moved on quickly to imply that the competing interests were Black and white: 'We are a multi ethnic, multi cultural society. . . . You cannot ask the police to hold down the lid on a boiling cauldron of anger and despair.' He said that 'problems', as he called them, arising from ethnic minorities were based in the main on socioeconomic or class factors, and had produced what many commentators refer to as an 'under class'. These 'problems' were behind the Brixton uprising in 1981. He moved on from this to cite the demands of the 'law-abiding majority' in defence of the action taken by the police.[40]

Newman liked the word 'heterogeneity' but not the idea. In the televised debate following the screening of May the Force be With You,[41] he argued that the problem with society today is that people in positions of power cannot agree. In another lecture, he said, 'Policing works best in a cohesive homogenous community where there is general consensus about norms and values.' In such a community, he argued, '*conformity*' (our emphasis) is achieved not so much by law enforcement but by informal means through the family, the school and other cultural initiatives. In such communities, policing can be applied with a low profile and a light touch.[42] By implication, we have only ourselves to blame for coercive policing and consultative panels who are asked to inform on 'problem' individuals and families in the name of community polic-ing. The Multi-Agency Approach was a debt to Newman's experience as head of the RUC in Northern Ireland where it was first introduced, for information-gathering purposes.

Interestingly, for a Metropolitan Commissioner, Newman betrayed a distaste for what he called 'the squalor and misery of life in the inner city'.[43] Among the 'social and economic pressures' he identifies are not only poverty but 'child in-discipline at school and home, one-parent families and racial conflict'.[44] Not, we should note, racist attacks, not men's violence against women at home and on the streets, nor men's violent and sexual abuse of their own and other children. His choice of evils betrays right-wing attitudes and a rural ethos – harking back to an idea of villages of happy families. Where are women in his analysis? They are 'villains' as single mothers, or paragons in their husbands' homes, disciplining their children.

During Newman's term, we witnessed abuses of police power, for example, at Broadwater Farm, at Wapping and in Brixton. We saw the effect of arming the police with riot equipment and the build-up of police shootings. Policing by consent became a slogan of the broad left in criticism of this kind of policing. Newman smartly reinterpreted the notion of policing by consent to apply to the citizen's obligation to uphold the law and the obligation of the police to enforce the laws laid down by parliament in a democracy.[45] In this again, he allied himself with the Tory government who have enacted repressive legislation and whose electioneering battlecry has always been law and order. He said 'Even if the police are applying coercion, they are policing by consent provided they are acting within laws passed by parliament.'[46]

Black youth, the recipients of much coercion, are set against 'the law-abiding majority'. Most Black people, said Newman, are law-abiding, but – and then he cited the exception which proves the stereotyping rule: 'Throughout London there are locations where unemployed youth, often Black youths, congregate; where the sale and purchase of drugs, the exchange of stolen property and illegal drinking and gaming are not uncommon.' Black people's complaints now became special pleading. 'We cannot,' said Newman, 'have the law enforced unevenly.'[47]

Newman equated communal safety with public order and told us that 'We should not forget that an over-regard for individual liberties can put at risk that sense of order and security without which no community can truly be free.'[48] Newman even used the excuse of the overcrowding of the prison system to argue for stronger social control measures, arguing that this could be achieved by liaison between government departments in the same way that Multi-Agency Policing involves liaison with different social agencies and institutions.[49] No doubt, this is not the last we shall hear of this.

Throughout this book, women have criticized Multi-Agency Policing. Newman's own statements are another indication of the real as opposed to the professed thinking behind it.

Peter Imbert succeeded Kenneth Newman as Metropolitan Commissioner in February 1987 and was welcomed as a man with an 'open-doors' approach to the media. He had authorized the television 'Police' series in which the episode exposing the police treatment of rape victims appeared. In practice, he has distinguished himself by calling, on behalf of the police, for the removal of a suspect's right to silence in the police station – a proposal the government is to introduce legislation to effect – which will mean, as the NCCL have said, an end to the first principle of British law that a person is innocent until proved guilty. (See also chapter 27.) No doubt as with Newman, his years in anti-terrorist work in Britain and Northern Ireland have influenced his thinking.

The police at a senior level have identified with their role as the front line of the government's repression of the rights of working people and minority groups. In return, they have won extended powers for themselves in the Police and Criminal Evidence Act. They have the government's ear. And they have now become overt front-line spokesmen for political changes in the law which would extend their powers still further and erode civil liberties traditional in Britain.

Notes

1. David Smith and Jeremy Gray, *The Police in Action*, Policy Studies Institute Report, vol. IV, 1983.

2. ibid, p. 91.

3. ibid, p. 114.

4. ibid, p. 128.

5. PSI Report, vol. IV.

6. *Guardian*, interview with Polly Toynbee, 19 May 1986.

7. PSI Report, vol. IV, p. 70.

8. ibid, pp. 71–72.

9. ibid, p. 91.

10. ibid, p. 94.

11. Interview with two women ex-Specials.

12. *Sun*, 13 December 1984.

13. ibid.

14. *Daily Telegraph*, 8 June 1986.

15. B. Whitaker, *The Police in Society*, Eyre Methuen, London, 1979.

16. ibid.

17. PSI Report, vol. IV, p. 246.

18. Bryant, Dunkerley & Kelland Report, from the Department of Social and Political Studies, Plymouth Polytechnic, 1985.

19. Mary Heller and Pauline McGill in *Police Review*, 15 February 1985.

20. Bryant, Dunkerley & Kelland Report.

21. Sandra Jones, *Policewomen and Equality, Formal Policy and Informal Practice*, Macmillan, London, 1987.

22. ibid.

23. Hansard, 17 December 1986.

24. Sandra Jones, *Policewomen and Equality*.

25. PSI Report, vol. IV, pp. 93–4.

26. *Independent*, 10 March 1987.

27. Industrial Tribunal Decision: Miss W.S. de Launay and the Commissioner of Police for the Metropolis and Chief Superintendent B. Wallace, 4 January 1984.

28. Bryant, Dunkerley & Kelland Report.

29. PSI Report, vol. IV, p. 110.

30. ibid, p. 128.

31. ibid, p. 115.

32. 'One Bad Apple?' *Searchlight*, no. 90, December 1982.

33. PSI Report, vol. IV.

34. ibid, p. 151.

35. ibid, p. 154.

36. ibid, p. 88.

37. *Daily Mail*, 24 January 1987.

38. *Guardian*, 17 March 1987.

39. *Guardian*, 19 November 1987.

40. Sir Kenneth Newman in the George Bean Memorial Lecture on the Scarman Report, 1983.

41. The Force of the Future, Channel 4, September 1986.

42. George Bean Memorial Lecture, 1983.

43. ibid.

44. ibid.

45. Sir Kenneth Newman's speech to the European Atlantic Group, 'Public Order in Free Societies', 1983.

46. Sir Kenneth Newman's James Smart lecture, 'Policing by Consent', 1984.

47. George Bean Memorial Lecture, 1983.

48. Speech to the European Atlantic Group, 1983.

49. ibid.

50. *Guardian*, 16 September 1987.

10. Broadwater Farm Defence Campaign

Into Our Homes

The Women of Broadwater Farm

During the night of Sunday 6 October 1985, the British public watched with horror and incredulity the scenes of violence on their television screens. Such was the scale of violence on the Broadwater Farm Estate, Tottenham, North London, that Deputy Assistant Commissioner Richards of the Metropolitan police said that this disturbance was the 'most ferocious and the most vicious riot ever seen on mainland Britain'. A week earlier, on 28 September, another 'riot' in Brixton, South London, had preceded that of Tottenham. The impressions that remained in the minds of the British public was one of burnt-out vehicles, looting and an abundance of missiles of every description being hurled at police lines by marauding bands of black youths, culminating in the death of a police officer.

The purpose of this essay is to provide an opportunity for the women of the Broadwater Farm Estate and its vicinity to challenge the British media's one-dimensional picture of the 'riots' as meaningless destructive violence. Thus, we will examine the death of Mrs Cynthia Jarrett and the police contribution to this tragedy in the context of black/police relations. Furthermore, because we are women residents or workers on the estate, who have experienced the full force of the 1984 Police and Criminal Evidence Act, we will highlight how this piece of legislation has been used as an unprecedented extension of the police's coercive methods against us and against similar communities.

Before the Uprising – the Estate and Black/Police Relations

Broadwater Farm Estate was completed in 1973. It consists of twelve blocks which are built off the ground and connected by raised walkways. There are 1,063 flats, housing approximately 3,000 people. Like most of the housing estates built at that time, Broadwater seemed to offer a solution to the borough's housing problems of unfit accommodation and housing short-age. The inhabitants were enthusiastic, welcoming the flats as spacious and warm:

> I love this flat . . . You can just go about in your T-shirt. That's how warm these flats are.

> There was a lot of peace there . . . especially at night when you sat on the patio.[1]

However, the condition of the estate began rapidly to deteri-orate due to structural defects and disrepair. Vandalism and burglaries increased, and there was a growth in the demand for transfers off the estate. As a consequence, Haringey Council began concentrating homeless families, unemployed youth and single-parent families on the estate. There was also a significant increase in the number of black people who were, in effect, dumped onto the estate. By 1979, it had become known as a 'problem estate' subject to sensationalist and racist reporting from the local press who claimed that the inhabitants were 'living in a subculture of violence' and that 'the sight of unmarried West Indian mothers walking about the estate aggravates racial tension'.[2]

Perhaps as a consequence of this adverse media publicity, the all-white Tenants Association demanded that a mini police station be set up on the estate. This suggestion incensed black youths and mothers. One of these formidable black women was Dolly Kiffin, who set up a meeting with the youths at which it was agreed to set up the Broadwater Farm Youth Association as an alternative, a centre where residents could play a part and 'see if life could be changed on the Broadwater farm'. The Youth Association caters for the whole community, bringing the young and the old people together. Furthermore, in order to ease the high unemployment on the estate and to provide much-needed facilities for residents, a number of co-operative enterprises, such as a launderette, a food and vegetable shop, a hairdressing salon, a sewing workshop and a photographic workshop, were established, in addition to a Mothers' Project and a Day Nursery.

In November 1983, the Broadwater Farm Neighbourhood Office was opened. It dealt with over 900 queries from tenants each month. The refusal rate (of people turning down offers of accommodation there) halved, repairs were completed faster than anywhere else in the borough and voids (empty flats) dropped from sixty to fifteen. The estate was clean with very little graffiti or vandalism. The crime rate plummeted.

However, despite the decline in crime in recent years, the police have continued to target the estate, and 'confrontational policing' has led to a series of incidents of which the following are typical.

On 1 November 1982, dozens of police officers, acting on 'a tip from a member of the public' entered the estate to arrest a member of the Youth Association for a burglary at a local social club. A crowd gathered outside Tottenham Police Station to protest, because it was known that the arrested man had been watching a film at the time of the burglary in the company of several youths in the Association. An Instant Response Unit (riot police) attacked the demonstration and arrested four other members of the Youth Association. On another occasion, in the spring of 1985, officers from three District Support Unit vans (for further information on riot units, see chapter 23) entered the estate and spread out in a show of force. It was later explained by a police superintendent that the units had been on patrol at a local football match and had not had enough to do. In these and many similar incidents, the community, especially the young black community on Broadwater Farm, has been continually harassed and criminal-ized. They demonstrate the effect of what the Gifford enquiry (the independent enquiry into the disturbances chaired by Lord

Gifford, QC) called 'the factor of racialism in the response of the rank and file of police'[3], together with the effect of the ambiguous new concept of targeting particular housing estates as so-called 'no-go' areas. In 1983, Newman's Commissioner's Report spoke of Broadwater Farm as one of: 'those areas identified as "symbolic locations" where black communities, often the young, come to view a particular location with something of a proprietorial attachment, resenting intrusion, especially by the police to enforce the law.'

Such a statement can only be viewed as racist in that it assumes that the black residents of Broadwater Farm do not want law and order enforced. More importantly, it provides justification for any incident on the estate to be policed in an over-excessive manner. It should be noted that the Special Patrol Group, the Instant Patrol Group and the Instant Response Unit have all been in operation on the estate, often for trivial offences.

The Death of Mrs Jarrett

Like the police shooting of Mrs Cherry Groce in Brixton a week earlier, on 28 September 1985, the death of Mrs Cynthia Jarrett during a speculative police search exposes the nakedly racist and sexist attitudes of the police force. In the case of Mrs Groce, ten armed police officers with dogs smashed down her front door, saying they were looking for her son Michael. Michael had not lived at his mother's home for three years. She was shot by a police marksman and has been paralysed from the waist down since. This incident led to the Brixton 'riot'. Likewise (as evidence heard at the magistrates' court and inquest revealed) four police officers illegally entered the home of Mrs Jarrett by obtaining her son's keys whilst he was in detention. Mrs Jarrett died during the raid, and her death led to the Broadwater Farm uprising. Although both these tragedies were the result of extreme police misconduct, as we have indicated, they were by no means unique instances. As black women, we believe that, had Mrs Jarrett not died and Mrs

Groce not been shot, these intrusions would each have been seen as 'just another raid'.

The events which led to Mrs Jarrett's death cannot be separated from the history of police targeting of the Broadwater Farm Estate. Mrs Jarrett's son, Floyd, had been an active member of the Youth Association for many years. On 5 October, 1985, his car was stopped by uniformed police; the reason was later given that his tax disc was out of date, but it is more likely that he was stopped for being a black man driving an expensive car. Floyd was arrested and then charged with assault. The magistrates later acquitted him of assault, awarding costs against the police, which indicated their belief that the charge should never have been brought. While Floyd was in the police station, D.C. Randall took his house keys to search the house for stolen goods.

Randall and his men let themselves in to Mrs Jarrett's house without knocking, in what the Gifford Report called 'a shocking violation of the privacy of the Jarretts' house'.[4] Mrs Jarrett was at home with her daughter, her grandchild and a neighbour's baby. The shock caused her can be imagined. Patricia Jarrett heard her mother say, 'Lord, Lord, there's some police in the house.' The men moved through the rooms including her bedroom, in spite of her protestations. As she stood in the doorway of the dining room, D.C. Randall brushed past her; she fell to the ground and died shortly afterwards of a heart attack.

At the coroner's inquest, the jury returned a verdict of 'accidental death' following the coroner's direction that this was the appropriate verdict if they were satisfied there had been accidental contact between D.C. Randall and Mrs Jarrett which had caused her to fall. In doing so they clearly rejected D.C. Randall's own evidence to the effect that there had been no contact at all between him and Mrs Jarrett. Randall had blamed Patricia and her brother, Michael, who had returned home during the police search, for causing their mother's fatal heart attack, saying that they had been abusive and disruptive to the officers, but this evidence was undermined by their own radio reports and a witness.

D.C. Randall was at no time suspended. No criminal charges were preferred by the Director of Public Prosecutions and no disciplinary charges were recommended by the Met. The Police Complaints Authority agreed with their recommendation.

The Gifford Report stated that the Police Complaints Authority had 'failed lamentably to grapple with the real issues'. In their view, the evidence of both the magistrates' court hearing into Floyd's alleged assault, and the coroner's inquest into Mrs Jarrett's death revealed serious misconduct which could have formed the basis of disciplinary action:

1.   That the officers who first stopped Floyd Jarrett made computer checks on his car, apparently for no other reason than that he was a young black man. At the magistrates' court hearings, Mr Solley, Floyd Jarrett's counsel had asked the officer concerned, 'Would you have checked me out if I had been driving with a tax disc five weeks out of date?' The officer said no. Mr Solley asked if he could give any reason other than that he was a black man driving a flashy-looking car – a BMW coupé. He could give no reason.

2.   That they arrested him and took him into custody on suspicion that his car was stolen, which had little if any reasonable basis.

3.   That they made a charge against him of assault which was found to be false.

4.   That they embarked upon a search of his family's home which appears on the evidence to have been entirely speculative.

5.   That a number of features in the evidence indicated strongly that the search was carried out without having obtained a warrant signed by a magistrate.

6.   That the officers took Floyd Jarrett's keys out of his property without the authorization of the custody officer.

7.   That they used the keys to enter (the premises) without having alerted the occupants by knocking on the door.

8.   That one of the officers lied to the occupants of the house in saying he found the door open.

9.   That distress was caused to Mrs Jarrett both by the sudden intrusion of the officers and by a quite unnecessary search of her bedroom.

10.   That one of the officers conducted himself so carelessly as to

push past Mrs Jarrett as she stood in the doorway and cause
her to fall.

11. That this push and fall, coupled perhaps with other upsetting
     features of the search, caused her death before it would
     naturally have occurred.

12. That after Mrs Jarrett fell and was clearly unwell the officer
     present expressed no concern but merely continued his search.

13. That after the event the officers told lies about the behaviour
     of the Jarrett family and covered up their own misconduct.[5]

The uprising on the Broadwater Farm Estate was the result
of outrage at Mrs Jarrett's death. Meetings between community leaders and police (who refused to suspend D.C. Randall,
even temporarily, as a gesture) were felt to be unhelpful, and so
was the resort by police to over-heavy policing of a demonstration outside the police station.

Following the uprising, and the regrettable death of P.C.
Blakelock, police operations on and around the estate adopted
a scale and ferocity which had never before been seen outside
Northern Ireland. The next day there were nearly 1,500
officers on standby for the estate and by the weekend this had
increased to 9,165. Between 7 October and 27 March 1986,
there were rarely fewer than ninety police officers actually on
the estate every day. By May, this had fallen to sixty.

In addition to the huge number of police in riot gear patrolling the estate, a mobile centre, a mobile incident room, a police
dog unit and a police helicopter fitted with an infra-red television camera and other sophisticated equipment, which
noisily circulated the estate, contributed to the oppressive
police presence. As one woman stated: 'I felt as if the estate
was under occupation. There was police everywhere. On the
balconies, on deck [the main shopping area], in the corridors
and at ground level.'

Women were particularly affected when, on the advice of
police, who said it would hamper their inquiries, postmen and
milkmen made no deliveries to the estate. We saw this as
intimidatory. It created immense anxieties for women, many of
whom rely on receiving their DHSS benefit cheques through
the post as the sole means of subsistence for themselves and

their children. However, the potentially desperate situation was averted when emergency supplies of food and alternative methods of payments were organized by the Youth Association and the Neighbourhood Office.

Raids and Searches

Some 271 homes (25 per cent of all the homes on the estate) were searched by the police. Eighteen front doors had to be replaced as a result of police kicking and sledgehammering them down in what Lord Gifford called 'the most horrific intrusion imaginable into the privacy of the home'. A climate of fear and anxiety was created for all women residents throughout the estate. As Ms G said:

> You just lie there and you would think, are they going to come and kick my door. What's going to happen to my children? Wherever you went, that's all you heard – am I next? . . . It was that horrible fear that you lived with day by day, knowing that they could come and kick down your door and come and drag you off and hold you for hours.

The following are extracts from statements made by residents between October 1985 and June 1986, supplied by the Legal Committee of the Broadwater Farm Defence Campaign and the London Borough of Haringey's Police Research Unit:

> On October 17 1985, whilst I was ironing, I heard my gate open and two people speaking. So I thought that somebody was coming to the front door and I looked. I did not see anybody at this stage. Then I saw something or somebody rush past my window. It was then that I saw a gun pointing up. I went over to another window and I saw another gun pointing to my bedroom. One police officer was also standing at the gate, with his hand on the trigger, pointing the gun straight at the front door. By the time I rushed up to my bedroom where my husband was still in bed, I heard my youngest daughter screaming. She was partly dressed in the bathroom and there were three armed police officers pointing guns at her. There

was a telephone call and when I answered, we were told by police, 'Mrs B, listen to me carefully. You are surrounded by armed men. Send a member of your family to the front door. If you do, you won't come to any harm'. Almost immediately, the doorbell rang and we were told, 'This is a gun. You must come out and walk down the path'.

My family and I did as we were told. Seven armed police officers entered my home. Three more were in the garden. There were more near the railway track and the alleyway was cordoned off by police.

Whilst waiting outside, I told a police officer that I was feeling ill . . . that I suffer from bronchitis. I was told to wait or knock on my next-door neighbour's door. My family and I remained in the street until the armed officers left. However, other police officers, both plain-clothed and uniformed, then entered my home. We asked whether they had a warrant. One officer pulled out a piece of paper. There was no name on it – only our address and the word 'firearms'. They didn't find any firearms. They took my food and my family's clothes . . . they broke into my trunk which had things in it that I had bought before my eldest son was born. They took all my knives and cutlery. They even took my family photographs. There were six policemen in my son's room. They took all his clothes, his complete wardrobe . . . I asked for a receipt but they bluntly refused to give me one. My son has had some of his clothes back. I have had nothing of mine. Not any of the food, nothing. Since the incident my doctor has told me to rest because of my nerves and bronchitis.

On Wednesday 8 November 1985, I received a phone call at 6.10 a.m. from the police. I was informed that armed police were at the front door and that I should put the lights on and come out slowly. There were thirteen plain-clothes policemen and five other policemen with guns who looked like the SAS. I was told to put my hands on my head and walk out slowly. I was told to walk ten steps before I was searched. I was then brought back into the house. Police removed pictures that I had taken whilst on holiday in Jamaica, trainers, shoes, clothes, social security book and £150 in cash. I was not given a receipt. Nor was I shown a warrant despite asking for one.

The above extracts provide examples of how the extended powers to search homes and seize property, enshrined in the Police and Criminal Evidence Act, have provided police officers with an authority to conduct 'fishing expeditions' in what Lord Scarman has called 'a breathtaking inroad on the individual's right of privacy and right of property'.[6] Moreover, the fact that women are being denied the right to read search warrants can only be interpreted as flagrant police disregard of the Codes of Practice under the Act.

As well as observing raids, we in the Campaign also witnessed police removal of personal papers, diaries, address and telephone books, and social security books. This can only be construed as a means of intelligence-gathering about estate residents. We are concerned that this information will be used as potential retrieval intelligence data.

On 13 October 1985, police began house-to-house enquiries. In addition to asking questions about the night of the disturbance, police questioned people about their nationality, place of birth, employment status and knowledge of their neighbours. There is a high percentage of ethnic minorities living on the estate; 42 per cent of residents are black (West Indian or African in origin), 3 per cent are from the Indian subcontinent, and others (among them Turks, Greeks and Cypriots) number 6 per cent. Accordingly, we are anxious that such questions will affect us as women who belong to ethnic groups. We feel that the questions are racist and are being used as part of the Multi-Agency Approach which, because of the expanding system of immigration control, may deny us and our children access to hospitals, housing and other welfare provisions. This is because black women with British nationality often find their claims to housing and welfare benefits held up while their immigration status is investigated. Delays can take up to two years. As British immigration law becomes ever more complicated and exclusive, more women are affected.

Arrest and Detention

Only 24 of the 354 arrests made by the police on and around the estate, since October 1985, have been of women. Most of the women arrested were young, black and living on the estate;

a substantial proportion of them were single mothers. It is crucial that the arrest and detention of these women is seen in the context of police harassment and criminalization of the community as a whole. Only six of these women were actually charged, five with handling stolen goods and one with threatening behaviour; only one was convicted. Most of the women arrested were predominantly questioned about the whereabouts of their menfolk on the night of the disturbances. It is clear that the main motives of the police in arresting them were harassment, intimidation and the extraction of information about men. For example, one woman was told that she had a choice of saying that her boyfriend came to her with bloody clothes and that she burnt them, or of being charged as accessory to murder.

Like the youths and men arrested, women also experienced prolonged detention and denial of access to a solicitor. An eighteen-year-old woman was not allowed to see a solicitor for forty-eight hours, from Monday night until Wednesday, when the solicitor was allowed to take in the first food that she had eaten during this time. Another woman with a five-month-old child spent a total of eighty-four hours in police custody before being released on unconditional bail. For forty-eight hours she had not been allowed to wash.

We, as women, are seriously concerned that the Police and Criminal Evidence Act grants police authorization of prolonged detention for the purpose of questioning until juveniles, men and women break down. This is a flagrant contradiction of the right to remain silent when questioned by police. Moreover, the Codes of Practice which state that access to solicitors need only be permitted by police as soon as is 'practicable' are evidently open to police abuse.

Effects on Women

The effect on all women, as upon the whole community, of months of police occupation and harassment has been immense. In addition, the mothers of those arrested, charged and convicted have suffered extreme stress because of the conditions under which their sons were detained and the severity of the sentences passed on those convicted. (Sentences of between five-and-a-half and eight-and-a-half years were given for affray, for which the previous maximum sentence was two or three years.)

Many women who have experienced police raids have said that the terrifying memory will remain with them for ever. They were always conscious of what happened to Mrs Groce and Mrs Jarrett in their own homes and feared that it might happen to them too. An additional pressure is put on the mothers of young children. One woman with children aged four and five said, 'My children now believe that the police are going to get me . . . If they see a policeman, they will want to run up and fight him.' A mother of a three-year-old girl whose door had been sledgehammered down by armed police said, 'It's not affected me, it's my daughter, because she saw everything that happened that morning and she was screaming when she saw the gun at my head'. Women lived with the fear or reality of being separated from their children, either if they themselves are arrested, with the likelihood that their young children will be left alone, or if their older children are arrested.

Although this essay has focused primarily on black women, it should be emphasized that a number of white women have shared the same experiences because they belonged to the Broadwater Farm community. These women have said that, had they not experienced the heavy-handed tactics of the British police in relation to themselves and their families, they would not have believed the accounts of police behaviour they heard from black people. Both white and black women have experienced raids on their homes and arrest and detention of themselves and their children. But black women have also had to bear the additional burden of police racism.

We would like this essay to act not only as a testament to our experience, but as a warning to other communities. White people must no longer assume that police intimidation cannot happen to them. It has happened to the white pickets of

Wapping and the mining communities across England, Scotland and Wales.

Law and Order

On the basis of the punitive sentences passed for riot and affray, we awaited the outcome of the Broadwater Farm 'murder trials' with grave apprehension. However, even we were shocked at the three convictions. The police had no evidence against any of the defendants except so-called and very approximate 'confessions' made under duress. There had been six defendants, three of whom were juveniles. Five of the six, including two of the juveniles, had been denied access to family and solicitors during their interrogation. The Old Bailey Judge, Judge Hodgson, threw out the cases against these two juveniles, expressing the strongest anger and frustration at the way they had been treated by the police. One of them, then thirteen, had been interviewed wearing only his underpants. He had been locked in a police cell for nearly forty-eight hours when he should have been released into community care. The other was severely mentally disturbed, with a mental age of seven. He had been arrested at school, without his mother being told, and questioned without access to his parents or a solicitor in circumstances that Judge Hodgson called disquieting and crushing.

Three youths were sentenced to life imprisonment for murder, with a recommendation in the case of Winston Silcott, that he should serve at least thirty years. The following day saw some of the most blatantly racist press reporting that this country has ever known.

A policeman died in the Broadwater Farm uprising and in the subsequent saturation policing of the estate, the dawn raids, racial and sexual verbal abuse and intimidation, and the everyday harassment of all tenants in the first few weeks after the uprising (caused by the heavy police presence on the estate, the police on horseback outside and police helicopter circling overhead), the Metropolitan police has avenged itself on our community. In addition, three youths have been sentenced to life imprisonment.

A black woman has died in Tottenham as a result of a heart attack suffered during an intimidating and humiliating police search of her home. The officer in charge of the operation, D.C. Randall (against whom complaints had already been made in connection with police searches in the homes of black people), has not had to face either judicial, or, so far as we know, internal disciplinary proceedings. Moreover, the abuses of procedure adopted by police in relation to the Broadwater Farm 'murder trial' and the Broadwater Farm trials in general, may have lasting consequences. Fifteen years ago, there was an outcry following the oppressive questioning of juveniles and people of low mental ability in the Maxwell Confait case. The irony is that this miscarriage of justice was one of the major concerns behind the passing of the Police and Criminal Evidence Act, which was supposed to provide safeguards to prevent 'a repetition of the false confessions which disfigured the Confait case'.[7] Broadwater Farm suspects provided a testing ground for this new piece of legislation; the extended powers it gives the police were well used and its safeguards were ignored.

Postscript

Sharon Raghip is twenty-one and the mother of a four-year-old child. She is the wife of Engin Raghip, one of the three youths sentenced to life imprisonment. Engin is illiterate. Without access to counsel, he was questioned by the police ten times for a total of approximately fifteen hours. He was convicted on the basis of a statement that he saw an attack, was armed with a broomstick, and tried to get into the crowd but was unable to do so. Sharon comments:

> Before Engin's case went to trial, I had faith that he would be cleared and the charges dropped. The prosecution evidence was weak. After he was convicted, I felt like dying. I cannot put into words how I felt that day. After I got home and had a good cry, I

thought that instead of feeling sorry for myself, I must not let them get away with it. That goes for Engin's family and my family as well. We know Engin is not guilty.

I go to a lot of meetings where I speak on behalf of my husband and others who have been convicted over Broadwater Farm. I go so that I can let people know the truth, rather than what they heard on the TV or read in the papers. I have been all over the country, speaking at rallies, women's groups, lobbying and campaigning. I won't give it up. Every night the last picture I see in my mind is Engin walking down to the cells, and the police laughing.

Notes

1. Dolly Kiffin, Broadwater Farm Inquiry.
2. *Tottenham Weekly Herald*, April 1976.
3. *The Broadwater Farm Inquiry*, Karia Press, London, 1986.
4. ibid.
5. ibid.
6. ibid.
7. Royal Commission on Criminal Procedure Report (Cmnd 8092), January 1981.

11. Nationalist Women and the RUC

Chris McAuley

When I was approached about writing a piece on women and policing in the North the first pictures that came to mind were of the RUC indiscriminately firing plastic bullets at women and children during peaceful protests and women continuously being left to count the cost of damage to their homes after an RUC/British Army search. I think of women like young Brenda Downes, left to bring up a little girl after her husband John was killed by a plastic bullet fired at close range by an RUC man; I see the face of Theresa Carroll from County Armagh who has had to bear the heartbreak of losing two sons, one killed by an RUC shoot-to-kill unit, the other assassinated by a UDR patrol. There are so many faces of women and so many tragedies that they have encountered over the past nineteen years that it almost doesn't bear thinking about. Yet each of their stories testifies to the fact that we are not living in a 'normal' situation in the six counties. We don't have a 'normal' police force engaged in impartially upholding law and order. Like thousands of nationalists I've come to this conclusion not through bias or hatred, but through bitter experience of the RUC's brutality and sectarianism, which we witness in our day-to-day lives.

While women universally suffer discrimination in all its forms in every society, nationalist women in the North are doubly discriminated against. We bear the brunt of bringing up children amidst RUC/British Army harassment. We can be arrested, interrogated, imprisoned and even be killed at any time, given the right excuse, by the crown forces. We are stopped in the street and ordered to open our coats in front of a leering patrol of soldiers and RUC. Our bags and personal belongings can be searched. We can be questioned about where we're going and where we've come from. The forces will question us about our families, about what members of the family work at, about where they worked at before their present job, or why they are not working, and therefore what they do all day. The questions can go on and on; you can be standing around in the street for an hour or more. It is very distressing and embarrassing.

If you refuse to answer questions to establish your identity then you'll be arrested and taken to one of the numerous RUC barracks which are dotted all over nationalist areas. They can hold you there for hours without informing anyone of your whereabouts. These military establishments are, in appearance and in function, very intimidating to any woman, whether she's a political activist or not. You can be held for seven days under the Prevention of Terrorism Act; for many women this can be a terrifying and traumatic experience, particularly if they have children. All personal items such as a watch, or jewellery, a wedding ring for instance, are taken off you. This is part of psychological warfare, the dehumanizing process which tells you that you are firstly, a prisoner and secondly, totally isolated and under the control of your captors. I have talked to countless women who have been verbally abused, and I don't just mean sworn at. I'm talking about a woman sitting in a small claustrophobic room while two RUC detectives shout gross obscenities into the woman's face about her sexual relationships, or a situation where a woman's body is made the subject of mockery and abuse, or women who have been physically assaulted during interrogations and threatened that if they tell anyone they'll be arrested again and receive more of the same. Sadly, women members of the crown forces quite often engage in as much sexist abuse of women as their male counterparts in the RUC, British Army or UDR. One of the most sickening aspects of such interrogations is that women with children are put under tremendous emotional strain to co-operate under threat that their children will be taken from them and put into care.

Women living in nationalist areas not only have to put up with bad housing conditions and chronic unemployment but with the day-to-day presence of heavily armed RUC officers and British soldiers patrolling their streets, crouching in their hallways and setting up roadblocks which cause tremendous inconvenience. If you are stopped at such roadblocks you can be ordered out of the car and left standing while the vehicle is searched, sometimes two or three times. You will be thoroughly questioned and if the army is not satisfied that you have established your identity you, whoever is with you, and the vehicle, will be taken to the barracks.

In nationalist areas there is no such thing as the sanctity of the home as far as the RUC or the British Army are concerned. House raids are very common occurrences and can disrupt family life for months. Women have seen their life's possessions destroyed overnight in such raids; they have seen their children upset because they've been lifted from their sleep in the early hours of the morning; they have seen their daughters, sons or husbands frogmarched to RUC Land Rovers or British Army Saracens and taken away without any reason whatsoever being given for their arrest. British soldiers may pound through the walls of your house with sledgehammers, shovels, drills and hammers or dig up the floors, tearing carpet and smashing items which you can't afford to replace. You are very often not allowed to move freely around the house while raids are in progress. The forces may put you under what they term 'house arrest' – that is you are not allowed to leave and no one is allowed to enter. 'House arrest' can arbitrarily mean 'room arrest' as well – that is, they will try and confine the family to one particular room, such as the living room. All this, of course, is totally illegal but most people, and particularly women, are intimidated into not protesting because they fear their family will be harmed or arrested.

British Army helicopters equipped with hi-tech surveillance cameras continuously monitor nationalist areas and have come to be a source of irritation with their constant noise. There is also constant surveillance of people's movements by under-cover units and the systematic monitoring of car registration numbers by cameras mounted on all major roads.

Individual areas can be targeted at any time for intense 'policing', which means more repression and harassment of the community. Divis Flats in West Belfast, where a high proportion of women are on anti-depressant drugs, is a favourite as are equally deprived nationalist estates like Ballymurphy, Turf Lodge, New Lodge and Ardoyne.

1969: The Turning Point

These experiences and many others were instrumental in forcing me out of a childish naivety about my country's political history, but in 1969, when I was thirteen, I couldn't understand why protestants were burning out catholic families in Bombay Street, close to where I lived in West Belfast's Lower Falls area. I knew my father had been threatened in Belfast Shipyard and forced to leave his job because he had 'turned his coat', as they say, and married a catholic woman, but we never discussed politics at home. He was always away working in England or in the South of Ireland and on that horrific August night when loyalists were burning down whole terraces of houses he wasn't there to see the sheer panic and fear of our neighbours and ourselves. My mother gathered what personal belongings she could and we joined hundreds of other frightened families and temporarily stayed with friends in Andersonstown. Others stayed in schools or community halls where conditions were cramped but at least people were safe. It was all very bewildering for me.

In school our history lessons had taught us about the 'glorious conquests' of English kings and queens, but little if anything about Irish history; nothing about eight hundred years of British interference and repression in Ireland. Nothing was put into political perspective, otherwise teenagers like myself growing up in the North would have known that in August 1969, what we were witnessing was the reactionary force of loyalism once more flexing its political muscle to curb nationalist discontent in the form of the peaceful Civil Rights Movement.

However, loyalist violence was a familiar reality for my parents and the older generation, who had bitter experience of the bloody pogroms, riots, sectarian attacks and murders both prior to and in the aftermath of Partition in 1921. This artificial boundary had split the protestant and catholic working class; protestants enjoyed a privileged position in terms of jobs, political patronage and housing in return for their loyalty to the state.

That August, when the RUC and the notorious B Specials[1] led loyalist mobs on attacks into nationalist areas, burning houses in their hundreds and shooting dead several innocent people, and my family fled from our home, was a turning point in my life. Little nine-year-old Patrick Rooney from Divis Flats in the Lower Falls was shot dead as he lay sleeping in bed. I remember thinking it could have been anyone. Any catholic was, and remains today, a potential victim of such sectarian hatred.

Like thousands of others, I began asking questions, and gradually found an answer: that the discrimination of the Orange State was merely a symptom of a greater discrimination, that because of Britain's selfish political, strategic and economic interests, the Irish people were being denied the right to self-determination. From then on, I could analyse what was happening.

An Alternative History Lesson

Phase 1: The British Army and the RUC

From 1969, when colossal numbers of reinforcements were brought in to join what had previously been a token garrison, the British Army quickly re-established itself in its historical role in Ireland: as an imperialist army of occupation. From a position of postured impartiality, the British government and its armed forces switched to open support of the Unionist supremacist position in order to protect British strategic and economic interests. Barricades initially erected in nationalist ghettoes to defend communities against loyalist attacks became the only means of keeping back soldiers lobbing CS gas.

It was the Lower Falls Curfew[2] in July 1970 which effectively catapulted large numbers of nationalist women into political and defensive action against the escalating repression of the crown forces. During the curfew, hundreds of families were held at gunpoint in their homes by the British Army. We were told we would be shot if we so much as put our heads outside the door. Deliveries of food supplies, particularly milk for young babies, were stopped, until a solid wall of fearless and determined women broke the curfew by marching into the ghettoes burdened down with armfuls of groceries.

During the subsequent years, the widespread raids on houses again brought women onto the streets in protest, banging binlids and blowing whistles. It became common practice for women, outnumbered and confronted by heavily-armed soldiers, to pull and free arrested teenagers from jeeps and saracens.

From street protests, many women began to take a more direct part in the national liberation struggle. This was not so much based on a family tradition of republicanism as born of the Civil Rights Movement, the ensuing loyalist backlash, and the increasingly threatening presence of thousands of British soldiers.

In the seventies, the RUC, better armed, equipped, trained and numerically stronger than the IRA, played a central role, alongside the British Army, in the attempted repression of the national struggle. RUC-trained interrogators participated in the physical and psychological torture of thousands of nationalists in various centres throughout the North. A high percentage of nationalists were convicted on incriminating statements achieved by force.

The RUC is not a civilian police force. It was formed after Partition, to replace the old Royal Irish Constabulary, and specifically to deal with crushing nationalist and republican rejection of the new state. Originally, it was to comprise 3,000 men, of whom a third were to be catholics. However, because of loyalist sectarianism and the force's political role in defending partition, it became an almost exclusively protestant and loyalist force and remains so today. Since its formation in June 1922, the RUC has been the iron fist of the state and, in reward, has received virtual immunity for its violent actions.

Phase 2: Criminalization and Normalization (Ulsterization)

Following several political attempts by the British government to reform the unreformable Orange state, which failed because the loyalists find it hard to tolerate any diminution of their power and economic stranglehold in the area, the British came up with a three-pronged strategy whose primary objective was to isolate and defeat the IRA. The aim was to portray the six counties as a 'normal' part of the UK which needed civil policing rather than military invasion. Instead of the primacy of the army in crushing nationalist opposition (whose evidence on the streets in great numbers made it difficult to pretend that there was not a war going on), the RUC was brought to the fore. Special category political status for republican prisoners was to end from 1 March 1976; the political struggle was now criminalized. We entered the era of the primacy of the RUC who were, in their turn, presented to the public by a willing media as the impartial upholders of law and order.

However, the contradictions in this policy were exposed and it failed. Criminalization foundered because republican prisoners refused to accept criminal status. They began a lengthy prison protest in the H-blocks and Armagh Women's Prison. Normalization failed as, during the two H-Block hunger strikes which culminated in the tragic loss of ten lives, international onlookers saw what was happening and asked *why*. The hunger strikes broke through the wall of misinformation and censorship and exposed the nature of British imperialism in the North of Ireland to the world.

As for the RUC, their terror tactics against the nationalist

minority during the hunger strikes guaranteed their unaccepta-
bility in that community. They fired thousands of plastic
bullets at peaceful demonstrators and targeted women and
young children in an attempt to intimidate them from walking
the streets.

Everyday Fear

I am terrified of plastic bullets. My terror, like thousands of
other nationalists', is born from experience, experience of
running in panic with my children when peaceful pickets were
broken up, of huddling in doorways with my heart pounding
so fast I couldn't breathe until the danger was past.

Nora McCabe, a mother of three young children who lived a
few streets away from me was shot dead by a plastic bullet on
the morning of hunger-striker Joe McDonnell's death. Her
'crime'? Going to the corner shop for a packet of cigarettes.
Senior RUC man, James Crutchley, admitted at her inquest
hearing that he had given the order to fire; evidence showed
that the RUC were in no danger. No criminal proceedings were
brought against Crutchley and, adding insult to injury for
Nora's family, he was promoted soon afterwards. He is now
Assistant Chief Constable of the RUC.

Kenneth Newman, who served his apprenticeship in the
North of Ireland before becoming Metropolitan Police Commissioner from 1983 to 1987, was not only an advocate of
stockpiling plastic bullets but of using them against British
people. He warned the British public after the Broadwater
Farm uprising that it was likely plastic bullets would be used in
a future public order incident. Sadly, it may be only a matter of
time before men, women and children in Britain too are
slaughtered by these lethal weapons.

On 24 September 1986, the RUC officer Nigel Hegarty, who
killed Belfast man John Downes with a plastic bullet during an
anti-internment rally on 12 August 1984, was acquitted. He
had been charged with manslaughter, not murder.[3] This verdict did not surprise Irish nationalists, but may have surprised
the hundreds of thousands, if not millions of people world-

wide, who saw the sequence of events that August on their television screens. What they witnessed was a pre-arranged, co-ordinated and totally unprovoked onslaught by the RUC on peaceful demonstrators, many of whom were sitting on the ground. Hegarty was merely the scapegoat. Scores of other RUC personnel involved in this RUC riot were absolved, as were their commanders and the political figures who sanctioned it. Indeed, throughout the countless incidents where nationalists have been shot by the RUC in controversial circumstances, particularly in their shoot-to-kill policy, only one member of the force has been convicted.[4] There is no independent complaints procedure relating to the RUC; all complaints are dealt with internally. Nationalists, needless to say, have no confidence in the internal complaints system.

Today, the RUC numbers approximately 13,000. It is well-armed with the latest weaponry and technology and its members are trained in a variety of repressive methods which are constantly being improved and refined. In Britain, these tested techniques of political control are already in operation, albeit in a more subtle way. Witness the heavy-handedness of the British police during the miners' strike, the vicious attacks on peaceful picketers, the targeting of leading local activists, the searching of houses and sealing-off of roads from flying pickets. Take note of the police's role during the Wapping dispute, or the harassment of Black people in the inner cities. Strip-searching, one of the most degrading and abhorrent tools of repression currently directed against the republican women prisoners at Armagh and now Maghaberry, has become a regular occurrence in women's prisons in London and Scotland. And women have now been strip-searched in British airports and police stations.

Meanwhile, in respect of the North, Amnesty International issued its third major report on abuses of human rights on 28 June 1988. The British government had refused to co-operate with the Amnesty investigation. The report gives considerable space to the killings in 1982 of six unarmed men, shot dead by members of a highly trained police squad, and the subsequent investigation by John Stalker.[5] It claims that the six possibly 'were killed with premeditation as a result of operations deliberately planned to this end'. It criticizes the decision by the Attorney General not to prosecute officers identified by Mr Stalker which, it says, has 'seriously called into question the British government's commitment to investigate fully disputed killings by its security forces, make public the findings and prevent the possibility of unlawful killings in the future'. It also criticizes internal police investigation procedure.

On 4 July 1988, Sir John Hermon, Chief Constable of the RUC, announced that twenty officers would face internal disciplinary charges in respect of the alleged cover-up. As at 1 July 1988 since 1982, forty-five people, nineteen of them unarmed, have been shot dead by crown forces. This is the police force that we as nationalists are supposed to accept with open arms, to respect and to recognize as the impartial upholders of law and order. The British may question the violence of the IRA and analyse the Irish situation as a civil or religious war. Yet the IRA would disappear tomorrow if the British government withdrew from Ireland. The IRA is only a symptom of a greater violence which the British public conveniently ignore: Britain's imperialist occupation of the six counties.

Notes

1. The B Specials carried out numerous atrocities on the nationalist community. They were disbanded in 1969/70 and replaced by the UDR.

2. The Lower Falls Curfew was imposed on several hundred families from Albert Street to the Grosvenor Road, known locally as the 'Lower Falls'. It lasted about three days.

3. In most cases of prosecutions against the RUC in respect of plastic bullet deaths, the charge brought is 'murder' not 'manslaughter' since the amount of evidence required to gain a conviction is far more stringent. In this case, the RUC officer was charged with manslaughter, which should not have been difficult to prove; however, he was still acquitted.

4. The one RUC man who was convicted received life imprisonment for the killing of Tony Dawson, a young nationalist from the Short Strand area of East Belfast.

5. John Stalker, then Deputy Chief Constable of Manchester, was appointed to head an inquiry into the shoot-to-kill policy, but met obstruction and obfuscation in his questioning of the RUC, from the Chief Constable down. On the eve of his return to Belfast, when he was due to question further the Chief Constable and tell him about his findings, he was officially removed from the inquiry and placed under investigation himself.

12. Lesbians, Policing and the Changing Law

Caroline Natzler

It is not unlawful to be a lesbian, but there can be few lesbians who do not *feel* criminalized in some sense, and few of us who readily turn to the police for protection from the criminal behaviour of others. Lesbians know that the police have all the prejudices found in society as a whole, together with the power of being the instrument of a patriarchal state that intentionally oppresses women, particularly lesbians. We are also constantly aware of discrimination against us in the civil law. Thus before considering the relationship between lesbian women and the police as enforcers of criminal law, it is important to look at how civil law discriminates against lesbians, both in the letter of the law and in practice. This is relevant because the police are often in fact involved in enforcement of civil law; it is also relevant in the context of the Multi-Agency Approach to policing whereby information may pass between the police and other agencies or individuals such as social workers. Subjectively, it is also important because it contributes to us seeing ourselves as marginalized; we are unable to see the police as fellow 'citizens in uniform' and feel that our lives are easily criminalized. Discrimination creates a climate for oppressive policing.

Family law is probably the best documented area of discrimination against lesbians.[1] Most lesbian mothers involved in custody disputes lose their children, regardless of their actual qualities as mothers and of the child's wellbeing. Lesbians cannot adopt as a couple[2] and girls may be taken into care simply because they are lesbians or associate with lesbian women, since this can be regarded as being 'exposed to moral danger'.[3] In the case of a man who kills his wife, the victim's actual or alleged lesbianism may be pleaded as 'provocation' to reduce the charge from murder to manslaughter. In the area of employment, industrial tribunals have said that an employer can be acting 'reasonably' in sacking an employee on grounds of homosexuality alone, since the employer would be acting on a prejudice widely held.[4] Cases include a woman sacked for wearing a 'Lesbians Ignite' badge,[5] a highly regarded care worker sacked from a children's home and a midwife who was sacked for being a lesbian. In the area of housing, a lesbian cannot succeed to her deceased lover's council tenancy under the Housing Act 1985,[6] and very few local authorities will rehouse a lesbian on the break-up of a relationship. Harassment from landlords is not uncommon and if a lesbian leaves her home because of this, she may find herself regarded as intentionally homeless and so lose any right she might otherwise have had to be rehoused.[7] Lifelong lesbian partners are not regarded as next of kin or dependants in areas of law or administration such as inheritance, rights to visit in hospital or the state pension scheme.

Under immigration law, many black women only have a right to come to Britain to stay on the basis of marriage, which can trap women in unhappy and even violent heterosexual relationships. The Immigration Act 1971 creates criminal offences e.g. overstaying, so this is an area where the police are directly involved in enforcing discriminatory law (see chapter 21).

Apart from the law, many bodies and pressure groups are intent on ensuring that lesbians are social pariahs. It has been clear for some time that the Thatcher government is prepared to persecute lesbians and gay men. In 1985 a Tory conference cheered a speaker who said, 'If you want a queer for your neighbour, vote Labour.' The 1987 election campaign lambasted Labour's attempt to redress discrimination against us; and in October 1987, Thatcher derided the notion of an 'inalienable right to be gay' and told *Woman's Own*, 'A nation of free people will continue to be great if family life continues and the structure of that nation is a family one.' Since family here obviously means nuclear, patriarchal family, 'free people' would appear not to include lesbians.

The Clause

At the end of the 1987 autumn session of parliament, David Wilshire, a Tory MP, introduced what was then clause 27 of the Local Government Bill. It subsequently became clear that this introduction was with Thatcher's personal support. The clause came into effect on 24 May 1988 as section 28 of the Local Government Act 1988. The relevant part reads;

(1) A local authority shall not –
    (a) intentionally promote homosexuality or publish material with the intention of promoting homosexuality;
    (b) promote the teaching in any maintained school of the acceptability of homosexuality as a pretended family relationship.
(2) Nothing in subsection (1) above shall be taken to prohibit the doing of anything for the purpose of treating or preventing the spread of disease.

'Promote' is not defined but a wide interpretation seems likely and was indeed accepted by MPs voting for the clause who had been warned by voluntary organizations of its potential implications. At the time these appeared to include an end to a range of services to lesbians and gay men, from legal advice agencies such as the Lesbians and Policing Project and the Lesbian Employment Rights to the provision of lesbian and gay literature in public libraries; an end to informed discussion of lesbianism in schools, fuelling hatred against lesbian youngsters and isolating the children of lesbian mothers; an end to heterosexism awareness training in local authorities (for example in Redditch and Camden) or police forces; and threat to much of the work of women's centres. Above all perhaps it was clear that the clause would exacerbate homophobia and lead to an increase in attacks on lesbians and gay men.

Some legal opinions obtained since the passage of the clause through parliament argue for a less draconian theoretical interpretation of the Act by local authorities and the courts; however, what is happening in practice is another matter. Michael Barnes QC's legal Opinion[8] for the Association of London Authorities (April 1988) counsels prudence to local authorities. He recommends that they should not fund organizations whose activities 'seek deliberately to further' homosexuality, nor publish material which does so. He interprets 'intentionally' as including knowing that a certain consequence may come about, even if it is not desired (by the local authority). However, his view is that 'discouraging forms of discrimination' is not 'to be equated with the promotion of homosexuality', and that many positive local authority decisions and actions concerning lesbians and gay men continue to be lawful. That does not mean, of course, that they will go unchallenged.

Another opinion by Keir Starmer (23 May 1988) emphasizes the ambiguity, absence of legal definitions, and illogicality of the wording of the clause and argues that there is no evidence that anything local authorities could do would promote 'homosexual inclinations' in people and that 'anti-discrimination measures and positive images would not fall within the ambit of promoting homosexuality'.

It is too soon to know how the courts will interpret the clause. In the face of alarm and criticism, the Department of Environment issued a standard letter to enquirers in the spring of 1988, stating that:

> There is no question of . . . a censorship of the arts . . . banning books stocked in public libraries as part of the normal library function . . . discouraging the balanced and objective discussion of homosexuality in the classroom; or providing any other service to homosexuals on the same basis as to other groups.

This is all theoretical. In practice, even before the clause became law, certain local authorities and police officers were using it quite blatantly to discriminate against lesbians and gay men. In January 1988 local police officers told the Greenwich

Lesbian and Gay Centre that they were in illegal occupation of their building because of the clause. The local authority dispelled this notion – which would not have been a criminal matter in any event – but obviously such actions contribute to an atmosphere of police intimidation. Again before the clause became law, a group of Tories in Haringey Council proposed a motion that the grant be withdrawn from a local community bookshop because 5 per cent of its stock was lesbian and gay literature. More recently, in Strathclyde, colleges have been told by their local authority that grants to students' associations should be conditional upon compliance with the clause. In East Sussex, the council withdrew a booklet produced by the National Youth Bureau because it contained a request for volunteers for the London Lesbian and Gay Centre. Wolverhampton Law Centre's grant is threatened because of the appointment of a worker to draw up an equal opportunities policy and its support for the Lesbian and Gay Rights Group. In London, Lespop (the lesbians and policing organization) has been refused refunding and the London Boroughs Grant Scheme has imposed a grant condition on voluntary groups they fund such as the London Women's Irish Centre, that the money must not be used 'for the purpose which constitutes the intentional promotion of homosexuality'. This is a direct attack on the equal opportunity policies of such groups which are an essential basis for the *effective* 'anti-discrimination measures' which legal opinions suggest should be exempt. A lesbian college lecturer has had her work curtailed because she mentioned the clause in the context of a lecture; and Brighton Women's Branch of the Workers' Educational Association has been told that they can no longer entitle a three-year course 'Lesbian Literature'. Women's studies teachers are already altering their courses and engaging in protective self-censorship, which means they can no longer explore the range of women's experiences and oppressions. Feminist publishers fear the self-censorship the clause will impose on bookshops, libraries and schools.[9] Self-censorship can also be enforced, as policy, as in the case of Ealing Council, whose employees have to undertake that advertising for events (leaflets and so on) for which they are responsible, will not promote homosexuality; the chief officer has had to sign a declaration that the work does not contravene the clause. Groups monitoring the clause report an increase in physical attacks;[10] the clause is evidently a licence to violent homophobia.

Though the clause has motivated lesbians into mass actions such as demonstrations and into ingenious direct actions, on an individual basis there is no doubt that it has already led to an increased level of fear, self-censorship and deceit as we go about our daily lives. It is once again respectable to view lesbians as beyond the pale; the difference in attitudes is detectable now that homophobia has been legitimated. It is evident even within 'liberal' organizations; in one London Law Centre, a worker suggested that the Centre's equal opportunities policy should be amended to comply with the clause.

It is in this context that we have to look at the relationship between lesbians and the police.

Whose Police? Lesbians as Victims of Crime

If a woman reports a crime, for example assault or burglary, and the police know or discover that she is a lesbian, she may find herself treated as if she were the offender. Lespop report that the police may discredit her statements, interrogate her as to her lifestyle and subject her to abuse and even assault. They may then charge her with a criminal offence. Black and Irish women are particularly vulnerable here, where racism compounds anti-lesbianism. Lespop report that they have cases of the police condoning male attacks on lesbians' property (for example, throwing bricks through their windows) and that where women fight back against assault they themselves may be charged and the men allowed to go free. Lespop cite a case where two white women were in a London pub discussing a lesbian club they had been to; the barman then refused to serve them and threatened them with violence if they did not leave immediately. He and another man attacked the women and called the police, who arrested the women, letting both men go free. The women were manhandled in the van on the way to the police station and told they would be charged with behaviour likely to cause a breach of the peace and criminal damage, and that if they did not make statements they would be kept in the cells overnight and their employers would be told they were lesbians. They were strip-searched within sight of male police officers. One of the women was involved in a custody case and her ex-husband did not know of her lesbianism. She was worried about leaving the police station in time to collect her child, so rather than tell the police that she had a child (and have them arrange for her to be collected) and risk her lesbianism emerging in the custody case, she made a statement admitting the charges. However, the court welfare officer preparing the report for the custody case a few months later appeared to know a lot more details of the alleged offence than would have emerged in formal documentation of the charge, and the woman suspects that the police informed the social work agencies of her lesbianism.

Not surprisingly, lesbians may think twice before reporting crimes to the police. There is the experience of male violence, common to all women living without men, which may make us wary of having male officers in our households. There is the danger of becoming known to the police as lesbians. Once such information is on the police national computer it can be summoned up at any time, possibly for prejudicial use against a woman. For the same reason, many lesbians feel reluctant to come forward as witnesses.

The following story, told in the words of one of the young women it happened to, is frighteningly clear. Perhaps it is no accident that it happened in mid January 1988 when awareness of the government's endorsement of homophobia (in clause 27 of the Local Government Bill) was high:

'I was coming home with my lover from a nightclub in Liverpool on 18 January 1988; we went to get a burger and there was a gang of youths outside the burger bar who started threatening and hassling us. They mentioned my leather jacket; I thought they were going to mug us for it. I said to my lover, "Let's make a break for it," and we ran to the police station round the corner. The youths gave chase but stopped off when they saw us going into the police station. We ran into the station and I said, "There's a gang of youths outside who've been threatening us." The desk sergeant said, "Fuck off, lesbian, and take your lesbian friend out with you." I just stood there; I couldn't believe what he'd said. I said, "Have I just heard you correctly?" He said, "Yes, you did, you fucking queer. Get out with your filthy dyke friend." I said, "Just because I've got short hair, a leather jacket and Doc Martin shoes, does that mean to say I'm a lesbian?"

'He called for assistance and five other policemen materialized behind the desk; two of them grabbed my lover and literally threw her out of the door – her feet didn't touch the ground. Then two of them grabbed me and pushed me out. They locked the police station doors on us and told us to go off and get what we deserved, which was "a fucking good meat injection". In a rage, my lover kicked the police minibus.

'Next minute, all five came out, jumped on top of us and pushed us into the back of a transit. Two of them went back into the station and the other three got into the transit with us and insulted us because of our sexuality. Then they told us they were taking us to Southport, which is a long way from Liverpool. We asked why they were taking us there and they said, "because it's a fucking long walk home". It was half past midnight. In fact, they just drove us round the block a few times, keeping up this stream of homophobic abuse, and we ended up in another police station where we were charged with being drunk and disorderly.

'The desk sergeant there showed us a piece of paper with our rights on it, at the same time saying that we were too drunk to inform anyone (friends or solicitor) of our arrest. We kept insisting that we weren't drunk and we wanted to inform at least a friend of where we were but he persisted with the line that we were too drunk and abusive to be talking to anybody. They put us in separate cells and wouldn't even allow us a cup of water which we were pleading for because our throats were so dry from arguing with them.

'We were held from 1 a.m. to 6 a.m. in the cells, being

insulted. They kept opening the hatch in the door of my lover's cell, saying, "Oh, are you the fucking lesbian then?" I was making a lot of noise and they kept telling me to shut up; each time they said, "Shut up," it was followed by one or other of the terms of abuse men use to degrade women; they went through the whole repertoire. In that five hours, I was dragged out of the cell four times because I refused to co-operate with the police because they wouldn't co-operate with us over our basic rights. They were trying to find out my date of birth which I refused to give them. Each time I was dragged out, the desk sergeant became more frustrated, irate and abusive toward me, calling me a "blasé fucker" and alleging that I must have been arrested many times before because I wasn't showing any signs of being intimidated by them. I could sense that he and one of the others wanted to hit me. They became even more angry when I refused to give them my correct address and because I had a political perspective. I was saying I thought the way they were behaving was a gross abuse of power and that it was no wonder people in Liverpool didn't trust them. I said I wondered how they treated black people if they'd treat a white woman like this.

'I'd given them two addresses, one of which was my lover's and the other my mother's. They sent an officer to interview my mother at 4 a.m. When this officer came back he dragged me out of the cell and told me my mother had said she hadn't seen me for four years and I was a lying bastard. I said I found that hard to believe as I'd had tea with her a couple of days ago.

'I subsequently found out that my mother had been asked whether she was the mother of a woman of twenty-four whose name sounded similar to mine. She'd said no; that was not my name and I was thirty years old. But this was the line they were taking, and, in their last round of intimidation against me, it worked. They told me I fitted the description of a woman wanted for a serious crime committed in Middlesborough, and they would be taking me there for interviewing, at 5.30 in the morning. They started revving up the transit van outside and shouting, "We're ready for the filthy fucking queer. Let's go now!" I just became completely freaked out and I gave them my date of birth.

'A couple of minutes later, they decided I was clean. They told my lover she could go but they took me down to the main Bridewell police station, next to the magistrates' court, where I was searched. They did not abuse me at Bridewell but they did put me in a cell with about six remand prisoners from Risley who hadn't been searched properly and were all shooting up. They kept asking me if I was queer and saying queers in Risley get beaten up. I was very worried.

'We appeared in the magistrates' court at about 10.30 a.m. and were charged with being drunk and disorderly. (We'd each had three pints; we had not been drunk and disorderly.) My lover pleaded guilty. I had no idea why. I followed suit. The court usher led me to believe that the fine would be £30–45 plus costs, and asked if we had anything to say. We both said that when we go into a police station requesting help because of being intimidated, we expect to be given assistance, not insulted, abused and locked out of the police station. The magistrates had a discussion and fined us both £10 and waived the costs.

'We would have liked to make a complaint against the police but felt we needed legal help and our Liverpool law centre were too busy to take it on. My lover was not prepared to get into a court prosecution because it would have jeopardized her relationship with the Home Office who is her employer for the bulk of her teaching work. We both dismissed the idea of making a complaint on our own because we were scared the police would come around and intimidate us.'

There are several very disturbing features about this incident. In the first place, there is the contempt the police showed for their duty; they did not begin to take on board the women's complaint; the police felt that the women, as lesbians, had forfeited their right to protection. In the second place, there is the 'retaliatory charge' of drunk and disorderly when the women became indignant about the treatment they received. In the third place is the aspect of taking punishment into their own hands (for a crime which so far does not exist). The police felt entitled to 'punish' Mary and her lover for their sexuality, not only by the formal detention and charge, but informally by physical and gross verbal abuse. They also seemed to feel no compunction about denying them the rights of 'suspects' held in police stations.

Social Control and the Policing of Lesbians

Lesbians are seen as a threat to men, to the patriarchal order which determines the particular structure of 'the family', and are viewed as generally out of control. The lesbian feminist lifestyle is threatening to the social order, not because we are 'different', but because we have extended the feminist principle of freedom from male control and protection. The backlash against lesbians which the clause represents is part of a movement against feminism, and has implications for all women.

However, the oppressive policing of lesbians should not just be seen in the context of anti-feminism; it is also part of a vicious campaign against gay men, who have been blamed for the AIDS epidemic. At the same time, there is a police onslaught against black people, strikers, the poor and so-called 'hippie' travellers. For many groups who are not part of the Thatcherite norm, the rights of free association, free expression and the right to walk the streets without fear and feel safe in one's home are under attack, both from the law and from police strategy. Lesbians, of course, belong to many communities and may suffer multiply, for instance from racism.

The police make no bones about seeing policing as an aspect of social control. This view has been expressed by ex-Chief Commissioner of the Met Kenneth Newman (see chapter 9) and less soberly by Chief Constable Anderton of the Greater Manchester Police. Others such as ex-Chief Constable of South-East Yorkshire, Basil Griffiths have commented: 'In every community there is a large minority of people who are not fit for salvage ... The only way in which the police can protect society is, quite frankly, by harassing these people.'[11]

The policy of targeting and surveillance of certain groups, operates, for example, when a lesbian is arrested for an offence unrelated to her sexuality or sexual politics and then questioned and harassed in relation to her lesbianism. Lespop report a black lesbian arrested for a minor traffic offence who was held in police custody overnight, not allowed a phone call or a solicitor, subjected to racist abuse, interrogated about her women's group and threatened with a drugs charge if she did not answer. She refused and was not charged as threatened, but when she got home she was told by her neighbours that people had been in her flat. She discovered that her belongings had been gone through, though money had not been taken.

It is the experience of women that the police make a link between lesbianism and political dissent, and may use 'lesbian' as a label for female protest which must be suppressed, as well as a term of abuse (see chapter 13). This appeared to be so in the case of Ms Dewhurst who was arrested during an anti-apartheid demonstration in 1986 and charged with assault and obstruction. After being cleared she took proceedings against the Metropolitan Police for assault, false imprisonment and malicious prosecution. She alleged that she was strip-searched, watched and verbally abused by male officers; that references were made to 'fucking' her and that she was called disgusting, a slut and a lesbian. Defending, the police cited their view that she was a 'determined and committed' campaigner, hostile to the police and a 'fraud'. The jury acquitted the police, to the shock and distress of Ms Dewhurst and those involved in her case.

The sort of random, unjustified arrests which seem to be an aspect of social control policing are particularly evident at protest marches and lesbian venues. Though lesbian clubs may not be raided with the same frequency as gay men's clubs, Lespop reports that the women's night at Merlin's Cave, King's Cross has been affected by police action, and in September 1987 the police started to make moves to close Frolic, a mixed lesbian and gay club in South London. The police declared, as reported in the local press and *Capital Gay* (a free newspaper for lesbians and gay men in London), that their object was to close the clubs because they were not for heterosexuals and that 'gays' belonged in the West End. But they used the excuses of a query on the licence and complaints from local residents to justify the raids, though when the club invited residents to complain, none did. The police doubts about the licence were not substantiated at the time. During one raid, a lesbian member was attacked by a police dog when she inquired why the club licence holder was being manhandled by the police. When another woman tried to pull the dog off she was arrested. Both women were punched and knelt on by the police, but the charges were dropped on condition that the women agreed to be bound over to keep the peace. One of the women is currently taking a complaint against the police. It appears that the police attempt to close Frolic was successful since the harassment has deterred the licence holder from pursuing the matter in court.

In December 1986, Ms King, two other lesbians and nine gay men were arrested at a protest rally against South Staffordshire District Council leader Bill Brownhill, who remarked that 90 per cent of gay people should be gassed. The group were charged with assault on the police and offences relating to public order. Ms King and others were held in custody for a week over Christmas simply because the Crown Prosecution Service claimed that their names and addresses had not been verified. All charges were, of course, dropped before the court hearing date. Ms King and two of the men are now taking High Court proceedings against the police and the Crown Prosecution Service, claiming damages for the period they spent in custody, on the basis that their names and addresses *had* been verified and they should therefore not have been refused bail. Ms King is also suing the police for assault against her by two officers.

As with the miners in the 1984/5 coal dispute, it is not uncommon for charges in such situations to be dropped, indicating that the arrests were for the purposes of social control rather than for enforcement of the criminal law. Arrest and detention in custody serves to intimidate the lesbian community and it is these events of course, not the dropping of charges, that figure in the popular media, stoking prejudice.

On 9 January 1988 about 12,500 lesbians and gay men marched in protest in London against clause 28 of the Local Government Bill. The policing of this demonstration was worrying from the beginning. For large sections of the march there was absolutely no evidence of any police escort to protect us from attacks by the public or the National Front, and at Trafalgar Square a lesbian steward was pushed by a car trying to break through the march. When she eventually found a policeman, leaving other women standing in front of the car, he told her it was nothing to do with him. But the police were there all right, ready to make 'indiscriminate arrests' as the Gay London Policing Group (GALOP) put it. A number of people were arrested at Downing Street and when the march reached Harmsworth Park for a rally the police arrested two women, apparently for kissing! Other people were arrested outside the park area when they tried to stop the police taking the women away. Mounted police appeared on the scene, overlooking the peaceful rally within the park and only left when lesbian leader of Lambeth Council Linda Bellos, in whose area the rally was held, pointed out the provocation of this sort of policing.

The police arrested people on charges which could not be sustained. In several cases, the charges on which people were originally arrested were later reduced, a hallmark of social control policing. Two charges of actual bodily harm were dropped to assault, and three of carrying an offensive weapon (banner poles!) were dropped to charges of threatening words and behaviour. Even the charges on which defendants were eventually brought before the courts were without adequate foundation. Of the twenty-eight cases known to GALOP, eight were dismissed for lack of evidence; in two cases charges were dropped, presumably for similar reasons; in one case the defendant was found not guilty and awarded costs against the police; and in nine cases the defendants were bound over to keep the peace, often an indication of the weakness of the police case. Of the seven women arrested, in six cases charges were dropped or dismissed for lack of evidence. At the time of writing (July 1988) there had been five convictions and one case was still outstanding. The policing of this demonstration has alerted many women to the current tendency of the state towards trying to criminalize lesbianism.

The policing of later demonstrations against the clause and of the Lesbian Strength and Gay Pride marches in June 1988 was low profile and without obvious incident, perhaps partly as a result of the counterproductive nature of the policing of the January demonstration. Whatever relief we may feel about this, as lesbian women we need to remain alert.

Although on the whole the charges relating to the January march seem to have been the traditional ones used in the policing of demonstrations (for example, obstruction, or threatening words and behaviour) there were four charges of 'disorderly conduct'. GALOP's information suggests possibly three other charges under the Public Order Act 1986.

Use of this Act has important implications for lesbians. Section five creates the arrestable offence of 'disorderly behaviour' (or conduct) which is behaviour likely to be threatening to anyone or likely to harass, alarm or distress them. It seems unlikely that the targets will be men harassing women with sexual approaches in the street, but they might now include a group of women singing in the street and wearing lesbian badges.

What Do We Want? Accountability versus Liaison

In the light of all this it may seem too sanguine to discuss what we should be demanding of the police. But many lesbians have been working hard in this area and are not going to be discouraged. Although Lespop reports that police monitoring groups are often hostile to lesbians, some groups like local authority Lesbian and Gay Units have been working in police liaison groups. In London, Hackney police have asked lesbian and gay groups to help with training recruits. Association of London Authorities (ALA) and other non-statutory groups had a series of meeting during 1987 with Scotland Yard Community Liaison Officers and the Equal Opportunities Unit to discuss the possibility of a non-discrimination policy; and GALOP and the ALA are submitting proposals for non-discrimination and equal opportunities policies as well as enforcement mechanisms.

It may be, as Lespop has claimed regarding Police Consultative Groups, that such liaison meetings between the police and lesbian and gay groups are merely public relations exercises on the part of the police and involve the groups in questionable compromises. Also, since the Metropolitan Police did not create an equal opportunities policy unit until a report[12] showed they were in breach of sex and race discrimination laws it seems unlikely that they will introduce a policy of non-discrimination against lesbian women and gay men now, when there is nothing in law to prohibit such discrimination, and much to encourage it. Many people also question whether anything can be achieved while the Met remain unaccountable and other police forces only partially so through local police boards with very limited powers. Finally, if the police are part of a patriarchal order to which the existence of lesbian women is in itself a threat, what possibility is there of 'reform'?

I do not believe we have a choice; we cannot simply *wait* for political structures to change, for police accountability, for a society of real choice, open to different forms of social organization and the liberation of women. In the face of the array of forces against us, we must maintain the pressure for change on all fronts, towards, at the least, equal rights for lesbians. It is vital that lesbian women remain visible and are not cowed by all the current forces towards criminalization of lesbianism. We are out and we are staying out!

Notes

1. See especially Jackie Forster and Gillian Hanscombe, *Rocking the Cradle*, Sheba, Feminist Publishers, London, 1982. Also Rights of Women Legal Custody Group, *Lesbian Mothers Legal Handbook*, Women's Press, London, 1986.

2. Children Act 1975, s.10(1).

3. Children and Young Persons Act 1969, s.1 (2)(c).

4. LAGER (Lesbian and Gay Employment Rights) quote Saunders v. Scottish National Camps Association Ltd (1980) IRLR 174, (1981) IRLR 277 as an example of this kind of thinking.

5. Boychuk v. H.J. Symons Holdings Ltd (1977) IRLR 395, EAT.

6. Harrogate BC v. Simpson 1984 17 HLR 205 C.A.

7. That is, if she falls within one of the 'priority' categories created by the homelessness legislation.

8. Information about Counsels' opinions from Law Centres Federation Lesbian and Gay Sub-committee, Duchess House, Warren Street, London W.1.

9. *Observer*, 8 May 1988.

10. Information from LCF Lesbian and Gay Sub-committee (see note 8).

11. Basil Griffiths, quoted by GALOP for Legislation for Lesbian and Gay Rights Conference 1986.

12. The Policy Studies Institute Report, *Police and People in London*, available from Policy Studies Institute, 1–2 Castle Lane, London SW1E 6DR.

Acknowledgements

Except where otherwise specifically stated, the information for this article has come from published papers and conference papers of the Lesbians and Policing Project, the Gay London Policing Group, the Community Affairs Division of Lambeth Council and articles in the newspapers *Outwrite* and *Capital Gay*; from my own experience as a lesbian and a solicitor, and from the experiences of my friends. I should also like to thank Louise Christian, of Christian Fisher, Solicitors, Christina Dunhill who actually assembled much of the written information, and the London Strategic Policy Unit.

13. Greenham Women

The Control of Protest

Rebecca Johnson

As circumstances at Greenham changed, so did police attitudes, partly because Greenham women represented a challenge to stereotyped views of feminine behaviour. As long as we could be viewed as mothers protesting on behalf of our children, our role was acceptable, even if our activity was 'misguided'. In the early days the police patronized us; this was the avuncular phase. But women surviving without men in harsh physical conditions, whilst disrupting the United States Airforce (USAF) with persistent success and ingenuity, were something else.

With the change in perceptions, the name-calling began. 'Lesbians' was used pejoratively; it fitted with traditional police (and social) prejudice. Besides, many of us were. Calling us 'slags' and 'whores' was more contradictory, as what incensed the police most was our independence. Once they could convince themselves we were not 'real women', we were also denied the general protection supposedly provided by 'law and order' for all citizens; further, we seemed to become particular targets for punishment and abuse, to bring us back into line.

Our use of nonviolence is not synonymous with passive resistance, for in intervening to prevent violence, we challenge the militarists and those carrying out government orders, confronting them with their personal responsibility for what they are doing, whether they are planning for war, building silos, driving cruise missile launchers or policing the bases. In nonviolence therefore, we choose to take responsibility for not acquiescing with or contributing to personal violence or violent systems established and sanctioned by the government. Thus, in addition to demonstrating, we've blockaded bases, cut open the fences that strangled common land and left painted messages on 'secret' convoys. We've also painted porn shops and the premises of commercial collaborators in the violence of rape and apartheid, as part of our peace work. Revolutionary nonviolence challenges the conditions that give violence its power over us. It is therefore deeply threatening to the military and to the police force, who rely on threats of violence to maintain control.

When 35,000 women arrived to 'Embrace the Base' on 12 December 1982, the policing was low key. However, when 5,000 women stayed to blockade the gates the next day, the police arrived in paramilitary squads. Women from the Camp especially were picked out, and suffered concussion, severe bruising, torn ears and cuts. We watched, astonished, as police arrived suddenly in vanloads, jumped out and stood in formation, rhythmically slapping their thighs to gee themselves up for the order to charge. On the order, they ran forward and hurled us from the gates to clear a passage for the fleet of vehicles attempting to enter the base.

The press portrayed the blockading women as screaming harridans, contrasting us with what they had presented as the nice, well-meaning middle-class mothers and grandmothers the day before. Yet it was not the women who had changed, but our activity. 'Embrace the Base' had been a nonviolent demonstration of public disagreement with the decision to site Cruise missiles in Europe. It took place on a Sunday so that the base could be surrounded without much inconvenience to the military. 'Close the Base', on a working Monday, was also nonviolent, but it was a direct action to prevent military and construction work being carried out, at maximum disruption to the base. Women who took part on both days viewed the demonstration and the direct action as complementary activities to raise public awareness, but the policing was much rougher on the second day, as the blockades brought the base virtually to a standstill.

Since then, there have been many more blockades at Greenham, including one lasting for a week in July 1983, and sudden unplanned blockades of Cruise missile support vehicles and launchers going out to Salisbury Plain. Sometimes the police made arrests. More often the officer in charge would decide that there were not enough officers or vehicles to transport women to the local police station. Occasionally the police would be prepared to arrest large numbers, especially if Newbury Racecourse was free for use as a holding area while the detainees were processed. (Processing involves giving name and particulars to the police, being searched, sometimes photographed or fingerprinted, then charged and either bailed or remanded in custody. It can take from an hour to three days.)

Often a local officer would indicate the 'resident' Greenham peacewomen who would be picked out and arrested as presumed ringleaders. Because there would not be enough police to hold the other women, they, angered by these tactics, would return to blockade again and again, stretching police resources and forcing them finally to arrest far more women than they had intended or had facilities to deal with. Release without charge for almost everyone usually followed after some hours.

When 50,000 women surrounded the Greenham base in December 1983 after the first missiles and launchers had been flown in, many women incorporated direct action into their demonstrating by taking down sections of the perimeter fence. Soldiers from the base struck at our hands with metal rods while Thames Valley police twisted and karate-chopped fingers and wrists, pulled us from the fence by our necks and flung us into ditches and trees. Mounted police rode their horses straight into crowds of demonstrators. When one woman tried to remove barbed wire from the path of a police horse she feared would get hurt, her photograph became the basis for a frenzied attack which ran the headline, 'Horse Whipped With Barbed Wire.' Police acknowledgement that this hadn't actually happened was delayed until after the press coverage. Headlines screamed of this fabricated outrage and ignored the many injuries, including broken bones, that women had suffered. The few arrests made that day were for cutting wire. It would seem that putting women out of action through injury rather than arrest was the preferred (and no doubt most economical) method of policing that day.

Policing the Cruise Missile Convoy

The first Cruise missile launchers were taken on exercise in March 1984. Over fifty police arrived to surround twelve women at Blue Gate at 1 a.m. As one woman ran to her car to alert Newbury supporters, she was tripped and her car keys were wrenched from her and flung into some bushes. The police held the women in a huddle face down on the ground until the launchers had passed. Then they jumped back into their vans and sped off. As women arrived through the night in response to the Camp's call, a couple of hundred police were brought in to police the convoy's return a few hours later.

Since then, the missile convoy has been taken on exercise almost once a month. The numbers of police brought in varied with the number of protesters they expect, but at Greenham and certain key roundabouts they aim to swamp us with hundreds. Often there have been more police escort than United States Airforce (USAF) vehicles in the convoy. Beforehand, the Ministry of Defence, the CID and the civilian police comb the route by car, motorcycle or on foot, with powerful searchlights. They are looking for Greenham women or Cruisewatchers who may be waiting with paint or banners to mark, halt or simply witness the nuclear procession. (Cruisewatch is a locally based network of peace protesters, living along the dispersal routes, committed to protest and nonviolent direct action every time Cruise is taken on its dispersal wargames.) If they find us they call in reinforcements to surround us, often forcibly preventing us from standing on the roadside, despite the fact that peaceful protest with banners is not illegal.

Usually, the convoy leaves Yellow Gate. Vanloads of police move in just before the event and block major roads to all traffic. They run up and line the roads, pushing visible protesters behind tight cordons. Accompanying them is a Thames

Valley Communications van which attempts to jam our legal CB transmissions. A police wrecker/tow truck is placed menacingly near our vehicles. Women are pushed and shoved and prevented from crossing the road. Sometimes, police try to tear our banners away or wrench car doors open to grab the CBs. They have tried to break aerials and have smashed car windows and windscreens. Keys have been confiscated and thrown into the undergrowth, or if you are lucky, returned later. Some women have been knocked to the ground and forcibly held down until the convoy has passed. Women who have blockaded the convoy on roundabouts have been thrown against railings and injured by police bouncing heavily on their backs as they lie on the ground immobilized and virtually unable to breathe.

Cruise is usually taken out at night, when the numbers that the police wear are rarely visible. If after experiencing or witnessing an assault by police, we attempt to see a man's number, worse violence is used to prevent us. We are knocked out of the way, thumped in the chest or grabbed by other police officers. If we persist we risk arrest. It is now increasingly common for women who have been badly hurt to then be themselves arrested and charged. This seems to have the dual effect of neutralizing the protesters' complaints and stifling the media's ability to report the injuries, because the whole incident is then regarded as sub judice.

One woman who had been assaulted and badly bruised by a police sergeant was subsequently charged with criminal damage to the shoulder section of his jacket for a half-inch tear just by the number he wore, which he was trying to prevent her from seeing. Her own clothes had been badly torn and a police surgeon who later saw her in the police station had to prescribe painkillers for her injuries. These were significant enough for the dose to be doubled two hours later by the police who still refused at that time to let her make a complaint. Six friends were refused permission to wait for her inside the police station and had to wait for five hours that night in the station car park, although it was snowing.

Arrest

On being arrested or removed, we have often been dragged long distances by arms, legs or hair, regardless of whether we are willing to walk or not. One result of this is that our clothes get torn or displaced, sometimes leaving us partially unclothed. Officers have refused to stop so that we can cover ourselves and have also made offensive and threatening sexual remarks. In addition, many women have complained of their breasts being deliberately touched, held or viciously twisted during police grabs or arrest. Sometimes a detained woman has been held on her own in the back of a police van with eight to ten policemen discussing her body and what they would like to do to her. Because the police may have orders to guard the Cruise convoy on its whole route, an arrested woman may have to be shut in the van with these men for over an hour until the launchers have gone to ground at their dispersal site, usually Salisbury Plain, after which she may be taken to a local police station for processing.

One young woman was dumped out of a slowly moving police van when the police decided they couldn't be bothered to charge her after all. She fell into the path of following vehicles and only just avoided serious injury. She had to be treated in hospital for shock and concussion.

Harassment

In addition to blocking roads, police also used stop procedures to harass Cruisewatch and Greenham women from preceding or following the United States Air Force Cruise convoy. Drivers are stopped and questioned, required to produce documents, sometimes searched and checked and often prevented for a period from continuing along public roads.

When a USAF vehicle ran into a Greenham car in 1986, the police issued a public statement to the press blaming the woman. This was done before checking the facts and was inaccurate and misleading. Eventually the Greenham driver received an apology and acknowledgement that the military driver had been at fault, but too late to counter the damaging publicity. He was not charged. Police also declined to charge the military driver who deliberately swerved to hit a woman at Blue Gate and drove on, leaving her screaming in pain with a broken leg.

Evictions

During the first three years, the Greenham Camp was evicted every few months in a glare of publicity with hundreds of police. Since its byelaw changes, Newbury District Council now sends in its bailiffs (renamed 'commons wardens'), accompanied by police, almost every day; for some months, this became several times a day.

The bailiffs are authorized to remove camping structures and put out fires. They are not entitled to take personal belongings or to punch, kick or hit women trying to hold on to their sleeping bags or rucksacks. However, instances of bailiff lawbreaking are numerous, ranging from assault, removal of unopened mail, threatening behaviour and abusive language to dangerous driving. The police have told us that though they cannot arrest the bailiffs, they do 'take them aside and have a quiet word'. But in fact, the police have watched various incidents without intervening and refused medical help to women seriously injured as a result. Only a few of the officers involved ever intervened to stop the bailiffs assaulting women or taking personal belongings. When asked why the bailiffs are not charged, the police have replied that it is a civil matter and that they are only there to prevent a breach of the peace. For some police, however, this function extends to harassing and ticketing women for parking offences as we load the cars with women's belongings to save them.

Women have been arrested for refusing to co-operate during evictions of the Camp and then released after the bailiffs have gone. We've argued that it is not the police's role to be Newbury Council's bullyboys. If we are committing an offence, then the police should bring us to court to answer charges. If not, then the police should not abuse their powers of arrest.

Conclusions

Official complaints about police behaviour seem to get no-where. After a year or so, the stock reply 'insufficient evidence' is received. A woman who has been manhandled, beaten or sexually terrorized by police will either have been on her own with no witnesses, or her witnesses will be outnumbered by police witnesses who will swear that no such thing happened.

We only register complaints about gross violence or abuse (such as someone being thrown, concussed or sexually molested) and not about the hundreds of incidents we experience of police using illegal, improper or intimidating behaviour. Our complaints represent only a fraction of police abuses of power and the law associated with Greenham, yet we are treated as timewasting nuisances. Station officers have sometimes tried to refuse complaints and refused to give us the required forms for registering a complaint. Women who have been injured and need to see the police doctor, especially necessary to substantiate a complaint, have sometimes been kept waiting for hours and intimidated until they give up trying.

Consequently, many women regard official complaints as at best pointless and, at worst, a further ordeal in which they will have to relate and relive a frightening or painful encounter about which nothing will be done.

In the early days of the Women's Peace Camp, older women and those who looked 'respectable' could expect to be treated with more deference by the police. However, women identified as Lesbian were picked on for verbal abuse and often for extra harsh treatment both by police and in prison. When Black women came to the Camp, they experienced racial abuse from British soldiers and the police. During one of the big demonstrations, for example, police arrested only one out of a large group of women pulling the fence down, a Black woman.

Because of the racism in court procedures in general and in

prison, Black women face harsher treatment; thus the consequences for Black women of taking nonviolent direct action are likely to be more severe than for white women. Black women are more likely than their white counterparts to be sent to prison for a first offence. Racism in prison reflects the racism in British society, which adds a further burden to Black women serving sentences. Black women and working-class women, perceived by prison authorities as somehow 'belonging' in prison (as opposed to middle-class women who are regarded as 'out of place'), are also more likely to be patronized and subtly co-opted whilst inside.

Lesbians, if 'out', suffer from the prejudices of lawyers, magistrates and judges: thus their 'deviation' is tacitly added to the charges and reflected in heavier sentences than for heterosexual mothers and women judged to be of good character (that is, misguided rather than criminal). Though many prison officers are themselves Lesbian, the issue of sexuality is frequently used to persecute 'out' Lesbians, who are far more likely to be punished for the prison offence of 'Lesbian Activity'. This covers things like hugging or sitting on someone else's bed and is used to prevent close friendships between inmates, whether sexual or not.

Because of the different pressures and treatment women face in the penal system, it has always been an important commitment at the Greenham Peace Camp for all women to support and validate individual women's own choices about whether or not to include direct action, and the risk of arrest, fines or imprisonment, in their peace work.

Over the years — and especially since the Public Order Act was passed — it has increasingly seemed that all protesters involved in nonviolent resistance to war preparations and injustice are to be criminalized. Confronted at times with visitors' shock and outrage at the behaviour of police, I began to realize that at Camp we had come to take for granted a degree of police violence and abuse that formerly would have horrified us. We have all become habituated to a level of violence which is beyond police codes of practice and which would amount to assault or worse if committed by non-uniformed civilians.

Not all police use violence. A number have shown restraint and consideration – even kindness – in carrying out their duties with an integrity that must, in the circumstances, take considerable personal courage. Sadly, these individuals are an exception. In general, local police on their own patch may harass but are less likely to be really violent than forces brought in to police an event. Some may privately express disquiet at the behaviour of outside forces brought in for Cruise convoys or big demonstrations. It was certainly our experience that where police from the Met or Thames Valley, Wiltshire and Hampshire were brought in as a large anonymous force, their behaviour was more likely to be violent, in a way akin to 'mob' violence. However, on a one-to-one basis or in small groups, it has been sometimes possible to break down some of the macho roleplaying. For example, for two months after the eviction at Yellow Gate on 4 April, between eight and twenty-four civil police officers maintained a permanent twenty-four hour patrol of the Camp. At the beginning, they used fire extinguishers to put out campfires every fifteen minutes and followed us everywhere. But gradually they became shamed or bored by this destructive and pointless use of their time and, by the end, a reasonably sympathetic communication had been established. It is in situations where the police are hyped up or rendered less accountable (such as in night time convoys or blockades when they whip themselves into a frenzy before charging), that the worst abuses occur.

Violence is often selective. Policing changes markedly if there are cameras and press about. If they are not being observed, they are openly rough, but if cameras are recording, they use other techniques. They bend thumbs back and tightly pinch nerves in protesters' necks, shoulders, arms and ankles when moving us from blockades. This is intensely painful but can't be seen and seldom leaves bruising. Moreover, the cameras show a woman with her face contorted in agony or writhing to get free. She looks hysterical, while the police appear calm and reasonable.

At first, women who were predominantly white and middle-class and unused to political activity were horrified at how quickly the police could be turned into an attacking force, fuelling rather than defusing potential conflict, behaving lawlessly and selectively applying their powers to arrest nonviolent protesters and protect vigilantes. I remember the real shock of hearing them lie under oath during trials. Childhood conditioning to respect and trust the police had gone deep, and acknowledging the reality caused some painful readjustment. However, a necessary part of our politicization through Greenham has been the recognition that civil liberties only ever really existed for white middle-class heterosexuals who were not politically active. For a long time, some police have used the brutalizing tactics that have now become familiar against minorities identified by their race, politics or sexuality. Our peace activities have simply made greater numbers of white, generally middle-class people visible to the police in the same way.

By codifying past stretching of police practice into law, the Police and Criminal Evidence Act has pushed back the threshold and will enable even greater abuse to go unchecked. Rising poverty and unemployment combined with increasingly repressive laws will result in even larger sectors of the population becoming criminalized and consequently included among those the police apparently consider outside the protection of the law and police accountability.

The consistent disruption of all Cruise missile exercises by Greenham women and Cruisewatch resulted in the recognition by the USAF that Cruise was not a feasible weapons system, and substantially contributed to the eventual agreement to sign them away in the INF treaty with the Soviet Union in December 1987. But it remains a severe indictment of the police that there is hardly an active Greenham woman or Cruisewatcher who has not been assaulted and hurt, although we have always deliberately avoided using violence ourselves.

14. Women in the Welsh Mining Communities*

Jill Evans

The history of the South Wales valleys in this century revolves around the mining industry. Close-knit communities grew up around the pits, and the series of disputes over working conditions, non-unionism, scab unionism and wages forms an integral part of its people's history and experience since the turn of the century.

In literature and on film the strength of the women of these communities in feeding and clothing their families under extreme and adverse conditions has frequently been portrayed, albeit in a sentimental manner. But their active political role outside the home in times of industrial dispute has rarely been recognized. The fact that the women's support groups that arose during the 1984–5 strike were seen as a new phenomenon of women's politicization substantiates this. In fact, the women were following the tradition of their foremothers in struggling against injustice.

As press reports from 1926 reveal, women appeared in the courts alongside miners on charges of unlawful assembly, rioting, attempting to cause disaffection amongst the civilian population and intimidation. Women were involved in twelve major prosecutions in the twenties and most were fined,

---

* The interviews with women involved in the miners' strike are all extracts taken from *Striking Back* published by the Welsh Campaign for Civil and Political Liberties and the NUM (South Wales Area), April 1985.

although a few refused to pay and went to prison. Much of the press coverage of the 1926 disputes records the presence of both women and men in mass demonstrations, and at that time too, the involvement of the women was described as 'strange'![1]

The role of the women in the miners' strike of 1984–5 was evidently not a new or unique feature of mining disputes. On the contrary, it was a response rooted in a political tradition. Most of the South Wales valley pits were shut down during the sixties and early seventies, and so the economic dependence on mining had diminished. Yet the loss of other industries in the area and the alarming increase in unemployment in the early eighties meant that these communities could not afford to lose a single job. Local services were being run down and cut; local businesses such as shops were battling to survive in the economically depressed areas. The very existence of the mining communities was threatened. Thus, from the start, the miners' struggle was everyone's struggle; at its heart was the future of the valleys and the promise of hope to the young people growing up within them. This was a much broader issue than the future of individual pits, and the formation of the Wales Congress in Support of Mining Communities drew in people from all walks of life: trade unionists, women's groups, peace groups, churchgoers, councillors and pensioners – all united in challenging the right of those in London to make decisions which would have such a devastating impact on our lives. The struggle became a question of people having control over their own lives and determining their own future or 'community socialism in action', as one woman put it.

Whilst industrial struggle was familiar to the people of the South Wales valleys, it is important to remember that most individuals involved in the year-long miners' dispute, and the women in particular, had themselves never before come into direct conflict with the authorities or the police. Indeed, a few months earlier they would not have believed it possible that they would be challenging either the actions or authority of the police. As one woman reported on returning from the first women's picket at the Port Talbot Steelworks:

There were about twenty police there, but within half an hour there were twelve vans full. It was unbelievable. I've never experienced anything like it in my life. I've always had respect for the law. As it is today I've got no respect at all for them. My attitude towards the police has changed. I've got no respect for a uniform.

Collective community support for the miners on strike was threatening to the police; they tried to counter this by treating non-miners, including the miners' families, as if they had no right to become involved. The miners themselves were constantly portrayed by the media as members of a union who were blindly following their leaders, and the women as unfortunate, misled victims of the whole dispute. The general attitude of the police was that the women should be at home and not interfere in the dispute. The presence of the women confused the issue. The police constantly referred to 'your men' when talking to the women and the frequent references to money suggested that the women themselves should see their husbands and partners as the breadwinners in the home, and further as failing in their duty to provide for the family. Given the economic circumstances of those families on strike, this may have been a deliberate attempt to create a rift between the women and men and to undermine the general morale by generating dissatisfaction amongst the women. The police recognized the crucial role of the women in the dispute, but did not appreciate their depth of political awareness, or their commitment to the struggle for their own sakes and for those of their children.

The strikers and their supporters were forced into an 'us and them' situation with the police which was to create a deep bitterness and a feeling of betrayal that even caused rifts between police and miners within families. There was a clear attempt to destroy the morale of those on strike, and the police tactics and strategy was the key to this. The police were on one side and the miners and their supporters were on the other. The police were not impartial, and their bias showed itself in a number of ways.

Firstly, and most obviously, there was the strong contrast between their treatment of working and striking miners. The scab miners were given protection, were transported to and from work (although in pits where there were only one or two scabs there was no work for them to do anyway), were given police escorts and at all times kept away from the legitimate picket lines at the workplace. The striking miners, on the other hand, were treated from the start as criminals. Picketing was not and is not illegal. Yet miners were stopped at roadblocks all around Britain, their buses and cars were searched, they were questioned as to their destination and they were frequently ordered to return home, on penalty of arrest if they refused. The legal right of the police to act in this way was challenged on many occasions, but they seemed neither to know or to care that they were exercising powers they did not have. The orders were coming from higher up.

Secondly, overall police policy was the mass criminalization of the miners and their supporters by arrests and charges such as criminal damage, riot, breach of the peace, assault and obstruction. The whole strike was treated as a 'public order situation' rather than an industrial dispute, and the police were in control. In a nine-month period during the strike, 509 people in Britain were charged with unlawful assembly and 137 with riot. This figure is higher than the total number found guilty of such charges in the previous three years.[2]

The courts, too, played a part in this strategy. People often appeared before magistrates' courts in groups and were dealt with collectively, with no allowance for individual circumstances. Bail conditions were handed out almost mechanically, to men and women alike, preventing them from attending pickets or protests. Their background or previous good character was not considered, the purpose being to weaken the strike by taking people out of the front line.

But perhaps the greatest single factor that aroused anger and resentment towards the police was their attitude towards striking women and men. From the start they treated them as criminals who had no right to be taking the action that they were. Many of the strikers attributed the violence that sometimes flared up on the picket lines to the fact that the police would not allow them to maintain a peaceful and orderly picket. They were prevented from talking to those who were entering the workplaces and this naturally led to frustration. The behaviour of the police suggested to those who didn't know the truth that picketing *was* illegal.

There were numerous incidents of police provocation and intimidation on the picket lines. A woman who had been present at the Port Talbot picket recorded:

> We hadn't been on the picket line before. Our men had come back with all these stories of police violence and provocation and we thought maybe it was an exaggeration. But we found it wasn't. You see a convoy coming out and you're seething with rage. I did a V sign to one of the drivers and a policeman told me I could be taken away for that. So I just turned my fingers around the other way. But the drivers made signs like that at us and no-one threatens to arrest them.

The fact that scab lorry drivers were able to behave as they liked was substantiated by numerous women:

> I'm beginning to see how the violence happens. Coming back from Birmingham we were on the motorway and we ended up in the middle of the coke convoy from Port Talbot. Lots of the lorry drivers saw us and made rude signs at us, showed their union cards and waved money at us. It drove us mad in the back of the bus. We regard ourselves as law-abiding people but we were really furious. I can see why our boys get so angry on picket lines and sometimes lose their self-control. When you've been out for nearly five months and someone taunts you like that it drives you mad.

Taunting and sneering at the women and men was a common feature of the policing during this strike. Much of it was petty, but nevertheless designed to provoke a reaction and cause unrest. For example, on a women's demonstration in Barnsley the police would not allow the women to use the public toilets. On a demonstration in London one woman remembered,

> '. . . because we didn't have our men with us the first thing this sergeant told me was "Where are your men then? Drinking their picket money in the pubs, is it?" '

In what was, for the families on strike, a most difficult and stressful period financially as well as emotionally, much of the police taunting took the form of remarks about the money the police were earning on overtime because of the strike. The following were examples:

> The police laugh at you. They do provoke a lot of trouble. They tell you what they're doing for their holidays and all the overtime money they're getting. One time they waved money out of their coach window at us.

> They say, 'Keep it up, we like the money. I'll pay for my house'. They want it to carry on.

> They instigate a problem to create overtime for themselves. They goad you, saying 'All right for you boys, but I've got to go to France or Spain for my holidays' or 'I've got to change my house now because I can afford to buy a new one. You carry on boys, we don't mind when it ends'.

Although at first the police were rather nervous in their handling of women on picket lines, they soon became accustomed to it and dealt with them in the same way as they dealt with the men. There were many reports of pushing and shoving, and some incidences of actual violence:

> I saw an inspector hit a woman in the mouth after she said something to him. He immediately disappeared behind police ranks and we have not seen him in the line since. Nobody was able to get his number.

> They were rude to me and attempted force to take our photographs. I had my right arm forced quite painfully up my back and my hair pulled, also painful, so they could pull my face away from my left hand, which was covering my face . . .

The latter incident was experienced by a woman who had been arrested on the picket line and had her photograph and fingerprints taken by force and without her permission. This again was a common story, and yet another facet of the process of criminalization: treating the strikers and their supporters as dangerous criminals.

There is limited space here to cover the very many frightening and unprecedented aspects of violent police conduct during the year-long dispute. I have tried to select a few representative examples of the ways in which the abuse of power and position by the police officers at this time affected the miners, their families and supporters, and in the long term caused such bitterness and resentment. The miners' strike failed, not because the miners did not have a just and powerful case nor because the government had the support of the majority in their planned programme of pit closures. The strike was lost because the miners battled against the amassed strength of the authorities, epitomized by the bloody and brutal scenes at Orgreave in May 1984. The government could not win a political or moral victory, and so they responded with sheer brute force. They were supported by the police, the media and the establishment generally. The women and men of the mining communities were having to fight on all fronts.

All of this contributed to the bitterness that remains long after the end of the strike. There is no evident hostility towards the police (although the police are rarely seen on the streets these days to deal with everyday crimes like burglary, whereas during the strike there were thousands of police on the picket line every day). However, a total lack of trust in the police force prevails. The women and men of the mining communities have seen how the police work, who they work for, and how quickly they can be used to control the population. When there are incidents of people coming into conflict with the police, or allegations of police misconduct or fabrication of evidence, the people in these communities are neither surprised nor doubtful. They have now made links with and offer support and solidarity to radical movements such as the Welsh Language Society and the peace movement; they can understand and empathize with the feelings of black, lesbian and gay communities who have, like them, long been victimized.

It is true to say that the women of the mining areas were changed by the strike. Many of them live now as they lived before, but their attitudes are different and they have a new strength and confidence in themselves and their abilities.

They have become part of a tradition of women challenging authority, a tradition that will continue as long as governments attempt to impose their will by force, ignoring and dismissing the rights of the people to control their own future.

Notes

1. For further details see Hywel Francis and David Smith, *The Fed, a History of the South Wales Miners in the Twentieth Century*, Lawrence & Wishart for Llafur, 1980.

2. It is important also to note that no police were charged in relation to complaints brought against them during the strike.

15. The Inappropriate Women

Chris Tchaikovsky

The police, like most men, tend to stereotype women according to their conformity to certain conventional feminine models: for example, as mother, daughter, sister, wife. The young woman with a Mohican haircut, wearing jeans and Doctor Martin's can expect different treatment from the police than the woman wearing the uniform of the 'proper' or 'appropriate' woman: skirt, high heels and make up. But not too short a skirt, not too high heels, not too much make up.

The judge who applied the concept of 'contributory negligence' as mitigation for a rapist, was merely restating the male convention that women who defy curfews, or get into cars with men they don't know, or dress inappropriately are 'jail bait'.

In the criminal justice system which closely mirrors everyday assumptions, the concept of guilty victim is widely applied to women by police and judiciary, whereas only certain men – for example, certain black men, gay men, and an 'under class' of the very poor or destitute – are similarly affected.

Male dominated society imposes conventions of appropriateness on women: appropriate dress, appropriate work, appropriate roles, appropriate attitudes and even an appropriate time to be on the streets. Police attitudes to – and treatment of – women reflect these conventions of appropriateness. Women on the receiving end are obliged to take police expectations into account. The cases that follow show a range of police attitudes from the trivial and everyday, to a situation that ended in a woman's death. (All these women are white. Police attitudes to black women are likely to be further complicated by racism as is shown in other articles in this book.)

Anne

Anne appeared to be a conventional woman, and was treated accordingly.

> About four o'clock in the afternoon I was racing down Trinity Road, because it's a fast road and there was very little traffic. I had my friend's baby with me; he was asleep and strapped into his car seat. A policeman on a motor bike passed and waved me down. He looked me and the baby over and then gave me what he obviously thought was a good talking-to. It was ridiculous really for such a young man – he was very stern and patronizing. Then he said, 'I know, you're rushing home after a good natter with your friends to get your husband's tea.' I gave him an acquiescent 'how-did-you-guess' look and he told me not to speed again, as next time I might not be so lucky. I laughed all the way home to my lesbian lover at this young man's vision of a world consisting of negligent nattering women tearing up the highways to grill hubby's tea on time. I suppose I reinforced that view too, but I didn't want a fine or an endorsement!

Ellen

Contrast this with the treatment of Ellen, who worked in a nightclub and returned home around 3 a.m.

> I got off the night bus at Clapton Pond. I had to walk straight down the road to Mandeville Street by Hackney Marshes. It was about a fifteen-minute walk, but there were no other buses that went nearer. The road ran beside a new council estate; it was downhill and well lit. I kept getting stopped by the police. The first time they asked 'What are you doing out at this time of night?' They were friendly, just a bit patronizing, but that changed when I told them I was coming home from working in a pub with a late licence. One of them asked me suggestively if I was still working now. I didn't realize what he meant at first, and when I did I was really shocked. I mean I'm not naive or anything but I was horrified that this

policeman had said that to me. I felt totally vulnerable. They must have registered that because they said they would see me safely home. Then they kerb-crawled me to my door. That was horrible too. Thank God they didn't offer me a lift home though, there is no way I'd get in that car with them. They scared the living daylights out of me.

I was stopped every other week or so, and although it was different policemen it was always the same questions. Some were more suspicious of me than others, but their attitude always changed from patronizingly friendly to suspicious, over-familiar and contemptuous when I told them I was coming home from work. Obviously in their heads working in a pub with a late licence means you must be on the game. After a while I got so fed up I'd tell them I'd been at work and it was quite legal, and I wasn't considering robbing the factory down the road. After those first experiences I wasn't going to be too polite to them. Why the hell should I?

The police were implying that Ellen was a prostitute who would not admit it. She was a target for harassment.

Paradoxically, the attitude of the police to certain women can be more tolerant and flexible where the women accept a label, as Stella does.

Stella

I've been a hustler for something like eight years now. I work in Paddington but I may go back to King's Cross when things have died down there ['Saturation policing' of the King's Cross area began in January 1983]. I preferred it in King's Cross. I knew the police and they knew me. They were pretty good really. They would tell me up front when they were going to nick me and that was a help. I'd be working the square on a Wednesday and they'd say, 'Be here Friday, all right.' We would fix a time in advance and that would give me the time to get the fine and arrange for my sister to pick up the kids. I never gave the police any trouble – why should I? They had their job to do and I had mine. The police here aren't friendly like that, but they don't know me yet. When they do and they know I'm no trouble I'll probably fix it up. But I'd rather go back to King's Cross, it was much better there.

Stella can fix a deal with the police because she is in a recognizable (to the police) police/villain relationship. She co-operates because, as a prostitute mother, she is especially vulnerable. But where a woman is unco-operative as well as unconventional, she can become a target for abuse.

Spikey

Spikey views the police as nothing but trouble and, as she puts it, 'I give as good as I get.' She has a Mohican hairstyle and wears shredded jeans, large safety pins, chains and heavy steel toe-capped boots. Spikey has a clearly defined view of society and her place within it.

It's all a con, all this talk of wasted youth and people caring. They expect us to take whatever they dish out, and give them respect when they don't deserve it. Teachers, police, they're all the same. I've been stopped a few times by the police. I expect it, looking like I do, I intimidate people. Last time I was stopped in Ladbroke Grove. Two of them in a car. At first they just took the piss out of me. I didn't care, they were so busy falling about at their Mohican jokes ('Lost your way back to your tepee, Sitting Bull?' and all that), they didn't notice me chuck my sulphate. I just sat on the wall and watched them laughing and dropped the gear.

Then they told me to empty my pockets, and I told them I had nothing in my pockets. I had no money, no smokes, no nothing. They asked me if I had identification, like a bus pass or something. I asked them if I looked like I'd have a bus pass or a season ticket to get me to my brain-surgeon work on time. They got nasty then and told me, 'enough of the lip'. I didn't care, I'd got rid of the gear. Then one of them pulled me and turned me around and pushed me against the car really hard. It took the wind out of me and hurt my ribs. Then he twisted my arm up and told me that if I wanted a lesson in manners he'd give me one. It hurt me that, not what he'd said, but my arm. I thought he was going to break it. It was all twisted against itself and felt like it was coming out of its socket. I said, 'all right, all right' and turned out my pockets. When they saw there was nothing in them, they said I was lucky they weren't going to search me, but they didn't want to get their hands dirty, and they didn't want to see me on the Grove again or they'd nick me for carrying a tomahawk. They thought that was really funny, they fell about again and got into the car and took off.

I had the last laugh though. After they went I got my gear back. My ribs and my arm hurt for a bit, but I got the better of them – they could have nicked me.

Because of her appearance and attitudes, Spikey was attacked by the men who should protect her and thus doubly forfeited her safety on the streets. But it is women who are drug and alcohol dependent, who, because they are furthest from models of female control, receive the worst treatment.

Gilly

The first time I was hit by the police was after we had been stopped in a car on the way to Coventry. A policewoman tried to pull me out of the car and I pushed her away. They arrested us and we were taken to the local police station. I was eighteen at the time and when the police sergeant, he was big, asked me for my name and address I told him to 'fucking find out'. He came over and fisted me right out of my chair. He hit me so hard I was banged right across the room. I was withdrawing at the time and they didn't get me a doctor. By the time I got to court I could hardly speak. I remember telling the court that this sergeant had hit me but they didn't believe me.

Another time I was arrested on the street. I was screaming and carrying on, I admit. I wanted to see a doctor, I was hysterical. I was only in for soliciting – an overnight stop. Three or four policemen came into my cell. One put his hand over my mouth and told me, 'you'll get fuck all in here.' They were holding me down and pushing me around the cell. I don't remember any bruises but there must have been. I was too sick to notice or care. I kept on regardless, ringing the bell all night. The doctor came in to see me in the morning and gave me two Tuinal barbiturates. It was just before I went into court; I was so sedated I didn't know what was happening. I couldn't get out of the dock. I couldn't move. It was in the local paper, in the court report. They said: 'This woman says she needs help not punishment.'

Two weeks ago I needed drugs so desperately I had to get picked up to get some sedation at least. I went to Highbury Corner and started shouting and carrying on. Eventually a police van pulled up. These were the worst I had ever come across, but I had to have some drugs . . . anything. When they picked me up they said, 'You belong in Friern Barnet [a local psychiatric hospital], you're a fucking nutter.' One of them said to me, 'If I had my way I'd shoot people like you.' They threw me into the back of the van and left me there alone for ages. I was sectioned and taken to St. Clement's psychiatric hospital the following morning. I had a lovely psychiatrist, she was really really nice. She said there was no need to section me at all and they let me go in an hour.

With Gilly, the police felt no compunction against openly expressing their disgust for women dependent on drugs. This took the form of physical and verbal abuse. For Wilma, the same attitude had far more serious implications.

Wilma

Wilma Lucas had been a chronic alcoholic for many years. She was a qualified radiographer who lived with her husband in a green-belt town in Surrey. At the end of 1983, she had been put on probation for two minor drink-related offences. On Friday 10 February 1984, Wilma was arrested for a breach of the probation order. In the late afternoon she was brought before Chertsey Magistrates' Court. She was unsteady on her feet, but able to stand and reasonably lucid. As her probation officer later testified at the inquest, Wilma had no visible facial bruising at this time. Wilma was remanded in custody, but as it was too late in the day to take her to Holloway, she spent the night in police cells at the local police station.

That evening she was visited by her GP, who found her fit to be sent to prison, rather than (as had happened before) to hospital for detoxification. He did not notice any bruises on her at that time. Later, Wilma's husband called at the police station to bring her some clothes. The desk sergeant advised him not to see her.

At noon the next day, Wilma was transferred to Holloway prison. She could not walk properly and had to be helped out of the police station. As she was urinary incontinent, they put her on the floor of a transit van, handcuffed to the side of the back seat. The policewoman who should have escorted her travelled in the front of the van.

Wilma arrived at Holloway at around 2 p.m. She was carried into reception face downwards because, the police testified at the inquest, she kept 'falling down'. She was examined by a prison doctor, who found that she was covered with bruises. He believed that her condition was more serious than mere 'alcoholic bruising'. A member of the prison religious staff said afterwards that in all her years in the prison service she had never seen such extensive bruising before, and that Wilma had obviously had 'a terrible battering'.

Wilma was taken to Whittington Hospital where a house-man examined her and gave her an X-ray. Finding no fracture, and thinking her condition was due to alcoholism, he returned her to Holloway. By the next day, her condition had deteriorated and she was deeply unconscious. She was transferred to the Royal Free Hospital. The doctor who examined her there, said later that in his opinion Wilma had been 'badly assaulted'. He testified that a blood clot at the base of her brain revealed by a brain scan had been caused by a blow to the back of her head. It was this that had caused the falling down and incoherence which both the prison staff and the houseman at the Whittington took to be the effects of alcohol – although by this time she had not had a drink for over twenty-four hours. Surgery removed the blood clot but Wilma did not recover consciousness. She died the next day.

An inquest was held on her death in June 1984; the jury returned an open verdict.

According to the pathologist, the fatal injury to her head must have occurred not more than three days before surgery. The ride on the floor of the transit van could not have caused it, he said, as the effects would not have shown themselves so immediately, Wilma had one hundred and forty-four separate bruises on her body including 'gripping' (fingertip) bruises on her arms.

If Wilma's bruises were caused by her falling down repeated-ly while in police custody, which is unlikely, this only confirms what the medical correspondent of the *Sunday Times* called 'a catalogue of official indifference, ignorance, incompetence and downright callousness'.

All women are directly or indirectly coerced by male notions of a proper femininity, but it is no excuse for the police to say that they have the same prejudices as other male members of the public. They have powers which set them apart from the public, and they have an equal responsibility to all members of the public. The police are not even-handed in their approach; they are sexist and racist, and their culture institutionalizes rather than challenges these prejudices. We can see the dangerous implications of these attitudes in police treatment of certain women who forfeit police protection and become targets of police hostility.

The police tend to represent and defer to the more conservative, narrow and authoritarian side of public opinion. This tendency increases the more they are cut off from the community they serve. Recruited at a young age and sometimes accommodated in purpose-built flats, they mix almost exclusively with each other both on and off duty. This spawns a deeply rooted occupational and social culture which has an insulating effect, reinforcing an unworldly elitism. Living outside the community, their own behaviour policed only by themselves and with no formal independent accountability, they are a law unto themselves. Until this isolation and the inflexible, self-protective and authoritarian attitudes which spring from it are acknowledged and changed, the police will not be responsible to the whole community. In particular, their bigoted and limiting notions of what is acceptable dress and behaviour will, to a greater or lesser extent, affect all their dealings with women.

16. Protecting the Honour of Innocent Men

Susan Edwards

Historically, the law on prostitution and allied offences (kerb crawling, procuration, living off immoral earnings, and brothel keeping) has focused on prosecuting the street-walking woman. Although there is a growing awareness of the degree of violent coercion that prostitute women are subject to from those 'exercising control'[1] over them and profiting from their earnings, this awareness has not resulted in legal change. The most salient features of the law and the public attitudes that support it are still surveillance, cautioning, arrest and prosecution of women working as street prostitutes.

The police regularly pick up street-walking women for 'loitering'. This is the only aspect of prostitution in respect of which they are able to gain straightforward convictions. It is clearly the case that there is sometimes abuse of police power involved here, but it is also evident that the law is the real problem. The law has been deflected away from its real target and its licence to do so has come from public opinion, which will not or cannot afford to look at the real nature of prostitution and its organization by and for men.

Coercion and Exploitation

In 1985, a report made by the Criminal Law Revision Committee, Prostitution, Off-Street Activities,[2] recognized that, 'All too often, those who practise prostitution are likely to become the victims of exploitation.' The report made several recommendations to redress the balance of the present law (the Sexual Offences Act, 1956) by tightening up the provisions in respect of living on the earnings of prostitution, 'exercising control', brothel keeping and procuration.[3] However, these proposals have not been heeded and there has been no consequent change in the law.

Prostitute women are deliberately exploited by pimps, many of whom are violent and coercive. But, as the nature of coercion indicates, it is unlikely that the coercers will be brought to justice as it is difficult to secure prosecution evidence sufficient to gain a conviction. Women living in fear of their pimps will not give evidence against them. As part of my research* into the law on prostitution, I interviewed thirty-five women in Marylebone Magistrates' Court while they were in custody. The women were very frank with me about all aspects of their work – with one exception. They would not talk to me about their pimps or ponces. Many of them had been assaulted by the men they worked for; a woman in Paddington had recently been murdered by her ponce.

The Sexual Offences Act 1956 requires women to give evidence to secure a conviction in respect of 'living on immoral earnings' or 'exercising control', yet a prosecution for loitering needs only the word of a police officer. The few cases of pimping that do come to court indicate a level of coercion. In the case of *R. v Parker* 1985, the defendant pleaded guilty to living on the earnings of prostitution.[4] He had been violent to the woman and had threatened to report her to the social services so that she lived in fear that she might lose her child. He had also forced her to have intercourse with a dog, with a view to giving demonstrations. She had tried to run away from him on several occasions. At the end of the day, however, there are very few such prosecutions and the organizers and controllers of prostitution tend to go free, while the street prostitute (who earns much less) is prosecuted. In 1986, there

* This research was supported by the Nuffield Foundation, 'Prostitution, Policing, Employment and the Welfare of Young Women', at Ealing College of Higher Education in London.

were 561 prosecutions for procuration and 120 for brothel keeping in England and Wales, compared with 9,404 prosecutions for loitering.

A major concern of feminist activists and campaigners in recent years has been to expose the inequality in the treatment of prostitutes who operate on the street and those who do so behind closed doors.[5] Prostitution in clubs, saunas, clip joints and brothels is not so often prosecuted as it is when women walk the streets; and even when it is, rarely does the 'tout, the bully or the protector' come before court as the law intended.[6] Instead, it is the 'passive ponce' – eighteen-year-old son, the brother or the boyfriend who is easily identifiable as dependent on the woman because he lives with her, who is prosecuted. Where brothel keeping is concerned, it is often women like Cynthia Payne (who exercise no coercion) who are prosecuted,[7] rather than women who genuinely exercise control.

As case law shows, it is not prostitute women who make a profit from prostitution but the owners of brothels, those who rent apartments to prostitutes for exorbitant fees, and the pimps or ponces. Consider for example the case of Robinson in 1984,[8] where the owner of a sauna grossed over £220,000 per year. Again, there is the case of Kelley and Purvis in 1983[9] owners of the Celebrity Sauna in Charlotte Street, which illustrates the vast profits that can be made by the organizers and controllers of prostitution. In cases such as these, where there is no coercion, the sentences of the court have been a fine and/or a short term of imprisonment.

The Innocent Punter

A further concern for feminists is the legal inequality between prostitute and male client. Traditionally, the male punter or client has enjoyed freedom from legal or police restraint. In September 1985, a new Sexual Offences Act received Royal Assent. For the first time in history, the conduct of kerb crawlers – men who solicit prostitutes on the street – was to be criminalized. The Act was the result of pressure brought variously by feminists, residents' associations and husbands and parents worried about wives and daughters being kerb crawled. Interestingly, in its earlier stages, the Bill had included provisions to criminalize general sexual harassment by men of women on the streets. These were dropped because it was acknowledged that women would not be prepared to go to court to act as prosecution witnesses when the defence tactics would obviously be to suggest that women led the men on, or were in fact prostitutes, and women would find themselves on trial. The final Act reads in Section 1(1):

> A man commits an offence if he solicits a woman (or different women) for the purpose of prostitution:
> (a)   from a motor vehicle while it is in a street or public place, or;
> (b)   in a street or public place while in the immediate vicinity of a motor vehicle that he has just got out of or off persistently . . .

The prosecution and conviction of male kerb crawlers has been widely reported. In February 1986, Colin Hart-Leverton QC was prosecuted by the Metropolitan Police in London for kerb crawling in Bayswater. He was convicted by magistrates at Wells Street Magistrates' Court on 19 February, and fined accordingly.[10] Hart-Leverton appealed to the Crown Court in Knightsbridge. He said the police had lied and that he was in the red light district of London to visit his late father's home. The Crown Court preferred this version of the night in question and quashed the conviction, finding insufficient evidence against him.

Despite the publicity that has surrounded this and other cases, actual prosecutions for kerb crawling have been very few indeed. The record of criminal statistics for 1986[11] shows a total of 189 prosecutions and 161 convictions in England and Wales. Again the comparison for this is with the 9,404 prosecutions of women for loitering; the different treatment of prostitutes and clients could not be more blatant.

Taking the London area as an example, the Street Offences Squad operating in Westminster reported two kerb crawlers for prosecution and warned forty-nine others during 1986.[12]

By contrast, almost one third (equalling about 3,134) of all prostitutes prosecuted in 1986 were the result of prosecutions originating from the London area. But the police reluctance to prosecute the kerb crawler, does not emerge out of a spirit of levity. Indeed officers of the Street Offences Squad were unanimous in their condemnation of the kerb crawler. Kerb crawlers were seen as a nuisance and a traffic problem! Officers in the Street Offences Squad when interviewed by the author and male co-worker pointed to the hypocrisy implicit in the system when women are prosecuted and men are beyond the law: 'I thought it was dirty old men in raincoats driving battered Ford Escorts, but they are a wide section of the community, a hell of a lot of respectable men ... bank managers, directors ...'

The reluctance of the police to report cases is due to the procedural and evidential requirements of the recently established Crown Prosecution Service. Officers in London explained: 'The problem is the law ... the law requires two overt acts. You can have a ten-page statement and have followed him for one-and-a-half hours and he still can get off.' Another officer remarked, 'I mean the law is so unworkable it has made our job very difficult.' Another officer said: 'It's a complete nightmare! The evidence required is so overwhelming. The Crown Prosecution Service says that we have to get a verbal admission if we can't get a plea of guilty!' Again, officers themselves pointed to the double standard as regards prostitutes and punters: 'The thing is people don't think much of prostitutes, but if somebody is going with a Tom, it's all nudge nudge, wink wink ...'

The criteria for prosecution in kerb crawling cases have been laid down in a Home Office Circular[13] where for the offence of kerb crawling to be proven, the courts require the conduct to be 'persistent' or likely to cause annoyance. The circular states that the test of 'persistent' will be for the courts to decide, although the guidelines suggest as a yardstick 'the soliciting of at least two women on the same occasion'.

The 'persistent' qualification emerges as part of the parliamentary concern to ensure that innocent men are not prosecuted, and the Home Office circular reinforces this sentiment:

> During the passage of the Bill through parliament, attention was
> drawn to the particular need for care in deciding to charge
> individuals with offences under this Act because of the possible
> implications for the reputation and family circumstances of a man
> accused of seeking the services of a prostitute.

Unfortunately, the Home Office has not found it necessary to express similar concern for the reputation and family circumstances of prostitute women.

The Sexual Offences Act 1985 was not intended to affect the lives of street prostitutes, but in fact it has increased the risks they run, in that women have to get into cars quickly and have little chance to assess their clients (see chapter 17). In addition, women cannot carry anything to defend themselves because this might lead to prosecution for possession of an offensive weapon (under the Police and Criminal Evidence Act), if they were arrested for loitering. Ninety per cent of the women I spoke to had been assaulted by punters. When I asked them whether they carried anything for their own protection, they said they used to, but they don't any more.

The circular indicates the possible use of cautioning in these cases whilst the Code for Crown Prosecutors[14] states more generally:

> When the circumstances of an offence are not particularly serious,
> and a court would be likely to impose a purely nominal penalty,
> Crown prosecutors should carefully consider whether the public
> interest would be better served by a prosecution or some other form
> of disposal, such as, where appropriate, a caution.

Prosecuting Street-walkers

The prosecution of the street-walker has never been difficult. The evidential requirement is proof of 'loitering' on the sworn evidence of two police officers. Once a woman is known to the police as having a conviction for prostitution it is assumed that even the most innocent activity on the street, for instance picking up a child from school, may provide an opportunity for loitering. The evidential requirements for loitering are far less stringent than they are for soliciting, as one officer explained.

> There are two offences; one is loitering and the second, soliciting. The first is loitering as a common prostitute in a public place. This is quite easy really, because you know most of them. The second offence is of soliciting, technically that is talking to a punter; but the courts want evidence of conversation, we can't get the evidence for that.

Thus, prostitutes are rarely charged with soliciting. What is the attitude of the police to prostitute women? Many studies including the major study from America by Skolnick in 1966[15] have observed harassment and intimidation of prostitutes by police officers. By contrast, the prostitute women I interviewed in 1988 reported no intimidation. Officers we interviewed from the London Street Offences Squad in 1987 saw 'nicking Toms' as just a job. Male police officers said they regarded prostitutes as simply a nuisance. On the whole, police officers looked on arresting prostitutes as 'shit work'; arrests are not seen as a move toward promotion in the same way as other arrests. But one male officer argued that the squad actually protected women from pimps. In fact it was women officers who held negative attitudes toward prostitute women, calling them 'greedy, filthy slags'.

Increasing Prosecutions

It is not only the problem of the inequality within existing laws regulating prostitution that is a cause for concern but also the sensational increase in the number of women prosecuted for prostitution over the last few years. These women are coming into contact with the police, the criminal justice system and sometimes imprisonment (for nonpayment of fines) for the first time. Despite the withdrawal of imprisonment as a routine sentence, women can be detained overnight in a magistrates' court, under the Police and Criminal Evidence Act. Under

Thatcherism, prosecutions for prostitution have increased by nearly 300 per cent. In 1979, prosecutions for prostitution in England and Wales totalled some 3,167; by 1983, this number had soared to 10,674 and by 1986 9,404 women were prosecuted.[16] The figures for 1983 especially reflect an increase in police activity, particularly in the King's Cross area of London. This 'get tough' policy represents part of a wider orchestration of the right-wing reformist movement towards more regulation and control of vice and street behaviour. The female prostitute has fallen victim to this zeal because of her high visibility; the pimps and organizers working behind closed doors have not come under such scrutiny. Notwithstanding the effect of greater control and regulation of prostitutes on prosecution rates, the dramatic rise is also due to the increasing downward spiral of women's economic position in employment together with the radical erosion of welfare support. Certainly, the erosion in women's employment opportunities and the gradual demise of state welfare has placed an increasing number of single parent mothers below the poverty line. These economic policies increase women's vulnerability, especially at the point of the break up of a permanent cohabiting relationship.

There is also a link between prostitution and domestic violence. Women may be forced into prostitution when they have no support after leaving home to escape violence from a partner. (They are likely then to find themselves in another domestic relationship in which violence from their pimp is a feature.) With the onslaught by the government on family income and on public and private maintenance, women's poverty has increased, and more numbers of women turn to prostitution out of economic necessity.

Most prostitute women working in London are unemployed and poor. Frequently they have come from cities outside London. If they are arrested and have no London address, they are refused bail and remanded overnight in police custody pending a court appearance the following morning. However, there are a small number of prostitute women working in the Shepherd's Market and Mayfair area of London whose motives for prostitution cannot be reduced to poverty alone. They have their own flats, charge higher prices and attract 'a different class' of clients. Many of these women own their cars and it is they who kerb crawl or wait for clients. But, whether operating in Mayfair or Soho, all street prostitutes become the victims of policing and of a criminal justice system to a greater or lesser degree. The going rate for fines at the time of writing (November 1988) is £50 per conviction. Inevitably this forces women to prostitute further in order to pay the fine. Those who cannot pay, inevitably the poorest, face a term of imprisonment for fine default. In 1986, over 200 women had spent some time in prison because they were unable to pay the fine imposed by the court (this included 163 women over 21 years and 48 women under 21 years).[17]

Discriminating Against Prostitute Women

The legal inequality between the prostitute and the punter or client is no accident. The legislation reflects social attitudes and popular ideology about appropriate models of male and female behaviour. Historically this division has persisted over the years. The bourgeois myth promulgates the view that prostitute women become 'bad' – although men do not forfeit their virtue by paying for intercourse with them. As a result, at various levels of jurisdiction, prostitute women have been denied certain rights and protection. Consider for example, that victims of rape and domestic violence forfeit their right to protection if they are 'known prostitutes'. This differential treatment is enshrined not only in police and public prejudice but in the very rules governing evidence and corroboration. According to Section 2 of the Sexual Offences (Amendment) Act 1976, a victim's past sexual experience is considered irrelevant to the issue of consent in a trial for rape. This ruling, however, does not extend to prostitute women, where the fact of prostitution becomes of supreme significance to the defence case. In addition, jurors are unlikely to believe the evidence of a woman who is a known prostitute; thus in corroboration warnings to the jury, judges frequently make reference to the moral character of the complainant which in law they have every right to do.

Yet another example of this differential treatment before the law can be seen in an application made to the Criminal Injuries Compensation Board (CICB) by Marcella Claxton, a surviving victim of Peter Sutcliffe. Marcella Claxton fought for seven years until the CICB finally made her an award. Until then, they had refused her applications because of their assessment of her moral character and way of life.[18]

Prostitute women not only receive different treatment as victims of rape, violence and murder, but also in family law over custody and similar disputes. Prostitute women are typically considered 'unsuitable as mothers'. The recent High Court decision by Mr Justice Schiemann sets a precedent which further reinforces this notion.[19] Janet Harriott had tried to conceive for several years without success so, as part of her attempt to have a child of her own, she joined the waiting list for the *in vitro* fertilization programme at St Mary's Hospital in Manchester. She had also applied on several occasions to Manchester's Social Service Department with a view to adoption. She had been repeatedly turned down on the basis that she had a poor understanding of the foster-parent role and had in the past had convictions for brothel keeping and soliciting. The staff of the fertility programme were made aware of her adoption application to the social services department and of the reasons for its refusal and decided to remove her from the infertility programme, telling her this decision was taken because of an infection in her husband's sperm. The High Court decision upheld the right of the infertility clinic to refuse her. This case further illustrates how at various levels women's perceived 'moral character' and sexual behaviour compromise their rights in other areas of social and legal life.

Street prostitute women are hardly criminal offenders or the state's enemies. They are instead in part created by the state through its economic policies, its criminal law and administration of 'justice'. The treatment of the kerb crawler by contrast rather than introducing some equality into our sex law, reinforces the already entrenched double standards of a sexist and bourgeois hypocrisy whose first commandment is to uphold and protect the honour of men, who are characteristically regarded as innocent. It is this hypocrisy which continues to uphold the inequalities in the existing system.

Notes

1. 'Exercising control' is a legal term for what is popularly called pimping or poncing. Strictly speaking, a pimp is a man who touts for business for prostitutes on the streets, and a ponce is a man who lives with a prostitute and takes money from her. In fact, the word 'pimp' is now commonly used for both categories and is used in this way throughout the article.

2. Criminal Law Revision Committee, Seventeenth Report, 'Prostitution: Off-Street Activities', Cmnd 9688, HMSO, London, p. 2.

3. 'Procuration' is the term used for the incitement of a woman into prostitution, for example in exchange for a flat.

4. *R. v Parker* ENGGEN 19 July (1985).

5. E. McCleod, *Working Women: Prostitution Now*, Croom Helm, London, 1982; C. Smart, 'Legal Subjects and Social Objects' in J. Brophy and C. Smart (eds), *Women in Law*, Routledge and Kegan Paul, London, 1985.

6. cf *Shaw v DPP* (1961).

7. G. Walker and I. Daly, *Sexplicitly Yours*, Penguin, London 1987.

8. Robinson (Cr APP Rep) (S) (1984) at 55.

9. Kelley and Purvis Q.B.D. (1983) at 663.

10. *Guardian*, 20 February 1986.

11. Criminal Statistics England and Wales, Cmnd 233, HMSO, London, 1986; Supplementary Tables vol. 1, HMSO, London, 1986.

12. The Report of the Commissioner of the Metropolis, Cmnd 173, HMSO, London, p. 46.

13. Home Office Circular 52/1985.

14. Code for Crown Prosecutors, p. 4.

15. J. Skolnick, *Justice Without Trial*, John Wiley, London and New York, 1966.

16. Criminal Statistics (1979) England and Wales; (1983) England and Wales; (1986) ibid.

17. *Prison Statistics*, HMSO, London, 1987.

18. S.S.M. Edwards, 'Contributory Negligence in Compensation Claims by Victims of Sexual Assault', *New Law Journal*, December 9 1982, pp. 1140–42.

19. *Guardian*, 21 October 1987.

17. Working Relations*

Christina Dunhill

It is evident that women working as street prostitutes are doing one of the most dangerous jobs in the world. When they pick up men in cars, they have to make a snap decision as to whether to take the man on; this could in the last analysis be a life or death decision. The five women interviewed here were working in the context of a recent spate of attacks in Manchester in which a number of women had been badly beaten up. All of them were aware of the risks they took and spoke of having to make instantaneous decisions based on instinct and experience. For example, they said, 'It's the way he looks at you'; 'It's a feeling you get'; 'We look for older men.' One woman spoke of having a friend with her who, she made clear to punters, was taking down their car number. However, the women said that they worked in a situation which was basically outside their control.

In addition to the danger from male clients is the regular harassment women suffer from the enforcement of the law, in terms of arrests by the police and appearances and fines at the

* This article is based on information given by five women working as prostitutes in one particular area of Manchester. The women spoke with two researchers, Rochelle Phillips and Maxine Sullivan, from Manchester Aidsline who had drawn up a questionnaire on the basis of questions we had discussed. Unfortunately, it was impossible within the scope of this book to commission a wider response. Responsibility for the interpretation of the five women's accounts given here is entirely mine.

magistrates' courts. One woman said she was arrested almost every night and she couldn't afford the fines; she thought she would be in prison soon for nonpayment. The women need to make enough money to pay for fines, as well as their other expenses; the police officers in their turn need to make arrests for their career prospects.

In spite of the strain caused by the conflict between the jobs of the police and the prostitutes the women did not, on the whole, *blame* the police. All of them, given a choice between describing police officers as 'sympathetic, indifferent, unfriendly, hostile or other' described the attitude of the police towards them as 'indifferent'. These women did not seem to feel that the police had internalized social strictures and were victimizing them. They felt that the police were only 'doing their job'. One woman said that all policemen, whether vice squad or uniformed, would always say that they didn't think prostitution should be illegal, if asked. (She added that she had a client who was a policeman.) They blamed the law, the courts and the magistrates for the problems in their situation.

Significantly, none of the women felt that their work placed them outside police protection. Except in respect of clients who refused to pay, the women said that they would call out the police if they or one of their friends was in trouble (if they had been beaten up, if one of them was missing, or if a punter had stolen from them). They expected the police to pursue the offender with a view to prosecution. But while three of the women thought they would personally be treated satisfactorily by the police, two of them did not.

Within these two broad principles of not blaming the police and not feeling themselves outside police protection, the women had a number of criticisms. One woman remarked, 'most of them are bastards'. Three of the five women reported abuse, in one case verbal, in another case of a young woman, of forcing her to return to a Children's Home which she had left, and in another of sexual harassment when a member of the vice squad told her she'd be arrested if she didn't have sex with him.

It is evident that their vulnerability on the streets makes women dependent on their personal relationships with the police. As part of the businesslike relationship they described, deals are struck up which the women are under every pressure to comply with, in a situation where all the power is on the police's side. Every one of the women reported that the police used them to try to get information about drug dealers, and would promise to let the women off prosecution in return. Three of the women said that the police kept to their side of the bargain in this sort of deal; one said that they didn't, and one said that she had never entered into such an agreement. Two of the women reported police officers suggesting that they might offer them sex in return for not being put up for soliciting. Three women said that the police would make accommodating arrangements with them, such as allowing them to return the following day to be arrested so that they could plan alternative child care. However, the woman who reported that she never made a deal with the police also said that she was not able to make working arrangements with them, and so did the woman who said that the police arrested her nearly every night. She said that her face 'didn't fit'.

Two women volunteered the remark that women police officers were 'worse' than their male counterparts and this seems to tally with the remarks of policewomen quoted in Susan Edwards' article (see page 199). On the other hand, one woman said that a community policing exercise with a WPC had seen an improvement in relations with the police; this had made everyone feel much safer. At that time, a number of women had been beaten up by punters and the exercise had been discontinued after the attacks had ceased for a time.

Asked if they thought there were ways of improving relationships with the police, two women replied no but, one added, 'It's your relationship, it's the way you handle it that matters.' One replied that progress could be made by community policing; this exercise, when it was in operation, was reported by the women to have made a real difference in terms of a feeling of protection. Another said no, simply because they *were* working women and the other woman said, only if you were a grass.

What all the women called for was an end to the criminalization of prostitution. The police do not, in all cases, regard their duties in relation to policing prostitute women objectively. It is perhaps predictable that a police officer may choose not to arrest a particular woman if she can instead be persuaded to part with information that might lead to an arrest of greater career value for that officer. However, it is disturbing that, in some cases, male police officers seem to consider that their duties afford them the right to free sex as an alternative to making an arrest.

In a situation where the number of arrests made affects an officer's promotion prospects, relationships of individual women working as street prostitutes with the police may be crucial. As a result, a great deal of strain may be placed on women who are unwilling, for whatever reason, to form working relationships with the police. 'I get nicked twice a week, it's OK', but another woman feared she would soon be in prison because she was arrested every night, and could not afford the fines.

Women, as ever, are paying the price for the double standards of sexual morality in our society. As even many police officers agree, the laws against street prostitution should be repealed.

18. MIND

Women and Section 136 of the
Mental Health Act 1983

Alison Faulkner

Section 136 of the Mental Health Act 1983 represents a somewhat controversial meeting point between the psychiatric services and the police. Approximately 10 per cent of compulsory admissions under the Mental Health Act are made under section 136. This represents a small proportion of mental hospital admissions; however, the section has become an increasing source of concern owing to the controversial involvement of the police in this part of the mental health arena.

Under section 136, police officers are authorized to remove a person they believe to be mentally disordered [1] and in 'immediate need of care and control' from 'a place to which the public have access' to a 'place of safety' (usually a police station or a hospital). The purpose of the section is for the person to be assessed by a doctor and an approved social worker, [2] with a view to making any arrangements thought to be necessary for that person's care. Although a maximum period of detention of seventy-two hours is allowed under section 136, it is intended that the person be assessed as soon as possible and released if found not to require hospitalization. The important principle behind the section is that it should only be used in emergency situations occurring in public places. Incidents leading to the use of section 136 are almost always reported to the police by members of the public, and often involve minor offences such as criminal damage or breach of the peace.

Women and Section 136

Men are more frequently detained under section 136 than women, in a ratio of approximately 3 to 2. This makes the section unique among forms of admission to mental hospitals. A possible explanation for the fact that more men than women are detained under section 136 is that these incidents take place in public and often involve violence; Phyllis Chesler suggests 'it is safer for women to become "depressed" than physically violent'.[3]

The following points for discussion, which have particular implications for the detention of women under section 136, have been identified by the campaigning organization, Women and Mental Health,[4] and through research carried out by MIND:

1. The allocation of WPCs to women detained under the section.
2. Arrests from private premises.
3. Racism in the police operation of section 136.
4. The implications for women of a procedure which excludes a social worker's assessment.
5. The implications of present procedures – and the lack of co-operation between the services – for women as carers.

Some of these issues, such as detention from private premises and the absence of social work assessments, also affect men. However, their implications are often greater for women, either because of their family responsibilities or because of their added vulnerability in the face of a largely male police force.

The Research

In response to considerable public criticism of the provision, MIND undertook a three-year investigation into the use of section 136. One of our main concerns has been the potential increase in contact between police and people with mental health problems as a result of the closure of large psychiatric hospitals, and the implications this may have for community care. We did not specifically aim to investigate the problems faced by women detained under section 136, and there are therefore limitations to the information that can be offered here. In addition, much of the research relied on the retrospective accounts of police officers and therefore has to be viewed with some caution.

Only two of the three stages of the research have so far been analysed. The first involved the examination of case records in three different places of safety: a hospital, a police station and an Emergency and Assessment Unit (EAU). This is the study upon which most of the following results are based.[5] The second stage involved interviewing police officers who had been responsible for detaining people under section 136, and provides much of the following background information here. The third stage involved interviews with psychiatrists and police officers associated with section 136 detentions, as well as a number of people detained under the section, but this stage is yet to be analysed at the time of writing.

The Allocation of WPCs

Our research suggests that WPCs are allocated to approximately one woman in three detained under section 136. It is clear that the small proportion of women in the police force (10 per cent of officers) must have some bearing on this. The police appear to recognize this problem officially, since the Metropolitan Police Standing Orders stipulate that whenever possible a WPC should be assigned to mental health cases involving women. However, it is clear that despite these orders, the majority of women are in fact detained exclusively by male officers. The failure of the police to allocate WPCs to incidents involving women may have considerable implications for women's distress.

Detention from Private Premises

As mentioned earlier, section 136 is intended for psychiatric emergencies which occur in public. Our research revealed eleven incidents (out of a total of one hundred) in which the police had contravened the conditions of the section by removing people from their own or other people's homes. Seven of the eleven incidents involved women. The procedure that should be followed when the police find someone they believe to be mentally ill on private premises is given in the Metropolitan Police Standing Orders, and states that a social worker should be contacted. (The social worker would then call out a doctor if she or he thought it necessary to consider sectioning the person.) However, during the course of MIND's research, many police officers complained that social workers would not come out to assess people thought by the police to be mentally ill and causing some kind of disturbance in their own homes. In two or three cases, police officers clearly felt that they had to do something in the absence of a social worker, and therefore invoked section 136. In addition, some police officers removed the person from private premises in the belief that there was no point in trying to call out a social worker.

In one incident, a PC said he was called to a house by a man who told the police that his wife had a ten-year history of alcohol abuse and that she had just drunk a bottle of vodka. He also said that she was receiving psychiatric treatment at the time. The police officer said that when he arrived the woman tried to hit both him and her husband; she then locked herself in the bathroom. The PC said that he intended from the outset to use section 136, but to get around the requirement that detention be from a public place, he arrested her for breach of the peace. He said that breach of the peace could be used as a 'convenience' in these circumstances, and that he was not prepared to call out a social worker because that would have meant waiting for three or four hours. He said that in this incident, the woman had to be carried out of the house.

In this particular case, the police officer made no attempt to invoke the proper procedure. It would seem that he thought the woman's mental state to be sufficient justification for his actions. The dangers for women (and men) of the police finding ways of arresting people from their own home under section 136 are clear. However, tightening up the police use of section

136 would also have to involve more co-operation between the police and the social services.

Racism

Allegations of racism in relation to the police's use of section 136 are based on a number of recent reports,[6] which have shown people of Afro-Caribbean origin to be over-represented in hospital admissions under the section. MIND's research also found a higher proportion of Afro-Caribbean people picked up under section 136 than would be expected from their proportion in the general population. This primarily involved black men.

In the majority of incidents, police respond to calls from the public. However, our research does suggest that the police approach incidents involving black people with different expectations from those which involve white people. In particular, the research suggests that racial stereotyping of black men as violent may well play a part.

It is also possible that the police are more likely to take some form of official action where a black person is concerned than to consider informal actions such as escorting the person to his or her home. In support of this suggestion, the report of the Policy Studies Institute,[7] found people of 'West Indian' origin to have 'substantially more contact with the police as offenders and suspects than members of other ethnic groups', and that these contacts were more often of a 'negative' kind. Our research suggests that incidents where section 136 is used fall in with this general pattern of encounters between the police and black people.

The Implications for Women of a Procedure which Excludes a Social Worker's Assessment

According to official DHSS statistics, 80 per cent of section 136 detentions occur in London. This figure is largely a result of the different procedure used in the city due to an historical anachronism. In London, the designated place of safety used is almost always a hospital, and the detained person is assessed solely by a psychiatrist. He or she is then usually admitted to hospital for the maximum seventy-two hour period. The detention will be recorded as a section 136 admission. Conversely, outside London where the police station is used as the place of safety, the person is assessed by a doctor and a social worker and, if it is considered necessary, will usually be admitted under a different section of the Mental Health Act. The advantages of this procedure are that the person receives the full assessment as intended in the legislation, and that alternatives to hospitalization may be considered.

The procedure operated in London, however, almost invariably precludes a social worker's assessment. Quite apart from the increased likelihood of being hospitalized against her will, a woman detained under section 136 in London runs the risk that her domestic responsibilities will be overlooked. If the police do not take this into account at the outset, it may be several hours before it is realized that a woman has children at home who are not being cared for whilst she is detained. In contrast, people detained under section 136 outside London are assessed by both psychiatrist and social worker at the police station, which increases the chance of domestic or social circumstances being taken into account at an earlier stage.

In one incident from the MIND research, a woman was detained from a GP's surgery after brandishing a knife. Although she expressed concern at the police station about her two young sons who she said were alone in the house, the police made no attempt to find out if they were being cared for until after she had been assessed at the hospital. The psychiatrist decided not to admit her (primarily on the grounds that she was pregnant), and was critical of the police for not finding out who, if anyone, was looking after her children. The police then returned her home and only at that stage (four hours later) did they decide to find out if the children were all right. Our research suggests that the police usually do contact social services or make informal arrangements with relatives or neighbours when children are present at the incident; however, they do not always find out whether child care is necessary in other cases.

The potential benefits of a social work assessment extend beyond the issue of child care, of course. The provision of a second independent assessment and the consideration of alternatives to hospitalization is of vital importance. In London, once a person reaches hospital, the alternatives under consideration tend to be either admission or discharge: admission to psychiatric hospital for three days or discharge back into the original situation, usually without any additional support. In addition, the tendency under this procedure for hospitals to admit people automatically for three days (the maximum time period allowed for section 136) means that the police are in effect being accorded more power than they would have if the section were being operated correctly. Essentially, the changes necessary in the operation of section 136 revolve around the need to re-emphasize, to all the services involved, its purpose as a means of providing emergency assessment, and not as a convenience of short-term admission to mental hospital.

The Effect of 'Community Care'

Statistics suggest that four out of every five carers of elderly and disabled relatives are women. Very often they are insufficiently supported in this role by the psychiatric and social services, and may be driven to call out the police in situations they find they can't cope with. One example from our research concerned a woman whose sister suffered from long-term mental health problems. She had tried the previous day to arrange for a psychiatrist and a social worker to assess her sister with a view to admitting her to hospital, but the social worker had failed to turn up. The psychiatrist told her that the best thing that could happen would be for her sister to wander out on to the street and be picked up by the police and admitted to hospital in that way. This is exactly what happened, and she was admitted under section 136. The interview with the police officer suggested that the police acted in response to the sister's genuine desperation, although they were critical of the psychiatrist for the advice he gave her.

Experience in the United States, where a programme of de-institutionalization has been introduced in the last few years, suggests that closure of the big mental hospitals leads to increased contact between the police and people with mental health problems. The implications of this for the move towards community care in this country cannot be ignored. Without adequate community facilities for dealing with mental health emergencies, the police will inevitably assume a higher profile in this area, an area with which they are not properly qualified to deal.

Section 136 of the Mental Health Act is essentially a way of dealing with situations that cannot be dealt with by direct recourse to the mental health or social services. As such, it is a necessary inclusion in the Act. However, the procedure followed in London gives the police greater power with which to detain and refer people, as a result of which both men and women tend to be admitted to hospital for three days following police detention, and are rarely assessed by social workers.

All women are traumatized by arrest and detention, but for women with mental health problems, the shock and distress caused by arrest, usually by male police officers, can be particularly acute. For black women, the situation may well be compounded by police racism. Women are particularly affected by the absence of social work assessments, in that arrangements for child care may be overlooked, but the implications for both women and men of incomplete assessments are considerable.

If 'community care' is going to adequately address emergency mental health situations, then a more suitable community based place of safety than either a hospital or a police station (with its particularly intimidating implications for women and black people) needs to be established.*

---

* Although I wrote this article as a result of our research work at MIND, the views expressed are my own and do not necessarily represent those of MIND.

Notes

1. As defined under the Mental Health Act 1983 to include 'mental illness, arrested or incomplete development of mind, psychopathic disorder and any other disorder or disability of mind'.

2. An approved social worker has undergone psychiatric training and is qualified to apply compulsory sections of the Mental Health Act.

3. Phyllis Chesler, *Women and Madness*, Avon Books, 1972.

4. Seminar on section 136, September 1984.

5. Anne Rogers and Alison Faulkner, *A Place of Safety*, MIND 1987.

6. For example, the Health Advisory Service report on Tooting Bec Hospital (1986).

7. See D. Smith and J. Gray, *Police and People in London* vol IV: *The Police in Action*, Policy Studies Institute, London 1983.

Case Studies*

Christina Dunhill

Case notes of advice workers at a London psychiatric hospital revealed one instance in which a woman had been taken in under section 136 after her husband attacked her in the street. Another case involved a woman who had called out the police to accompany her to another premises where she felt she would need police protection. In a third case, a woman who was separated from her husband called the police after her husband had kidnapped her daughter from the neighbour with whom she had left her. The police deceived her into accompanying them in their van and took her first to the police station and then to a mental hospital, without letting her put on proper outdoor clothing or locking her front door. The case of Ms S. is perhaps the most distressing. This is her story:

---

* Because Alison Faulkner's article is based largely on interviews with police and psychiatrists, I spoke to women advice workers at a London psychiatric hospital, about any contact they had had with women brought in under section 136 in connection with any possible abuse of police powers. I also spoke to one of their ex-clients in person.

I'd been in terrible pain for years. The doctors had done tests but they told me there was nothing wrong with me. I was drinking and taking pills to try and get rid of the pain. My husband was getting fed up and one evening in June 1986, he hit me and blacked my eye. In a temper, I went next door and phoned the police asking them to get him out of the house. When they came to my house, they said, 'We can't do that.' I said, 'If you don't get him out, I'll kill him.' I'd picked up a small vegetable knife. My husband took the knife away from me (he knew I'd never use it anyway). But two of the policemen tackled me. They got on top of me and pinned me down on the floor. They handcuffed me and then they took me out to the van, dragging me by my hair. (My husband gave a statement verifying this; my daughter-in-law witnessed it too.) All I had on was a short nightdress and underwear – nothing on my feet. They threw me on the floor of the van on my back. I asked if I could sit down. This officer just put his foot on my face, holding me down, and kept on laughing. The policewoman sitting next to him didn't say anything. Another policeman was holding me down with his foot on mine, but he wasn't hurting. They kept me like that the whole journey.

They took me to the psychiatric hospital on a section 136. When I got there, the duty doctor was shocked by the state I was in. I had bruises all over my back and shoulders and arms and a deep wound running from my knee up my thigh where I had been dragged over the gravel on the hospital grounds. They took photographs at the hospital.

Afterwards, I complained to the police and they are taking up the complaint. They said to me, 'If we've got bad officers in the force, and we have, these are the ones we want out.' Whatever happens, I am also going to sue the police, although it is very expensive. [Ms S. is working and has to pay a certain amount of the legal costs herself.] But it is a matter of principle and my solicitor thinks I have a good case. This year, I had two emergency major operations after the doctors identified what was wrong with me. Since then, I've been feeling much better. My mental distress was entirely caused by untreated physical illness.

The police treatment of Ms S. was gratuitously violent and contemptuous, a further assault on a woman who was already in extreme distress. It indicates that, in some cases, the police may severely abuse their power under section 136 of the Mental Health Act.

19. Policing Irish Women in Britain

Maire O'Shea

In Birmingham, on a Saturday night at Christmas time, four young people come out of a pub at 11 p.m. They are a twenty-one-year-old, second generation Irishman with a Brummie accent, his eighteen-year-old fiancée, and her two brothers who come from Belfast. They are singing an Irish song but are sober and not molesting anyone. Suddenly four policemen jump out of a 'paddywagon', parked outside the pub waiting to pick up drunken Irishmen. They grab the three young men, telling them that they are being arrested for being drunk and disorderly. In the course of the ensuing argument, a policeman asks the twenty-one-year-old what the effing hell he is doing getting mixed up with these Irish sods. The policemen throw the young men into the van and drive off, leaving the girl standing in the street.

Fearing for the men's safety, the girl decides to follow the van to the police station which is a mile away. She walks because she cannot afford a taxi. The police station is in a very sleazy area and she arrives tired, very frightened and suffering extreme discomfort from a full bladder. In the police station she hears shouts and screams. The policewoman on duty orders her to go home, adding, 'You must be up to no good hanging around at this hour of the night.' The girl says she will wait for her fiancé and brother, and that they haven't done anything wrong. The policewoman tells her she is wasting her time, waiting for those drunken Irish sods. A request to use the toilet is refused. She sits down and waits. After an hour she sees a young man being brought out of a cell whose face is so covered with blood that it is unrecognizable. She realizes that it is her fiancé. He is charged with assaulting the police.

An Irish woman with three children lives in a small grove on a council estate in Birmingham, where there are no other children. The children who are quiet and well-behaved, play in the peaceful road. An English neighbour is constantly ordering them off the road and when they carry on playing she calls them 'effing Irish brats'. Their mother intervenes, telling the woman that they have a right to play in their own street and to leave them alone. The woman calls her an 'Irish bitch' and tells her to go back to Ireland. From then on, whenever the mother opens her door she is met with a flood of racist abuse. When she eventually loses her temper and threatens her tormentor, the neighbour calls the police. She is taken to the police station and charged with threatening behaviour. No action is taken against the other woman.

High-level political policing of the Irish community in Britain occurs in waves, against a background of low-level, often invisible, incidents like these of harassment, provocation, discriminatory arrests and unfair charges. Anti-Irish racist policing affects women as well as men very directly; it also affects women indirectly, through their social and family relationships. Separated from menfolk who have been arrested, they are left to bring up children alone, and cope with hostility from British neighbours, traumatic prison visits and dealing with an unfamiliar world of lawyers.

The policing of the Irish community reflects racist attitudes deliberately inculcated during eight hundred years of British rule in Ireland. The Irish are stereotyped by the British as: 'thick', dirty, lazy, wild, treacherous, violent, ungovernable, given to tribal warfare and possessing inordinately long memories. They are seen as having an irrational attachment to Roman Catholicism resulting in very large families and sexual inhibitions. All this racist stereotyping has served as an excuse for the continuous process of colonization.

The origin of racism in Britain today lies in colonial oppression, an experience which the Irish share with black people.

The deep roots of anti-Irish racism can be understood only if it is remembered that Ireland is Britain's oldest colony. A long series of wars, two episodes of genocide (one by Cromwellian massacres, the other by famine), dispossession, internal exile, mass deportations and forced emigration have all failed to subdue the Irish.

In this century, following a war of independence during which an all-Ireland parliament was elected by over 80 per cent of the people, two partitionist states were established by Britain. One is an openly colonial statelet dominated by loyalist supremacists in which a part of the majority of the Irish people has suffered discrimination and military and police violence. The other is a neo-colonialist state with an impoverished economy subservient to Britain. One of the results has been widespread emigration due to mass unemployment in the twenty-six counties and in the six North-Eastern counties, as a result of state violence and discrimination.

In the mass emigrations of the forties and fifties, the Irish arrived in Britain disillusioned with native Irish governments. Having internalized the racism suffered by their parents, they felt inferior. In Britain they were faced with an alien society, and 'No Irish need apply' notices outside lodgings and factories. They ended up with the jobs which the British did not want, because the work was too hard, or too badly paid. The few Irish immigrants qualified to compete with the British for higher status jobs succumbed to pressure to assimilate; they distanced themselves from working-class Irish people and have not been available to give articulate support. The Irish government, glad to be rid of those it has failed, has given no support to victims of police racism. The majority of the Irish, submerged and made invisible, have not dared until recently to assert their separate identity or to raise the Irish question, even in the Labour movement. To preserve some of what was left of their Irish identity, Irish working people have gathered in churches, Irish pubs, clubs and dance halls in Irish areas, where they are easy targets for police attacks. 'Paddywagons' touring the streets in these areas when the pubs close have become a familiar sight.

The level of anti-Irish police racism in Britain has varied according to the state of Anglo-Irish relations at a given time, and according to economic and social conditions in Britain. It had a higher profile during the Depression in the thirties due to competition for low-paid jobs, the need to scapegoat the largest immigrant group for government failures, and due to a political bombing campaign. It became latent in a period of full employment in the forties and fifties when the Irish were needed to undertake work in the construction industry, in catering and in hospitals – jobs that were unpopular with the British. New immigrants from the Caribbean replaced the Irish as scapegoats for the system, and came under attack from the police in their turn. But since the late sixties we have seen a resurgence of anti-Irish racism in Britain and of police harassment and violence against Irish people. It began again as a kind of colonialist knee-jerk response when nationalist people in the six counties began to fight back against the violent attacks by the Royal Ulster Constabulary (RUC) on the peaceful civil rights movement.

Demonstrations in the six counties by the civil rights movement, who were pressing for equality in jobs and housing for catholic people, were brutally policed. In Britain, the fact that the civil rights movement drew a good deal of popular sympathy must have been seen as dangerous. Huge British demonstrations protested against the violent suppression of the movement, the subsequent random internment of nationalists and torture of suspects in police stations. And these British demonstrations themselves were policed with an aggression which was at that time unfamiliar on home territory.

On the Silent March in London in January 1972 mourning the thirteen innocent civilians massacred by British paratroopers on a peaceful civil rights march in Derry, I saw women being kneed and punched by the police. A bus driver was instructed by the police to drive his bus through the crowd, and the police knocked two of the thirteen coffins off the shoulders of the bearers onto the ground. On the following Saturday, over 60,000 demonstrators protesting against the Bloody

Sunday massacre were hemmed into Whitehall by the police. When permission to enter Downing Street to leave the thirteen coffins outside Number 10 was requested by the leaders, demonstrators were charged by police horses and attacked with truncheons. There were many women among the injured who filled the emergency departments of nearby hospitals.

A few months later the barricades protecting the nationalist ghettoes in the six counties from police and British army violence were crushed with enormous force in Operation Motorman. Military repression escalated; there was no chance of resistance. The IRA took the war to England out of desperation. The government responded with dawn police raids staged indiscriminately in the Irish areas of Britain's inner cities. The police smashed down the doors of ordinary homes, destroyed furniture and valuables, terrified children, and arrested men at gunpoint.

The whole Irish community in Britain was being punished, and women bore much of the brunt. They would be dragged out of bed during raids, wearing only nightwear, to face degrading sexist jibes. They would have to comfort their children who might be locked in a room with them, terrorized by the police dogs. In the days that followed, they would fear for their menfolk and suffer abuse and attacks from British neighbours. But they had to carry on with their lives and cope with their children in the ruins of their homes. Some blamed their husbands, believing that they might have become politically involved. The effect on the community was devastating. Families and friends turned against one another. Marriages broke up. At best, there was a climate of constant uncertainty and fear. When the wives and families of the six men framed for the Birmingham bombings in 1974 were attacked in their homes or burnt out by British people seeking revenge, they were refused police protection. Some who had been settled in Birmingham for many years were forced to leave.

After 1974, police surveillance of the Irish community escalated and has remained at a high level, with phone tapping and members of the Special Branch sitting outside doors in cars, watching. The right of the Irish to organize or to express their political views in public has been restricted. Since 1974, access to Trafalgar Square, the traditional venue for national political rallies has been denied to the Irish. The only exceptions have been for Ian Paisley, the loyalist supremacist (who advocates violence and has known links with paramilitary groups) and the so-called 'peacewomen' whose apolitical initiative in the early 1980s supported the presence of the British security forces in Ireland. Publicans and Irish club managers have been instructed by the police to refuse to let rooms to legitimate Irish political groups. Members of Irish political groups leafletting outside churches have frequently been questioned by the police.

In the case of political activists, trawling operations and intimidatory exercises are often disguised as investigations of particular bombings. After a small bomb was exploded in a nearby town in 1973, injuring no one, my house and those of the two other officers of the local anti-internment committee were searched by the Bomb Squad with metal detectors and sniffer dogs. As I did not live in an Irish area, six police officers, including one woman, came to see me not at dawn but at 10 a.m. to avoid shocking my British neighbours, and rang my door bell instead of breaking down the door. They were frigidly polite and behaved correctly, taking care to put everything back after they had searched all the drawers and the cupboards, lifted the carpets and gone over the rubbish bins with a metal detector. Significantly, they did not go into the loft where bombs might have been expected to be hidden. When I protested about the search and in particular at the removal of a list of names and addresses given me by people attending a perfectly legal meeting and of a shield presented to our committee by some internees in Long Kesh, I was instructed to make my complaint to the local police station.

The inspector who came to take my statement was apologetic and informed me that I would be visited by the Chief Constable of Hertfordshire. When I asked this eminent gentleman the reason for suspecting me of being involved in a bombing, he took from his pocket a bundle of cuttings of letters which I had written to local papers about repression in Ireland.

He pointed to one protesting about the conditions under which ten Irish people were being held on remand. 'Here you are,' he said, 'giving support to bombers.' He spoke as if the result of the case was a foregone conclusion. He spent two hours trying to persuade me to withdraw my complaint, which I would not do, and I heard nothing further.

The Prevention of Terrorism Act 1974

The Prevention of Terrorism Act (PTA), the most vicious piece of racist legislation ever enacted in this country, has given the police unlimited power to terrorize the Irish in Britain. Within a week of the Birmingham pub bombings, the Prevention of Terrorism Act was rushed through the House of Commons. MPs were persuaded to vote for it in spite of the serious restrictions on civil liberties it involved, on the grounds that an emergency measure was necessary to prevent a recurrence of a recent atrocity. Thirteen years later, it is still on the statute book. This legislation is not necessary for catching terrorists, who can be arrested and charged under the Explosives Act or with murder or manslaughter if there is any concrete evidence against them. There have been no more convictions of Irish people for terrorist offences in any year since the introduction of the PTA than there were in any year preceding it.

Over 6,000 Irish people are officially listed as having been arrested in England and Wales between 1974 and 1986 under the PTA; an average of 44,000 per year are listed in the Port authorities arrival reports as having been stopped for security checks. These are not listed as arrests if they last for less than twelve hours but in fact many are arrests, involving being taken to a police station, having one's property removed, being fingerprinted and interrogated. There are also so-called security checks at airports, railway stations and in the street, for which no figures are available. Since 1974, fewer than 200 people arrested under the PTA have been charged and of these the majority have been charged with trivial offences such as being 'drunk and disorderly' or withholding information.

Those arrested under the PTA can be detained incommunicado for forty-eight hours and for a further five days, with the approval of the Home Secretary, without access to a solicitor. They are strip-searched, fingerprinted, photographed and usually deprived of sleep, washing facilities, reading materials and proper food. Up until 1983, interrogation was invariably accompanied by physical brutality, since stopped because of widespread protest. Now, psychological torture in the form of verbal abuse, threats to the prisoner and his or her family, sleep deprivation, isolation and disorientation are used to extract incriminating statements. The PTA allows summary deportation without any obligation to inform the victim of the reasons for this and without the right to appeal before an appeal court. Men who are deported, having lived in Britain for many years, leave wives and families behind, the wives suffering the pain of separation and bearing the burden of bringing up children without a father.

The PTA has been very successful in silencing the Irish community. Only committed political activists who wish to use their experience to expose the true purpose of the PTA have sought publicity for their cases. In order to keep British people in ignorance of what is being done in their name in Ireland, the PTA is used to try and deter supporters of Irish unity and independence from speaking to British audiences. For example, Bernadette McAliskey (spokeswoman for the anti-imperialist movement, once the youngest MP in parliament) has been stopped for questioning (under the PTA) on her way to a speaking tour in Britain. The PTA is also used to deter members of British Labour movement organizations from visiting the six war-torn counties and finding out for themselves the truth about the Irish situation.

Women members of legitimate Irish political organizations have been arrested at gunpoint and taken to the notorious Paddington Green police station where Irish political activists in London are interrogated by the Irish Squad, (themselves Irish), to the accompaniment of beatings and threats. In intimidatory information-gathering exercises like these, women have been interrogated about their political opinions and usually detained for seven days before being released without charge. As a result of their experiences, many have suffered longstanding psychological ill-effects.

In one instance, three republican women were arrested on arrival in Scotland with a minibus full of children on their way to holiday with families in Scotland. They were detained for four days in horrific conditions; one who was menstruating was denied sanitary protection. They were also kept in ignorance of the fate of the children who had been in their charge.

In British police stations, the form of abuse most regularly inflicted on Irish women arrested under the PTA, is strip-searching. It is said to be carried out for security purposes but is undoubtedly a form of sexual harassment. The degree of sexual degradation involved is tantamount to rape. Like rape, it is a means of exerting total power over a woman. Irish Catholic women, many of whom have never appeared naked before another person, feel particularly desecrated. They are made to turn around slowly, with their arms above their heads. The soles of their feet are felt and their mouth and ears searched. A woman may suffer a running commentary about her body, with emphasis on any blemishes or deformities. Comments like 'What are you embarrassed about, you Irish bitch?' or 'What would Father think of this Holy Mary now?' are not uncommon. The women cannot resist, or express their anger; if they did, this might provide an excuse for police to overpower them by violence. Strip-searching is often carried out in the presence of, though out-of-sight of, male officers. The women are screened off but they are aware of the proximity of men, whose voices they can hear.

Another technique for sexual degradation frequently practised is denial of sanitary protection. Annie Maguire, one of the thirty-four Irish prisoners, wrongly convicted for the Guildford and Woolwich bombings now released in 1984 after ten years in prison, describes how, during interrogation, she was made to stand spreadeagled against a wall with menstrual blood flowing on to the floor, and was kicked whenever she tried to bring her legs together.

I myself experienced the horror of being held incommunicado in a police station when I was arrested under the PTA in

January 1985 in my own house in Birmingham. I had returned voluntarily from Ireland where I had been visiting my daughter and grandchildren, having heard from friends and neighbours that my house had been searched in my absence. I work as a psychiatrist and when I returned I found that my filing cabinet had been smashed up, and the highly confidential psychiatric reports which it contained scattered about the floor. A friend who, like me, belonged to the Irish in Britain Representation Group, a legitimate organization fighting anti-Irish racism for the rights of the Irish in Britain and a united Ireland, had been arrested. I knew I would be arrested myself, but not charged, as only about a hundred of the many thousands arrested in this way in the past have been charged.

After my arrest, I was held in the Liverpool Bridewell where I was given no edible food and had no washing facilities. I was dripping with perspiration, I believe because the heating had been deliberately turned up when it was seen that I was wearing a heavy jumper (which I could not change, not having been allowed to bring anything with me other than my handbag). My watch was taken from me. The only furniture in my cell was a two-foot wide wooden bench attached to the wall on which I was expected to sleep. Outside the interrogation room no one spoke to me except to give orders; if I complained I was told, 'You shouldn't have been naughty.'

I was interrogated in my unwashed state, was faced with two overdressed Special Branch officers with shining faces and shoes, one aggressive and threatening, the other ingratiating. I was threatened with life imprisonment as I had been 'less than truthful'. I can testify to the emotional turmoil and sheer panic I experienced while deprived of human contact. I was overcome by loss of identity and feelings of disorientation, helplessness and abandonment.

The techniques used by the police to frame a political activist are exemplified by my own case. I was charged with conspiracy to cause explosions in the UK on the basis of evidence which would not be admissible on charges other than conspiracy: associations, friendships and political opinions. Conspiracy charges are used when there is a shortage of evidence. They have been used over the centuries, in the words of Kitson, the Commanding Officer of British forces in Ireland 'as a psychological weapon to dispose of unwanted members of the public'. Having been an active member of organizations campaigning for Irish unity and independence for the whole of my thirty years in Britain, I must have been seen as an 'unwanted member of the public'.

I was refused bail by the magistrates because the police objected that I would abscond or interfere with ongoing investigation, and I was remanded in custody to Risley Remand Prison. I was held under Category A in solitary confinement without visitors apart from my daughter who is my only relative in Britain. When my son, who works in Paris, arrived in Dover on his way to a special visit to me, he was arrested under the PTA and held for four hours, missing the train which would have got him to Risley in time for the visit. It was only through the intervention of the Irish Embassy that he was allowed in to visit me.

At the weekly remand hearings, friends coming to court to support me were attacked by loyalist mobs. The police had discreetly spread the news that a 'Fenian' would be in court. After five weeks in prison, I was granted bail due to pressure brought to bear on the legal establishment by a leading churchman in Ireland, by MPs, MEPs and labour movement organizations lobbied by my daughter and many friends. The police agreed reluctantly to release me, under pressure from 'on high' and on humanitarian grounds, because of my age and disabilities.

During the long period leading up to my trial a year later, I suffered the fear of life imprisonment and of destitution. Having been refused legal aid, there was no guarantee that I would be granted costs (which amounted to £40,000) even if acquitted. My daughter and I were harassed by the Special Branch who followed us everywhere, interfered with our telephone conversations and questioned several of my friends and patients. My daughter was stopped and questioned in a railway station. My car, which had been taken away by the police for forensic tests, was so badly damaged as to be unusable afterwards. Three years later, I have not received compensation for the damage to my car, nor to my house and furniture during the police search. Nor have my personal papers taken been returned, in spite of repeated phone calls and the censure of the police for their behaviour in this respect by the trial judge. After a visit to my employer by the police, the sessions at a local psychiatric day centre which I had taken on following my retirement from my full-time NHS post were terminated.

The security drama surrounding my trial in Manchester for the purpose of convincing the jury that I was a dangerous terrorist cost the ratepayers one million pounds. Streets within a radius of half a mile of the court house were cordoned off by police with sniffer dogs who searched all cars in nearby car parks from 7 a.m. each morning. A helicopter hovered on the roof of the court house, and inside everyone moving from one part of the building to another was body searched. The sand-wiches in the cafeteria were searched. The court room was steel-lined; a bullet-proof screen had been erected in front of the dock; an armed member of the Special Branch sat beside the judge.

On the first day the police tried to have the trial held in camera by refusing admission to all members of the public, including relatives and observers from my union. My bail sureties were kept waiting for three hours outside in the snow. Only those press men who had been given special security badges by the police were admitted; they represented papers which could be counted on to 'find me guilty', even before the jury gave its verdict.

I was found 'not guilty' on all charges. I believe that this was only because I had certain advantages not enjoyed by my fellow countrywomen whom the police have succeeded in framing. I was well known to a great many people in several British cities through my professional work and my involvement in Irish and Labour movement organizations, many of whom gave evidence in my defence. A strong defence campaign was mounted from the day of my arrest by trade unions and observers to the trial. I had brilliant lawyers, and recent events had shaken the faith of members of the jury in the police.

At least thirty-four Irish people, including four women, who did not enjoy the same advantages, have been framed by the police and judiciary and are serving severe sentences, or bearing the burden of a criminal record.

20. Black Women Targeted

Olga Heaven and Maria Mars

Since the shooting of Mrs Cherry Groce in Brixton and the death of Mrs Cynthia Jarrett in Tottenham during police raids on their homes in Autumn 1985, attention has been focused on Black women and policing. As the story of Ms B. below demonstrates in particular, the relationship of Black women to policing practices should not only be considered in terms of the context of Black people in this country, but must also be analysed in terms of gender.

The development of policing of Black people in Britain has taken place in the context of various immigration acts which have been imposed to restrict Black people's rights of entry and citizenship. The 1962 Immigration Act legitimized public assumptions that Black people were a 'problem'. Some believe that this Act began the progress of modern institutionalized racism. As A. Sivanandan has pointed out:

> If labour from the 'coloured' commonwealth and colonies was needed, its intake and deployment was going to be regulated not by the market forces of discrimination but by the regulatory instruments of the state itself. The state was going to say at the very port of entry (or non entry) which Blacks could come and which couldn't, and where they could go and where they could live and how they should behave and deport themselves. Or else . . . There was the immigration officer at the gate and the fascist within. Racism was respectable, sanctioned, but with reason of course; it was not the colour, it was the numbers – for fewer blacks must make for better race relations.[1]

The police and other institutions (such as the education service and the NHS) were given a licence by the Act to be openly hostile to Black people. Thus began the process of criminalization of the Black community, one of the most significant aspects of which was that Black people became forced to protect themselves not only from racist attacks but also from those responsible for maintaining the 'Queen's peace'.

Since the early seventies, we have seen a movement away from 'preventative policing' to a more reactive policing. There have been changes in police organization and equipment. Special Patrol Groups have been reconstructed as the British version of paramilitary squads; an illegal immigration intelligence unit has been established as part of the Metropolitan CID, and the Special Branch has increased its size. There have also been major additions in police equipment: specially equipped vans, computers, helicopters and guns.

The SPG and other specialized units are armed and have been used in saturation policing of Black communities in Brixton, Peckham, Stoke Newington and Lewisham.[2] The development of policing methods has been more antagonistic to Black people than to others. Evidence of police misconduct against Black people is considerable and has been well documented.[3]

Since the late fifties, with the participation of women like Claudia Jones and Amy Garvey, Black women have been actively involved in the struggle against police brutality and injustice. Some may argue that our struggle then was mainly around supporting and defending Black men, but even then those of us who came into contact with the police did not escape police brutality and assault.

By the 1970s, Black women were becoming increasingly visible and active. We continued to organize alongside Black men as well as autonomously; and it was important for us to take up issues that neither Black organizations nor the white women's movement would concern themselves with. For Black women, issues of race, gender and class could not be separated.

We were responding to the growing criminalization of our

children. We found that the police were being called into schools to break up fights or minor incidents which we would have normally expected teachers to deal with. The 'sus' law provision of the 1924 Vagrancy Act further legitimized police victimization of young Black people.[4] The 'sus' provision empowered the police to arrest and charge anyone they considered to be behaving suspiciously. It was our children and our community who were victims of this law.[5]

Since the 'sus' provision was repealed, the police have used their powers to stop and search, augmented under the Police and Criminal Evidence Act (see chapter 24), disproportionately against young Black people. Even in connection with section 136 of the Mental Health Act, which empowers the police to remove to a 'place of safety' anyone found in a public place and judged to be dangerous to him/herself or to others (see chapter 18), it appears that the police use their powers disproportionately against Black people.[6] And the Public Order Act 1986, which came into force in April 1987 and enables the police to arrest anyone for 'disorderly behaviour', is being used, as we feared, particularly against young Black people.

There is little doubt in the Black community that the police have used the law as an instrument of oppression and social control. The drugs laws present another way of criminalizing Black people. All sorts of people smoke cannabis, which is generally accepted as less, or at least no more, harmful than alcohol. But you do not hear of many police raids on white people's houses and clubs to look for it. In *Police and People in London*, the PSI researchers found that enforcement of the law on cannabis was the one policing priority which the majority of Londoners disagreed with. But this law provides the police with a useful entrée into our houses and clubs.[7]

In the following statement, Ms D. tells of a raid on her flat that took two hours and twenty minutes. The alarming features of her story include: the abrupt and intimidating entry by police officers, the contemptuous disruption of the household, the strip-searching of Ms D., her detention in a police cell for eight hours with nothing to eat, routine questioning about her immigration status, use of her concern for her children to induce her to make an incriminating statement and misrepresentation of her boyfriend's response to questioning in an attempt by the police to get her to incriminate him. This is her account of what happened:

That particular morning, my boyfriend – my baby's father – was there. We went into the kitchen so I could give him something to eat before he went. I started frying an egg – I had one egg in the frying pan and one in my hand – and I thought I heard the doorbell. I went out to open the door and I just quickly took a look through the spyhole, not really paying much attention, and all I saw was this guy with a checked hat on. Within the space of peeping through the spyhole and turning the door, the whole lot of them were just standing there, and that's when I realized what was happening and I attempted to shut the door, but they put their foot in the way.

Before I had time to do or say anything, they barged their way in and were going towards the kitchen. At that stage I started getting upset and asked if they had a warrant to search my premises. I was very upset. I went to put the egg I was holding back in the fridge but they wouldn't let me. Eventually, the egg broke on the floor in the struggle because they were preventing me from going into the kitchen.

Then I said I wanted to go to the toilet because at that time I was on my monthly and they said that I couldn't until the toilet was searched, but in the meanwhile they would go into the bedroom and search me.

They [two policewomen] made me take off my clothes – everything apart from my knickers really – and when I got to my knickers, I said, do you want me to pull that down as well, and they said no. That satisfied them, and they told me to get dressed. I was going into the drawer to get a pad and the policewoman shut my hand in the drawer. When she saw what I was taking out she let go of the drawer, and I was followed to the toilet. I was not allowed to shut the toilet door.

Then they took me to the kitchen, while they took my boyfriend to the bedroom to search him and to search the bedroom.

Well, I usually keep some weed for my own use, and they found it in a little plastic bag. That was what they were waiting for, so that they could charge me. They told me that I intended to sell.

When the police came to my place, it was 9.40 a.m. and by the time they finished searching, it was after 12 o'clock. They took my boyfriend and me to the police station. I was locked up and honestly I never had anything to eat all day. I was kept in the cell from after 12 midday till 8.40 p.m. in the evening.

I asked the police if they could phone someone for me and they said yes. I gave them the phone number, but at that time I still didn't know if they had phoned or if no one was in. I was really worried about the kids [Ms D.'s three sons] because I took them to school that morning with the intention of going to collect them after school.

Eventually, at 8.40 p.m., they brought me into this room where there was a policewoman. They asked me personal questions like where were my parents and how long had I been in this country.

The policewoman asked me if I wanted a cup of tea so I said to her that I was told the canteen was shut. She brought me a cup of tea and gave me a cigarette. She took a Bounty [chocolate bar] out of her bag and offered it to me. I said, no, thank you. She sat on the desk while the sergeant and the other officers sat next to me, writing. Before going to the police station, my boyfriend had said to me, 'No matter what happens, don't say anything and don't sign anything'. Well, I thought that was easy, so when they asked me if I wanted to make a statement, I said 'no'. They said, 'If you don't make a statement, we won't let you out of here until 10 a.m. tomorrow morning when you go to court'. I got panicky, because I was worried about my children, I didn't know if they had been picked up from school. I said, 'I can't stay all night'. So, after all that, I took the blame for everything.

But they weren't satisfied with my story, they kept insisting that the weed belonged to my boyfriend and that there was more. My boyfriend had three fines for possession of cannabis and they really wanted him. They said that most of what I had told them was a cock-and-bull story. The policewoman got off the desk and said, 'I've had enough of this, after this morning I had sympathy for you but now my sympathy is gone altogether. I'm going to phone social services to tell them to put your kids in care'. She left the room and the other police officers left as well. I could hear them talking.

Soon the policewoman came back and said, 'You should be a fly on the wall, you should hear what he is saying next door, and here you are prepared to sit down and take the blame'. Eventually, when she saw that she wasn't going to get through to me, she started to frighten me and said, 'You know, you could get two years for that'.

Eventually, when I said, 'I told you the truth, I can't tell you nothing else,' she locked me back up again. After about another hour, they said I could go home.

When I appeared in court I was given a custodial sentence. My boyfriend was acquitted. He took care of the children whilst I was in prison.

Physical and Sexual Abuse

Many Black women have made allegations and complaints of physical, racist and sexual abuse against the police. Ms B.'s story of her three encounters with the police is a horrifying catalogue of such abuse. It also indicates how young Black women may be picked on and provocatively policed in the same way as young Black men (see also chapter 6). It tells of an apparently spontaneous assault by the police and their not uncharacteristic reaction of a retaliatory charge (a charge made by the police against someone whom they have given cause to bring a charge against them – see also chapter 13) of 'assault on a police officer' when the victim responds by fighting back. Ms B. also makes detailed allegations of assault, abuse and intimidation continuing in the police station, where it is perhaps also significant that she, who had received so much sexualized racial abuse, was also humiliated by strip-searching.

Ms B., a twenty-two-year-old Black British woman from South London, describes her experiences:

I first experienced police brutality when I was fourteen. I was attending an Educationally Subnormal school in London. I got in an argument with my headmaster. He told me to do something and I refused, he hit me and I hit him back with my hand. He was pushing me, so I ran outside and got two housebricks and told him that, if he touched me again, I would throw them at him. He called the police and I was dumped in the police van. I couldn't believe it; the police began to bully me, they pulled my hair and called me names – 'black bastard', 'black whore', 'Sambo' – and they told me to 'go back to the jungle'. I was scared.

When we got to the police station, they questioned me. I didn't answer, I was too scared. A young policeman said, 'Open your mouth, you black c—.' I still didn't answer and he said, 'You are going to stay here for a long time.' They bullied me. I didn't say anything. I just cried. My mother came to get me and I was allowed to go home.

When I went to court, I was found guilty of assaulting the headmaster and of carrying an offensive weapon (housebricks). I was given a one-year suspended sentence. I was also expelled from ESN school.

From then on, the same cops kept picking on me all the time. They would arrest me and sometimes charge me. They just wouldn't stop picking on me.

Another time, I was fifteen then, three friends (all roughly the same age, fifteen or sixteen) and I were walking along the street. A police van pulled up and the police got out and asked us what we were doing. We didn't answer, then one of my friends said something like, 'minding our own business'. A police officer said, 'all right, you are under arrest.' So we began to argue, saying, 'she didn't do anything'. There was a struggle. This policeman was beating up my friend so I began to hit him with my hand, so he would stop hurting her. Eventually they threw us all in the police van and took us to the station.

When I was in the cell, the police officers told me to take off my clothes. I said I wasn't going to take off my clothes in front of no man, and why couldn't they just search my pockets? They said that if I didn't take my clothes off, they would rip them off me. I refused to strip in front of them. They began shouting racist and sexist abuse. As they began to take my clothes off me, I began to fight them off. I was punched and kicked, my head was banged against the wall. In the end, I had to give in. Later, they charged me with assaulting the police officer who had been beating up my friend.

In court, I was found guilty of assault. My friends were also found guilty of assault. The magistrate never listened to us. The police harassed us, racially abused us and assaulted us, yet nothing happened to them.

The police harassment did not stop. I couldn't walk the street because the police were creating trouble. One day, they came to my house. I heard this loud knocking and I decided not to answer. The knocking became louder and I was scared because I was on my own. I went to the front door and asked who was there. A man said 'police' and that he had a warrant. I opened the door, otherwise he would have kicked it in.

When he came in, he asked who else was with me. I said, 'no one', I was alone. He then started to search my place, pulling everything out, and another police officer joined him. They went to the kitchen and accused me of stealing almost everything – washing machine, spin dryer, food mixer and so on. I said my things were not stolen, I had proof. The first policeman called me a 'lying Black bitch' and began to bully me. He shouted racist abuse and threw my things on the floor. He was now searching my bedroom, emptying the drawers and dumping my clothes on the floor. By this time I was angry and scared. I shouted at them to leave me alone, stop turning my place upside down and tell me what I had done. Suddenly, I realized that I was breathing fast and that I was having an asthma attack and needed my inhaler. He told me to shut up. He said I wasn't an asthmatic. I said I knew where the inhaler was, it was in the bedroom although I couldn't see it.

Because I was really scared, my breathing was getting worse. I tried to run through the front door but they caught me. I was dragged to the police van. In the van I was punched and kicked. I kept asking for my inhaler. I could hardly breathe. One of them said he was going back to look for the inhaler, otherwise they might have to take me to hospital. He went to the house and came back with it. He had to hold the inhaler to my mouth because by that time I was so breathless I couldn't do it myself.

I was taken to the police station and charged with conspiracy to forge. Once I was in the police cell, they sent for a police doctor. I showed him the bruises on my legs but he ignored me and said they were only grazed and not so bad. He gave me tablets and a new inhaler for my asthma.

At first, I refused to give a statement. I was told that I would not be given bail. I stayed in the police cell for five nights. It was pure torture. They kept pulling me out of the cell every hour to give a statement. One particular policewoman had it in for me. She kept coming into the cell and abusing me. At one point she hit me and I hit her back and ended up being punched and kicked again, even though she started the trouble. She kept kicking the door every hour, saying I had to come out and give this statement. I did give a statement but they said it was 'bullshit'.

I knew a few of the police officers from when I was arrested before. They just kept picking on me. I eventually gave them the statement they wanted. For five nights, I hadn't had a wash and I was taken to court without being allowed to wash myself. I was remanded in custody. When I arrived at Holloway, I felt like a tramp.

Police officers abuse their power. There is nothing we can do about it. They are the law. The women officers are as bad as the men; they hold your hands behind your back and the men punch and kick you. They really hate Black women.

Ms B. was remanded in custody for nine months and was eventually given a custodial sentence of a year. She has since had to change her address in an attempt to avoid police harassment.

Some Black women have claimed that they have been sexually assaulted by police officers but have felt completely unable to report the offence. Others who have tried to report an assault have often been threatened with being charged for wasting police time unless they withdraw their complaints. In January 1984, Ms Jacqueline Berkeley was found guilty of wasting police time after the magistrate had rejected her allegations that she had been raped by police officers while being held down by two women colleagues.

After hearing about Jacqueline's case, many Black women came forward and reported similar experiences of police violence.[8] For the most part, they remain silent because they are afraid that no one except perhaps their families and close friends will believe them. This is also because they have no faith in the police, who instead of offering protection, have used their power to physically and sexually abuse Black women.

The issue of police accountability poses a dilemma for the Black community and others who feel that they have been harassed and abused by the police. It is widely believed that the police do not enforce the law impartially and this belief has led to a considerable decrease in public confidence in the police. However, many of the victims of police violence are reluctant to make official complaints, simply because they are investigated by the police themselves. For example, Ms B. has never made a complaint. Victims who do make complaints experience great difficulties and often risk further police harassment and sometimes arrest. Victims who sue the police often have to wait for very long periods before their case is brought to court, although the outcome may sometimes be satisfactory.

In 1976, a Caribbean couple, David and Lucille White of Stoke Newington, were brutally beaten in their own home by police officers. It took them six years for a civil case to come before a high court. The couple were acquitted of assault charges and were awarded a total of £51,392 in damages by a High Court judge (see also chapter 29, in particular the cases brought by Mrs George and Mrs Lucas).

The police profess to consider that only a 'few officers' are responsible for racist policing, but many of us believe that racism and sexism in the police are quite pervasive. Lord Scarman argued in his 1981 Report[9] that Britain is not an institutionally racist society; he concluded, 'I find that the direction and policy of the Metropolitan Police are not racist. But racial prejudice does manifest itself occasionally in the behaviour of a few officers on the streets.' However, Lord Scarman failed to identify the way in which such racist officers are supported within police ranks. As P. Gordon has pointed out, 'there can be no doubt that police officers are racist. The police themselves accept that it is so, and argue that the police are only a cross-section, and therefore reflect the make-up of that society.'[10] The argument is, of course, put forward precisely to excuse the existence of racism within the police.

The police do not enforce the law impartially. Black women have experienced racist and sexist policing. The racism of individuals within the police force cannot be seen as the only or main problem, for the fact remains that they are operating within the context of institutionalized racism, where Black people and their cultures are defined as the problem. For Black women, the struggle against institutionalized racism and oppression must continue.

Notes

1. A. Sivanandan, 'Challenging Racism: Strategies for the Eighties', *Race and Class*, vol. XXV, 2.

2. J. Downing, *Now You Know*, WOW Campaigns Ltd, 1980.

3. D. Humphry, *Police Power and Black People*, Panther Books, 1972.

4. C. Demuth, *SUS: A Report on the Vagrancy Act, 1924*, Runnymede Trust, 1978.

5. B. Bryan, S. Dadzie, S. Scafe, *The Heart of the Race: Black Women's Lives in Britain*, Virago, 1985.

6. *Women and Policing* supplement to *Policing London*, March 1987.

7. 'Policing and People in London', Policy Studies Institute, 1983.

8. C. Burgher, *Black Women and Racist Attacks* (Black and Ethnic Minority Women, GLC Women's Committee).

9. Lord Scarman, *The Scarman Report*, Penguin, London, 1981.

10. P. Gordon, *White Law: Racism in the Public, Court and Prisons*, Pluto Press, London, 1983.

Bibliography

C. Gutzmore, 'Capital, "Black Youth" and Crime', *Race and Class*, vol. XXV, 2

M. Kettle and L. Hodges, *Uprising! The Police, the People and the Riots in Britain's Cities*, Pan, London, 1982

Policing London, 1 (July/August 1982), 2 (September 1982) and 19 (August/September 1985)

'The Policing Aspects of Lord Scarman's Report on the Brixton Disorder', *Policing London*, March 1982

Women and Policing supplements of *Policing London*, issue 4 (July 86) issue 5 (November 86) issue 6 (March 87)

Policing London is available from Lambeth Police Committee Support Unit, Lambeth Town Hall, Brixton Hill, London SW2 1RW

21. Joint Council for the Welfare of Immigrants (JCWI)

Women and the Immigration Law

Sue Shutter

There are two main reasons why women come up against the police in connection with immigration. The first is when the police have information, for example from the Home Office, that a woman is here illegally; the second is when the police suspect that a woman may be here illegally, often for no reason other than that she is black. The role of the police in immigration control is both to enforce the law and to show those who are here perfectly legally that they are under surveillance.

British immigration law and rules are both racist and sexist. Commonwealth citizens who had a parent born here are not subject to immigration control at all. Commonwealth citizens who had a grandparent born here may come to live and work in Britain without difficulties. EEC citizens have the right to come to Britain to look for and to take work, without other restrictions. Nearly all of these people are white, so they have few difficulties with immigration. Other people from abroad, who have present rather than past connections with Britain – for example a Jamaican woman whose children and grandchildren are living here – may find things more difficult. The rules about family reunion are very strict and there are long queues, particularly in the Indian subcontinent, of people who may have to wait years to join their families here.

Until 1 August 1988, the law was different for men and women. Commonwealth citizens and British citizens who were settled here on 1 January 1973 had the right to be joined by by their *wives* (our emphasis) and children under eighteen without having to satisfy other tests. This did not apply to *any* women living here, who have no legal right to be joined by their husbands; the rules regarding this have been changed six times in the past eighteen years. The 1988 Immigration Act has now removed these rights from men, in the name of sex equality. This is the government's response to the 1985 judgement of the European Court of Human Rights, which found that British immigration law discriminated against women and should be changed. All couples wanting to live here together, when one partner comes from abroad, now have to show that theirs is a genuine marriage, that they intend to stay together permanently as husband and wife, that the primary purpose of the marriage was not to obtain admission to the UK, and that they can support and accommodate themselves without recourse to public funds. Even if they can prove that, the person from abroad will only be given permission to stay for a year, at the end of which all these conditions may be checked again, before he or she is granted settlement.

Sex discrimination still continues in the immigration rules. Men here temporarily, for example as students or work permit holders, can be joined by their wives for the same length of time; women here temporarily have no chance at all under the law to have their husbands here with them.

Even coming to visit friends and relatives living in Britain or wanting to come to study here is very difficult for people from black and Third World countries, who may face difficulties with the immigration officials at British High Commissions abroad or at British airports. The introduction of visas in 1986 and 1987 for citizens of India, Pakistan, Bangladesh, Ghana and Nigeria, making it necessary for them to obtain prior permission to enter Britain before leaving their country, has added a further bureaucratic difficulty for all these people.

Black people and people with 'foreign-sounding' names within Britain are much more likely to be checked by the Home Office or by the police and action is more likely to be taken against them if there are any irregularities in their stay here.

Social Control

All women and men over sixteen who are not Commonwealth citizens and who have been allowed to stay in Britain for more than six months are required by law to register with the police. This means going to their local police station and giving the police their name, date of birth, address, marital status and occupation, and having this recorded in a 'police registration certificate' for which they had, in 1988, to pay £25. Any changes in their situation have to be reported to the police within seven days and it is a criminal offence not to do so. This is clearly a very strong means of social control and the condition to register with the police is only removed if the person is allowed to remain permanently in Britain.

The police are used by the Home Office to make inquiries into immigration status and into applications for British nationality. If a man has applied to stay here with his wife who lives here, the police may be asked to make inquiries as to the 'genuineness' of the relationship (see above) and to interview the couple about it. Stories of the police asking offensive and personal questions as to the details of the relationship are common.

The police are also often used to interview people to see if they have the 'sufficient knowledge of the English language' required of naturalization applicants. The police clearly have no training which would make them remotely appropriate to make these inquiries.

The records of the Joint Council for the Welfare of Immigrants (JCWI) include the case of a Pakistani postgraduate university student who had applied for naturalization but was so frightened by a visit from the police that she was unable to speak to the officer at all. Her application was refused on language grounds, although she clearly had a good command of the language.

Criminalization

The Immigration Act 1971 increased the number of criminal offences associated with immigration, the most common of which are knowingly remaining longer than the period allowed by the Home Office or immigration officers (known as over-staying), or failing to observe a condition attached to leave to remain (most commonly, working without permission).

The Act gives the police as well as immigration officers power to arrest without warrant anyone who has or whom they suspect may have committed an immigration offence. These very wide powers allow police to question women and men about their immigration status without any justification; often they have no more reason to believe that an offence might have been committed than that the person is black, or that the person looks worried when the police approach.

The maximum penalty for these immigration offences is a fine of up to £1,000, imprisonment for up to six months, and a recommendation for deportation. People appear before a magistrates' court; the police may give evidence against those charged. There is a certain amount of scope for abuse. A person who has been charged may not have had access to legal advice; he or she may find it difficult to understand court proceedings going on in an unfamiliar language. In some cases, people plead guilty straight away because they have been advised to by the police, when all the time a defence might have been found.

The police may also urge the magistrate, as part of the sentence, to recommend to the Home Office that the person should be deported. Only about a quarter of such recommendations are not followed by the Home Office making a deportation order. A particularly disturbing case was that of a Nigerian woman taken into Stoke Newington police station because she was wandering the streets in a disturbed state. Although she was unable to speak at all, she was charged with making a false statement to the police. She was conditionally discharged, but the court still recommended deportation. She was held at Holloway for the next two weeks until the Home

Office found that she was settled in Britain and deportation should not even have been considered.

Home Office Powers: Why Involve the Police?

There is, however, no need for the police to be involved in immigration in this way. The Home Office can make its own administrative decisions to deport people on the basis of its own information or inquiries if they have overstayed or worked illegally. When this procedure is followed, a person has the right of appeal to the immigration appeal authorities; this procedure may give him or her the chance to put forward a case against deportation; it also avoids some of the distress caused by being treated like a criminal. However, the 1988 Immigration Act restricts the right to appeal and only permits people who have been here for more than seven years to put forward reasons why they should not be deported. Within the criminal procedure set out above, there is neither the right to put your case against deportation nor to appeal against a decision to deport. The only recourse under the criminal procedure is an appeal against sentence (see chapter 22).

In the past, the Home Office procedure had to be followed when people had been overstaying for more than three years, as they were then time-barred from prosecution. However, there have been three separate government attempts to change this ruling, by making overstaying into a continuing offence, so that the police can continue to arrest at any time. The 1988 Immigration Act successfully made this change, so people can now be prosecuted for overstaying however long they have lived here. Obviously, the authorities wish to continue to criminalize people and make them more vulnerable to police questioning, and it may not be long before they are able to do so.

If a deportation order is signed against people whose whereabouts are not known to the Home Office, or who attempt to escape, their personal details are passed on to the police computer, so that they can be traced for deportation if they are questioned for any other purpose. So if, for example, a black woman is questioned about a minor traffic violation, the police may routinely run her name through the computer to see if she is wanted for immigration reasons. For most black women, on whom nothing will be found, this will be another form of harassment, but for a woman who may be in breach of the immigration regulations quite unwittingly, it is humiliating to be arrested and detained straight away if her name is on the computer.

Another way in which the Home Office can force people out of the country is by deciding that they entered illegally, alleging that they lied to an immigration officer on arrival or had not revealed their true intentions and have therefore gained entry to the country under false pretences. Often the only 'evidence' in such cases is a 'confession' by the person, usually obtained by the police or immigration officers as a result of interrogation, sometimes with threats and intimidation, when the person has had no access to legal advice and has no idea of the reasons behind the questioning. This interrogation often takes place in a police station, which adds to the pressure on the person concerned.

The reason for the continuing, and possibly expanding, role of the police in these processes may be that finding criminal 'offences' provides a way of short-circuiting the appeals procedure whereby people may be able to put forward full legal arguments about their status and right to be here. It is easy to overstay or breach a condition of stay inadvertently, whereupon the criminal process allows for deportation without full consideration of the case. Another reason may have to do with the continuing surveillance it allows the police to keep on all black people.

Raids and Harassment

As well as dealing with individuals, the police also organize immigration raids, in conjunction with immigration officers. Many workplace raids have received publicity. In London, for example, Bestways Cash and Carry, Main Gas Appliances and the Hilton Hotel were raided; but there are countless smaller operations, for example, against contract cleaners and 'sweatshops', where women are particularly affected. Raids take place either as the result of a tip-off or because the police have gained information from the immigration service. Police and immigration officers are complementary to each other. The police can investigate suspects for any other criminal offence (perhaps as a cover people may be told that a theft is being investigated, as they were at a raid on Liberty's department store); the immigration officers will have the more detailed knowledge of immigration regulations to know whether a person can be charged or whether they must be dealt with solely by the Home Office. Such police/immigration raids are terrifying experiences for those involved, even when they are here quite legally. People are questioned in detail about their immigration status and may be held for long periods while their statements are verified or documents produced.

Police harassment of black women often occurs because of their insecurity about their immigration status. As we have seen, the criminal law leads to the questioning of women who are in Britain legally. The case of the Nigerian woman, who was forced into sex with a police officer because he threatened to get her deported (see chapter 29), is extreme, but questioning and threats to women who are legally here is common.

Whenever a black woman needs police help, she is likely to be asked to produce her passport first. The police may try to take the opportunity to investigate her immigration status. Women have been arrested after going to the police for help in cases of domestic violence or robbery, or after the police have visited their homes (often in search of someone else as part of a criminal investigation) and asked all the occupants to produce their passports.

The knowledge of these practices clearly deters black people from seeking police help. The checks that the police constantly make reinforce prejudices – if they mainly question black people about their immigration status, they will find more black than white people who are illegal, and will continue to suspect all black people of being 'illegal immigrants'.

Conclusion

The present system of immigration control is in urgent need of overhaul and reform. One important change should be to remove the police from any role in immigration control. Police registration serves no useful purpose and should be abolished. The Home Office has its own powers to force people out of the country by administrative means; overstaying or breaking the conditions on stay should no longer be a criminal offence. If the police had no immigration role, one of the major sources of friction and hostility between the police and the black communities in Britain would also be removed.

22. Jane B.'s Story*

Protesting Deportation

Christina Dunhill

Jane B. is forty years old. She moved to Britain from an African country fifteen years ago. She works in local government and also does voluntary work in her local community, particularly with young people. She is one of hundreds of black residents who fall foul of British immigration law every year. The following is the text (with chronological updates) of what she told me when I met her about her experiences at the hands of the police, following a Home Office decision to deport her:

'Britain is my home. I was educated here and have worked here for the past ten years. I couldn't go back to the country of my birth because of my political involvements. I was lucky to have left when I did. Politics there is life or death. My father died in a prison cell. He had been a leading member of the opposition party.

'I came to the UK in August 1973 to study, but also to escape political tension. I applied for leave to remain but didn't hear from the Home Office. They didn't serve a deportation order on me until July 1984.

'In August 1984, three male police officers called at my flat at about 7.30 a.m.; they said they had come to arrest me because I had overstayed. There were no civilities; they were rude and threatening. When I said, "What about my passport?" which

---

* Jane's name and personal details have been changed throughout this article.

was still with the Home Office, they said: "Forget about that, we'll get you travelling documents." They were trying to make me feel guilty, as if I was a terrible criminal. They said, "You have been in hiding, breaking the law." I said "It's not up to you to pass judgment." They wanted to know if the flat was mine. When I said it wasn't, they asked about the furniture. "You can easily sell that," they said. I had some French visitors staying with me at the time who were also black. They interrogated them too and went through their papers to check whether they were in order.

'They took me to the local police station and left me in a room for half an hour. Then a WPC searched my bag and gave me a body search before more or less throwing me in a cell. My period came on and I asked for a pad. It was fifteen minutes before I got it. They brought me out again to take a statement. There was one particular detective who was really arrogant. He was the one who'd done most of the "telling off" before. But he mentioned to the others that my name was not on the computer, so they couldn't have been looking for me for years as he had told me. I asked what would happen to me and he said I would be sent to Holloway Prison, but that was nothing to fear. They had special private cells for women who weren't criminals and I would be well treated. In the afternoon the alien police came and took me to Holloway. When I got there I realized that what the young detective had told me was, of course, a fabrication. Conditions at Holloway are appalling for everyone, but deportees are at the very bottom of the ladder.

'I had spent five days in Holloway before I was allowed to see a solicitor. When I did, he was able to argue that I could gain British citizenship because of my impending marriage to a British citizen and I was released.

'In fact, after my release my relationship with my boyfriend began to deteriorate. He had been in exactly the same position as me – he came from the same country and had been a political opponent of the ruling party. But he had been granted British citizenship on this basis, as a refugee, which they were refusing to me. I had been pleased when he had come forward saying that we were going to get married, but now he seemed to think that I should feel indebted to him, to the extent that I should do whatever he wanted. He wanted me to be a subordinate wife. It wasn't what I wanted and it destroyed our relationship. And I felt bitter that I was being forced into marrying my boyfriend, when he had been granted citizenship in his own right. I determined not to go ahead with the marriage but to fight my case on its own merits.

'Two months after my release from Holloway, I was arrested again when I went to sign on at the police station – something I had been obliged to do every week since release. (I don't know if my boyfriend had told them we weren't getting married now or if they had acted on my marriage certificate not coming through. But I think they'd been watching me.)

'This time their treatment of me was worse. They made it clear they thought I was a criminal who had deliberately employed a ruse to mislead the authorities and escape my just deserts, which they seemed very pleased to be seeing I would now get. The same detective lectured me self-righteously; he told me I had messed them around and that I had no legal rights. He seemed personally vindictive and contemptuous. I was so frightened and upset that I had a stomach upset. The WPC who took me to the toilet said, "You're disgusting." She also tried to insult me further. She suggested that my credit card was stolen because it bears my African first name instead of Jane. I wasn't allowed to see friends who had spent the whole day waiting to see me. The police then took me home, bundled my things together and marched me off to Holloway Prison that afternoon.

'This time, I was strip-searched when I arrived, under my overcoat, by a prison officer, who was very abusive to me because she thought I had been deported on a previous occasion but returned to the country. She gave me another lecture about wasting police time and costing the state money. I was in Holloway Prison for a month and I was treated worse than any criminal. There are young women there who have been convicted of murder but are given privileges like working in the prison kitchen, which are denied to immigration prisoners.[1] All prisoners are supposed to get notice of visits from their solicitor, but I was never informed, not even when the Home Office interviewer was coming, so that I could prepare my case.

'Like the police, the prison officers told me I had no legal rights. It is as if all the authorities conspire to make people held on immigration charges feel as if they are at the bottom of the heap, unwanted intruders to whom civil rights do not apply. When he came, the Home Office interviewer told me there was no way I was going to leave the prison except to board a plane; the best I could hope for was that I would get a prison escort to pick up my things.

'But after a month I was transferred to an open prison where I was treated with respect and the welfare officer did everything she could for me. My MP took up my case and made representations on my behalf to the Home Office against my deportation, and I was released.

'Unfortunately, these representations were unsuccessful, but the Home Office didn't tell me; they wrote to my MP direct; he was on holiday and therefore I wasn't informed. Consequently, I was subjected to more intimidation from the local police who took to calling at my flat at odd times, day and night, and leaving notes to say that I should report to the alien police or be arrested. I went to my solicitor, who found out that the Home Office had turned down my appeal.

'Then my union took up my case and has organized my anti-deportation campaign. My solicitor applied for a judicial review of the Home Office decision and this has been accepted. The requirement for me to report to the police every week has been lifted at the request of my solicitor, but if I had not noticed the Home Office memo attached to my signing-on sheet, I might not have known. The police officer hadn't bothered to read it and told me it was none of my business, when I asked. At the time of writing, we are waiting to hear when the judicial review will take place.[2] I am living from day to day, waiting for the date to be announced. My health is suffering. I cannot relax and I cannot enter a relationship with a man in case he thinks I'm only doing so to secure my position.'

Notes

1. Immigration prisoners are treated like remand prisoners and so denied the 'privileges' of sentenced prisoners.

2. Jane lost her judicial review. She will be appealing the decision on humanitarian grounds.

Part 3

Stepping Up Control:
Police, Politics and the Law

23. Public Order:

Political Policing

Cathie Lloyd

Democratic and collective action has been constantly targeted as dangerous by the Thatcher government. The Public Order Act 1986 is part of the same overall political 'project' as industrial relations legislation, the outlawing of trade unions at GCHQ, attacks on local government and censorship of the media, more restrictive immigration law, benefit snoopers, cuts in public expenditure and privatization.

In 1986, the government enacted major changes in the forty-year-old Public Order law with the effect of criminalizing spontaneous protests. The nature and scope of this new law has made many people fear for the freedom of assembly in this country. In this chapter I discuss how the new law came about and suggest some of its implications, and then look at the technology which the police now deploy against protesters.

Public Order Policing

Policing can be roughly divided into two overlapping areas: the prevention and detection of crime and the maintenance of public order. Public order is the most obviously political aspect of policing because it involves the police in limiting and controlling public meetings and demonstrations. Since Britain has no written constitution or Bill of Rights we have no absolute right to assemble. This means that we can legally do anything which is not actually forbidden in law. Many people would dispute that the police should even be involved in the control of most demonstrations and protests except for traffic control and general safety purposes. However, the 1986 Public Order Act combined with other general and discretionary police powers, has hedged around the freedom to hold assemblies, street meetings and so on with many qualifications. In effect it is now up to the police to exercise their political judgement about our freedom to demonstrate.

Public order is defined by the state. It is about control. It is not about trying to establish an order which might be beneficial to us – keeping the streets safe for women and the elderly, for example (for the police, this falls under the general heading of crime prevention). Yet we could argue that fear for personal safety on the streets or freedom from assault in our own homes is a public order problem of far greater magnitude than a handful of demonstrators outside the South African Embassy. Today, public order is viewed by the state and the police as an issue of maintaining control of the streets and limiting what they see as threatening manifestations of dissent. And this militaristic definition of public order has been adopted by all governments this century, although the Thatcher administration has made it very much its own.

Public order is where the function of the police meets that of the army. It is the original raison d'être of the police forces established in England and Wales in response to the great parliamentary reform demonstrations of the nineteenth century, ostensibly to safeguard the highway and private property. The Metropolitan Police was established in 1829. The early police force was modelled on a military structure, with chief officers drawn from military backgrounds. There are echoes of this origin in the uniform and training of police officers today. Up to the beginning of the twentieth century, the police and the army shared responsibility for the maintenance of public order. Since the First World War, the police have taken on this role alone. In this there is a contradiction for the police: while they wish to retain this function they are trapped into organizing more and more specialized and militaristic riot control units, which have a tendency to become autonomous.

Recent Changes in the Law: Context

Almost as soon as Margaret Thatcher's government was elected in 1979, a review of Public Order Law was announced. The immediate cause was the events of 23 April that year in Southall, when a massive demonstration against a provocative National Front election meeting in the heart of the Asian community was brutally policed. The police protected the NF and cordoned off the town centre so that the meeting place was inaccessible to the protesters. The Special Patrol Group (SPG, elite riot-trained squad) was associated with violent attacks on protesters on that day, when one demonstrator, Blair Peach, was killed from blows on the head and the police mounted a punishing raid on the Peoples Unite Community Centre, truncheoning everybody inside.[1]

Rejecting demands for a public inquiry into what had gone wrong in the police operation, the government set up an internal police investigation which uncovered a few unauthorized weapons in SPG officers' lockers but failed even to discipline, let alone charge, any police officers for the killing or any of the acts of brutality committed on that day. This is despite a settlement with Blair Peach's family which has cost the Met £72,000.[2]

After the election, the new Conservative government set up a Public Order Review which deliberated for six years, while the police drifted towards specialist, more militaristic forms of Public Order policing (see pages 264–70).

The White Paper *Review of Public Order Law* was published in May 1985. It took account of the riots of 1981, events at Southall, earlier events such as those at Grunwicks in 1976–7,[3] the 1984–5 coal dispute and also demonstrations by animal rights protesters, the Stop the City Campaign, the anti-nuclear movement, the National Front and football hooliganism. These were all used to justify the new police powers it proposed. Significantly, it was the moral panic surrounding football hooliganism which the government used in its publicity for the new law. The opposition vainly argued that football violence could not be lumped together with political unrest and industrial disputes.

Public Order Act 1986: Summary of Provisions

Marches and Processions

- Organizers must give the police six clear days' notice, in writing, of their intention to march.
- Conditions such as time, route, restrictions on leafleting, use of loudhailers can be imposed in advance by the Chief Constable, his deputy or equivalent ranks in the Metropolitan police.
- On the day of the march the most senior officer present who could be as junior as PC, can impose any further conditions on a march.
- If the organizers fail to give proper notice of the march or do not keep to police conditions they risk arrest, conviction for an offence, and up to three months' imprisonment and a fine of £1,000.
- Participants in a march who break police conditions risk arrest, conviction and a fine of £400.

Bans

The power of a Chief Constable or their deputy to ban marches under the Public Order Act 1936 on the grounds of serious public disorder remains. People taking part in a banned march risk arrest, conviction and a fine of £400. It is an offence to organize a march in breach of a ban: on conviction up to three months' imprisonment and a fine of up to £1,000 may be made.

Static Assemblies and Pickets

- An assembly is defined as twenty or more people standing in a public place.
- There is no need to give the police notice of an assembly or picket.
- The most senior officer present can impose any condition on the location of an assembly, its maximum duration and the numbers of participants.
- Such conditions can also be imposed in advance of an assembly.

- Failure to abide by police conditions is an offence: penalty is three months' imprisonment or a fine of £1,000 for organizers and £400 for participants.

Trespass

The police can evict or arrest trespassers who intend to reside on land and who cause damage to property, have been abusive, threatening or insulting or have brought twelve or more vehicles onto the land.

The 1986 Act updates and extends the 1936 legislation. It redefines some old common law offences (riot and affray) and creates some new ones (violent disorder and disorderly conduct). The police powers to interfere with the detailed organization of processions by imposing conditions are entirely new as is the requirement to give advance notice, although this did apply before in some local bylaws.

The Ideas Behind the Provisions

While recognizing that most demonstrations were peaceful the government asserted that all involved in demonstrations, (organizers, demonstrators, their opponents, the public and the police), have obligations as well as rights. This said, the review then came down heavily on the side of protesters' obligations and proceeded to weave a tangle of duties around them so as to choke the freedom to protest.

Both the White Paper and the Act juxtapose demonstrators against 'the wider community'. Acknowledging that some degree of disruption is inevitable, the White Paper argued:

it does not seem right that the police should have no power to reroute a procession in order to limit traffic congestion . . .
pedestrians, businesses and commerce . . . to impose conditions on a procession in order to prevent serious disruption to the normal life of the community.[4]

This formulation is almost identical to that expressed by the Association of Chief Police Officers (ACPO) in evidence to the Home Affairs Committee on Public Order Law:

> Irrespective of the peaceful nature of the processions the numbers involved bring town centres to a halt, business is seriously disrupted and the public bus services thrown out of schedule. In short a general annoyance is created to the normal process of daily life.[5]

This phrase, 'serious disruption to the life of the community', is actually incorporated in the Act (section 12(a)). It provides the basis upon which the police are to decide what conditions to impose upon protest. It suggests that the legislators view political demonstrations as something quite outside normal community life.

Impact of the Law on Organizers

The 1986 law has altered the way in which people organize demonstrations. It makes it more important for organizers to anticipate some of the conditions which the police may try to impose. One group wrote an account of their experience of picketing the Old Bailey and advised organizers to follow a checklist of tasks to avoid unnecessary trouble:[6]

- *Check with the local police on the day of a demonstration in case of any new conditions*
- *Arrange observers and a phone number for legal cover in case of arrests*
- *Brief stewards on what do do when things go wrong*
- *Make sure any demonstration organized is well supported with the presence of well-known people and the press*
- *Arrange for photographs to be taken to show how the demonstration was organized; especially useful if you need to organize a defence campaign.*

Technical Fix

During the late 1960s the student movement and demonstrations against the war in Vietnam gave political protest more impetus. Demonstrations were seen by many on the left as an effective political tool. Since then police tactics have been transformed. By 1972 the standard methods of crowd control used during the Vietnam war protests and industrial disputes had become discredited in the eyes of police chiefs. Their inability to deal with mass pickets at Saltley Gates coking plant during the coal dispute of February 1972 dramatically highlighted the situation.

In addition to new legal powers, reviews of public order equipment and training since 1972 have led to a massive re-equipment programme. Paramilitary training of special riot squads has transformed strategy from 'containment' (using large numbers of police to push and shove demonstrators), to 'area denial' (which forcibly disperses protesters).

The new methods have been introduced by means of an internal drift in police strategies rather than as the result of open and democratic decisions. Technology has been prepared and made available on the sidelines and then wheeled on to the streets at moments of high drama. This has been endorsed by the government, courts and the press even when democratically elected police authorities have withheld approval or protested.

In August 1977 reinforced perspex shields were first used on the streets of London against anti-fascist demonstrators in Lewisham, and a few weeks later they were used again in a massive operation at the Notting Hill Carnival.[7] The previous year at Carnival, the heavy police presence (an incredible increase of 2,500 per cent over the previous year) sparked off a confrontation which lasted for five hours. Uniformed police officers, unequipped for street fighting, defended themselves with whatever came to hand, throwing building rubble at protesters. Sir Robert Mark, the Commissioner of Police claimed, 'There are not going to be any no-go areas,' and equipped the force with shields. The Carnival has since been used as a testing ground for elaborate surveillance equipment situated on the nearby Westway motorway flyover and other high buildings. Long-lens cameras with night vision monitor the crowd and helicopters patrol to give general or close-up pictures to the command centre.

After the uprisings in Brixton, Toxteth, Handsworth and many other areas in 1981 there was a full Home Office review of protective clothing and public order training. Improvements were made in the fireproofing of shields and garments and officers were issued with riot boilersuits. In 1982 the new Commissioner, Kenneth Newman, was appointed with a tough managerial approach to public order. As Deputy and Chief Constable of the RUC between 1973 and 1979 he had presided over the transfer of public order engagement in Northern Ireland from the military to the police. He had been in charge of a force which had been severely criticized for the way in which they had extracted 'confessions' from republicans in prison and which was forced to set up an inquiry after Amnesty International reported its concern.[8]

Technology

The theory behind police/crowd control weaponry is to inflict maximum pain on protesters while maintaining an image of public acceptability:

> It is preferred that onlookers do not get the impression that the police are using excessive force or that the weapon has an especially injurious effect on the target individuals. Here again, a flow of blood and similar dramatic effects are to be avoided.[9]

The police have a vast range of crowd control equipment. Even apparently defensive perspex shields (weighing 15 lbs) can be used to strike people. By November 1982, twenty-two of the forty-three police forces in England and Wales had acquired plastic bullets, and thirty forces had stocks of CS gas. All forces now have access to all weapons through mutual aid. The Home Secretary has recently ruled out the use of water cannon because of their unwieldiness and their frequent need to be refilled, but many other weapons are available.

CS gas fired in canisters causes a burning sensation in the eyes and severe irritation of the respiratory tract, causing sneezing and coughing, increasing to nausea and vomiting. Forces have special barricade-penetrating devices primed with

CS gas which were used, contrary to regulations, against crowds in Toxteth in 1981. These caused serious body injuries. More powerful gases such as CR are also available.

There is little knowledge about the long-term effects of CS gas, but in South Korea where it has been used on a university campus, plant life is dying and clouds of gas have drifted into nearby hospitals and other public buildings, causing serious health worries.[10] Gas canisters combined with explosive charges were used in France during the student demonstrations of 1986. Serious injuries were sustained when students kicked away canisters which then exploded.[11]

Plastic bullets replaced rubber ones in Northern Ireland in 1975 partly because of publicity surrounding the many deaths and injuries they had caused. In fact the plastic bullet is more accurate and has a longer range than the rubber bullet. It can be aimed directly at targets. Studies have found the new bullet to be on average four times more lethal than the one it replaced.[12] After the Tottenham uprising in October 1985 Kenneth Newman put the people of London 'on notice' that in the event of further disorder plastic bullets and CS gas would be used.

Stun guns firing tranquillizer darts are at present being 'evaluated' to tackle situations where the police would normally consider using lead bullets. The likelihood is that they could be used more widely to tackle other 'violent' persons. Stun guns are normally used to tranquillize animals. Veterinary experts are already concerned about the effects of the drugs used on the nervous system.

Vehicles may be driven into crowds at high speeds as at Toxteth in 1981 with considerable risk of injury. The police use vehicles which look innocuous, such as Ford Transit vans, but which are armoured, covered with wire grilles and sometimes with protective skirts against petrol bombs.

Riot Squads

After the 1972 coal dispute, the Tory government reviewed the role of police in civil disorder and rejected the 'third force' idea. Whilst accepting that a separate riot squad would relieve the police of a militaristic role and might improve relations with the public, it was thought that a separate riot squad would generate more hatred and counter-violence than the ordinary police. Thus a covert riot-squad element was built into every police force in the country.

The police manual of Home Defence (1974) outlined the role of emergency services in wartime and instructed police forces outside London to set up Police Support Units (PSUs). They were composed of ordinary officers who were specially trained in the use of shields and other crowd-control formations and techniques. PSUs were a reserve which could be called upon when necessary for Public Order duty. The officers involved spent the rest of their time in community policing duties. PSUs were to guard key installations (government buildings, police stations, courts, hospitals, etc) in national emergencies such as insurrection or war. Police forces are committed to going to the assistance of one another in 'mutual aid'; PSUs formed their basis, co-ordinated by Scotland Yard's National Recording Centre (NRC) under the command of the President of the Association of Chief Police Officers (ACPO).

While Thatcher was still in opposition there was rethinking of how to deal with resistance to new Tory economic policies. The Ridley Report, leaked to *The Economist* on 27 May 1978 discussed ways of countering the trade unions. Among their strategies was the development of large mobile squads of hand-picked police to deal with picketing. They were co-ordinated by the NRC and criticized as an embryonic national police force. At the end of the 1984–5 coal dispute, in which it played a key role, the NRC was renamed the Mutual Aid Co-ordinating Centre (MACC) to stress its administrative rather than operational role. Many people had surmised that the NRC was the basis for a national police force.

London's police already had a specialist unit to deal with Public Order. The Special Patrol Group was set up in 1965 as a one-hundred strong, all male anti-crime unit to aid police in London. It developed into a Public Order force in the context of Commissioner Robert Mark's 'fire-brigade' policing in the 1970s.[13] Explaining the development of the SPG, Mark wrote:

Some of the tactics adopted by the London police and later by other forces were those developed and used by the army and the RUC SPG in Northern Ireland. The introduction of 'snatch squads' and 'wedges' in demonstrations and random stop and searches and roadblocks on the streets were based on the Army's experience in Ulster.[14]

In a survey of all fifty-two Chief Constables' annual reports in 1979, State Research showed that twenty-four had already SPG-style units in addition to PSUs.[15] The size of these special units has increased since then and large sums of money are spent on their equipment and training. In 1986 the Greater Manchester force announced that it was to spend an additional £150,000 on protective clothing, equipment and the conversion of nine vans into fully protected personnel carriers.[16] It has built an £89,000 police riot training school in Manchester, taking the forces' public order expenditure to £500,000.[17] The West Midlands force trained 2,200 officers between September 1985 and 1986 in public order.[18] Senior officers from all forces were also given intensive training in public order tactics after the Broadwater Farm uprising.

When the Metropolitan police set up the SPG it comprised one hundred officers. By 1986 it had grown to two hundred and eighty and achieved notoriety. There was a public outcry at the SPG's brutal tactics which allegedly led to the killing of Kevin Gateley in Red Lion Square in 1974, their brutality at the industrial dispute at Grunwicks in 1977, and the killing of Blair Peach at Southall in 1979. An internal police inquiry after this incident unearthed illegal weapons in SPG officers' lockers. The unit was associated with the worst aspects of paramilitary policing. It was the swamping of Brixton with SPG officers on an intensive stop-and-search operation which led to the uprising of 1981. Nevertheless, despite cosmetic changes, the SPG was the model for an expanded public order policing in London and elsewhere.

In response to the 1981 uprisings in Brixton, Handsworth and elsewhere the Met set up Instant Response Units (IRUs) in each of London's twenty-four police districts, comprising some 1,100 officers. They were quickly renamed District Support

Units (DSUs) but never lost their contentiousness. In August 1983, a DSU was involved in the Holloway Road incident where police assaulted a group of young mainly black men. In 1986, the SPG and DSUs were dissolved to form a larger unit of 800 officers backed up by a command structure of 100 based on the eight areas of the Met. These units were renamed the Territorial Support Groups (TSGs).

Like the SPG, the TSGs are staffed by officers on permanent attachment for three to four years. Their basic unit comprises a police inspector, three sergeants and twenty-four constables. Women also serve in these units, and the average age is thirty. The units are on permanent standby to give support to local divisions in combating street crime and burglaries by uniform patrol and plain-clothes surveillance. London wide, they deal with terrorism, major incidents and public disorder. TSGs are given sophisticated training in firearms, the use of CS gas and plastic bullets. A Scotland Yard press release in July 1986 made it clear that in the event of future public disorder the TSGs would go in quick and hard as a 'first-wave response'.

Public Order Training

All police forces in England and Wales now have some public order training for their special units and PSUs. The Met have the most elaborate facilities at two training centres. Ten minutes away from Heathrow airport at Hounslow, they have built a small town with streets in which realistic exercises can be carried out. This has now taken over from the Greenwich centre.[19]

The training involves simulations in which officers in flame-proof overalls, helmets and shields confront 'rioters' hurling wooden bricks and even petrol bombs. Training is constantly updated aiming for 'maximum realism' with noise, smoke and confusion.

The police also practise the kind of tactics seen in the coal dispute: shield manoeuvres, forming cordons and preparing to advance against a hostile crowd with offensive wedge formations to split up the crowd and pull out 'ringleaders'.

Police public order training has become fairly standardized. Experiences in 'mutual aid' where officers from various forces work closely together, as during the coal dispute, encouraged this development. In August 1985, at the trials arising from incidents at Orgreave during the dispute, the police were obliged to disclose part of the secret ACPO 'Tactical Options Manual', which provides detailed guidelines for crowd control manoeuvres. It had been drawn up by ACPO after the uprisings in 1980 and 1981.

When the manual was released lawyers said that it contained instructions to commit assaults occasioning actual bodily harm – a criminal offence. The manual appears to breach official Home Office guidelines which state that truncheons should only be used by police as a last resort or in self-defence.[20]

> One manoeuvre, for example, involves officers running forward to disperse the crowd and incapacitate missile throwers and ringleaders by striking in a controlled manner with batons about the arms and legs or torso so as not to cause serious injury.
>
> (Source: Tactical Options Manual)

This amounts to an instruction to commit assault and makes no distinction between incapacitating ringleaders and using reasonable force to arrest them. Clearly it is impossible in the heat of the moment, to 'strike in a controlled manner'. Manoeuvres are designed to intimidate demonstrators. Mounted officers are told to disperse crowds rapidly by using 'fear created by the impetus of horses'. In one manoeuvre horses are lined up in a double rank and cantered into the crowd. The manual stresses the importance of appearance to create fear: 'To use the show of force to the greatest advantage officers should make a formidable appearance'.

Noise is used to intimidate. The manual recommends the rhythmic beating of shields. This was used during the coal dispute but was later banned by chief officers because of public criticism. However, in the Broadwater Farm trials in 1987 many defence witnesses described police beating shields.

Effect on Police Culture

In 1983 a report they had themselves commissioned found the Met to be a white, male preserve pervaded with racism, sexism and prejudice against those who do not fit their narrow stereotype of respectability. Researchers from the Policy Studies Institute (PSI) had conducted a two-year observational study with various groups of police officers all over London. The report highlighted the determining role of an aggressive and macho police culture on their work.

In particular the PSI investigators saw DSUs as a breeding ground for strong 'in-group' norms. Cooped up together for long periods in their transit vans, the men in the DSUs saw their mission as being to respond rapidly to disturbances. Over-response and over-reaction when pent-up energy was finally released are the hallmarks of this kind of unit. They regard dealing with provocation in a decisive manner as a matter of pride and resent tactics which involve placating the community. Strong ties between these officers develop so that they are unlikely to break ranks and give evidence against one another.[21] This was well illustrated in the DSU incident in Holloway Road in London, when the sergeant in charge of the team and four constables were convicted of conspiring to pervert the course of justice and of misconduct by failing to take steps after witnessing an assault.

Training and deployment of the police in present-day public order tactics exaggerates the macho culture underlined by the PSI report. Police involved in special units have themselves stressed that it is difficult for them to switch on and off and return to normal policing after a major incident. One specialist firearms officer said:

At Tottenham I was kitted up with gas mask, baton gun, flameproof suit and a crash helmet and put in the front line. I was in a very aggressive role . . . For some days after I was still on a 'high', still very hyped up and yet the next day I was knocking on someone's door to see his driving licence. I genuinely found it hard to be civil, because I was still on a 'high' from the previous day.[22]

Strategy

At Scotland Yard between 1982 and 1987 Newman set the pace for other police forces in England and Wales. He set up a Central Information Unit in the Public Order department of Scotland Yard to study the causes and likely locations for public disorder, using modern information management techniques with computers. Police officers passed on scraps of information about their beats to station collators who put it on computers for district and force-wide analysis. Categories of information to identify increased tension in an area were compiled using a 'causes of fear' index formulated by the US National Institute of Justice.

1. *Physical signs of crime, such as garbage-strewn vacant lots, abandoned buildings, graffiti, abandoned cars and broken windows.*
2. *Social signs of crime, such as groups of young males loitering on street corners, prostitutes soliciting customers, illegal drug sales and use in public view, loud shouting and music and other violations of public order.*
3. *Inadequate orderly pedestrian presence, such as shoppers going out to buy things, couples going for a walk, or other 'conventional' activities, as a ratio to the 'threatening' activities described above.*
4. *An absence of good news about crime, such as crimes prevented by police or citizen actions, crimes solved and persistent offenders given long sentences.*
5. *An absence of local news about crime, right down to the neighbourhood or block level.*
6. *Citizen feelings of powerlessness to affect the crime problem, the garbage problem, the order problem, or governmental responses to those problems.*
7. *Inter-group conflict across ethnic, religious, racial and (especially) age groups.*
8. *A generalized sense that no one cares, that the neighbourhood is out of control, that no one can or will do anything about it.*

9.   *Insufficient contact with police as the primary symbol of order and control.*[23]

Targeted Estates

These 'tension indicators' have been used by the police to compile a list of potentially riot-prone estates in London. They also added local criteria of their own and these demonstrate race and class prejudice quite clearly such as 'a high density of population and ethnic mix', 'hostility towards police manifested by incidence of complaints (against them)' and 'a high level of street crime in the surrounding area'. They also include environmental factors such as 'the design of flats with walkways and interconnecting alleys and lack of facilities'.

Speaking about what he sees as the 'most difficult streets' in inner city areas, Newman explained his approach which is in itself redolent of racism:

> These are at the centre of areas where crime is at its worst, where drug-dealing is intolerably overt and where the racial ingredient is at its most potent. In such places indiscriminate police action, however proper an enforcement of the law it may be, runs a real risk of provoking serious public disorder. These are the flashpoints of policing the inner city.[24]

In order to police these 'flashpoints' a combination of tactics have been developed to build up support for the police amongst the 'law-abiding majority'. A high level of visible policing with adequate back-up to deal with any disorder, and targeting of people who are the focus of crime, is proposed. Thus a network of neighbourhood watch schemes, police consultative committees and agencies like schools and social services departments has been built up to provide the police with intelligence about targeted communities.

This technique divides the population into the 'law-abiding' and 'others' on whom the police cannot rely. It fits into the picture in the 1986 Public Order Act, where demonstrations are juxtaposed to the 'normal life of the community'. The significance of this development is that the policing of political protest has now been incorporated into a more general system of social control.

Notes

1. M. Dummett et al., *Southall 23 April 1979, The Report of the Unofficial Committee of Inquiry*, NCCL, London, 1980.

2. *Guardian*, 8 July 1988.

3. The dispute at Grunwicks in 1976–7 in North London was an attempt by a workforce composed mainly of Asian women to secure trade-union recognition. Mass picketing in the summer of 1977 was countered by the police use of new crowd-control tactics like the flying wedge and snatch squads. See Dromey and Taylor, *Grunwicks: the Workers' Story*, Lawrence & Wishart, London, 1978.

4. Review of Public Order Law, p. 27.

5. Minutes of evidence, 18 February, 1980.

6. Irish Prisoners Appeal c/o Irish in Britain Representation Group (IBRG), 245a Coldharbour Lane, London SW9. A detailed account of experiences of organizing under the new Act for the Fight the Alton Bill Campaign in Police Powers: Public Order BBC2 28 July 1988.

7. Public Order Research Group Bulletin, July/August 1985.

8. *Guardian*, 19 April 1982.

9. Wargovitch et al., 'Less Lethal Weapons', Manchester City Council Police Monitoring Unit, January 1986.

10. *Financial Times*, 9 June 1987.

11. Senate Inquiry into the Student Demonstrations in France 1986, 'Étudiants, Police, Presse, Pouvoir', Hachette, Paris, 1987, p. 235.

12. *Sunday Times*, 17 May 1981, 'Less Lethal Weapons', op. cit.

13. 'Fire-brigade' policing was the term used for responding to incidents often in patrol cars rather than beat policing.

14. Robert Mark, *In the Office of Constable*, London, 1978.

15. *State Research Bulletin*, vol. 2, no. 13, Aug/Sept 1979.

16. *Times*, 22 November 1986.

17. *Guardian*, 17 May 1986.

18. *Guardian*, 1 August 1986.

19. 'Riot Policing in Greenwich', London Borough of Greenwich, November 1984.

20. *Observer*, 21 July 1985.

21. Policy Studies Institute, *The Police in Action*, vol. IV, 1983, p. 51.

22. BBC2 Out-of-Court Special, 'The Queen's Peace', October 1986, in *Police*, November 1986.

23. Kenneth Newman, Speech to the Cranfield/Wolfson Colloquium on Policing and Social Policy in Multi-ethnic Areas in Europe, September 1983, *Police*, October 1983.

24. Speech to the Society of Conservative Lawyers, 16 February 1987.

24. The Police and Criminal Evidence Act

Barbara Cohen

The Police and Criminal Evidence Act 1984 is the first comprehensive attempt by Parliament to regulate the relationship between the police and the public. Prior to the Act, police powers were set out in a confusing and often contradictory combination of statute, local acts, case law, Judges' Rules, Administrative Directions and internal police rules and regulations. This enabled regular and serious abuses of police powers to go unchecked and left the public vulnerable and unprotected. There was a wide consensus that legislation was urgently required; the fact that it was introduced as a central part of the Thatcher government's 'law and order' package gave it a particular shape and content.

A major factor was the Report of the Royal Commission on Criminal Procedure (RCCP).[1] The RCCP was set up in 1978 by the then Labour government to consider the varying demands being made by police, politicians and civil liberties groups for changes in the law and to respond to the growing concern over the miscarriages of justice, most notably in the Confait case,[2] as the police ignored the rules intended to safeguard suspects' rights. The Report proposed a comprehensive scheme of legal reform relating to police powers and criminal trials.

A second factor was the government's experience of successful repressive policing and severe restriction of individual rights in Northern Ireland which combined well with its growing paranoia about the 'enemy within' in Great Britain (embodied by peace protesters, trade unions, radical political groups and so on).

Thirdly there was a widening gulf developing between the police and the public. People who saw themselves as victims or potential victims of arbitrary police action were not willing to give the police the co-operation they needed. This was a central concern of Lord Scarman in his report on the Brixton disorders.[3] Without community support, the police were failing to solve many of the crimes which caused distress to members of the public, leading to a further loss of public confidence and support. At the same time there was a build-up of sophisticated systems for storage and retrieval of information within most police forces, creating a desire for even more information. New equipment for surveillance and for the 'control' of public order served further to broaden the gap between the police and the policed.

The government clearly chose not to use the legislation to tackle the widespread abuses of police powers or to provide the effective safeguards for suspects. Instead it strove to 'protect' the community by bestowing increased powers on the police. The Act confirms the shift which was already taking place from policing by co-operation to policing by coercion. It gave the parliamentary seal of approval to what is likely to be a permanent change to a more hostile relationship between the police and the public.

From its earliest pronouncements the government claimed that its package of increased police powers was what was necessary to equip the police to deal with rising crime rates, especially organized crime and street crime. Professional criminals were seen to be out-manoeuvring the police with their 'bent' lawyers and highly efficient information networks. Street crime, exaggerated by the tabloid press, was said to be gravely affecting the quality of life in inner cities. The powers which the government claimed as essential to tackle these target areas have now been approved by Parliament, and are available to be used at the discretion of the police in the investigation of any sort of crime involving suspects of any age, sex or background.

Equipping the police to combat increasing crime was the government's primary object, but it could not, politically, be seen to write them a blank cheque for greater powers. Thus there are some minimum, but non-enforceable, provisions to protect suspects. The government boasted of the 'balance' it had achieved. In fact, a reading of the Act will reveal how illusory most of the safeguards are and how far the balance has swung towards legitimating oppressive policing.

Similarly, although the police have stressed their desire to rebuild their crumbling public image and, since the Act, have complained of the burden of complying so meticulously with its formal requirements, there is no evidence of a real commitment to stamp out abuse. Defence lawyers regularly note that safeguards in the Act and the Codes are bypassed or ignored. Instead the police are utilizing fully their greater powers, ostensibly to investigate crime, but also to gather information more widely and, on occasions, to harass or demoralize particular individuals.

In framing the Act, the government seems, at least initially, to have considered women only as victims of crime, and not as victims of policing. But while the Bill was still being debated, the Policy Studies Institute published its substantial report on police and the public in London (see chapter 9) which documented the gross sexism and 'macho' culture which prevailed in the Metropolitan Police. In response, the government made only minor amendments to the legislation to deal with situations which might be embarrassing for women, for example a search carried out by a man.

In this chapter those provisions of the Act which have particular significance for women will be discussed together with some of the broader concepts which the Act embodies including wide police discretion, legitimation of the use of force and erosion of the right of silence.

Stop and Search: Formalized Harassment

The 'stop and search' provisions in the Act were the subject of long and heated debate. The RCCP had found a clear need for safeguards to protect people from random, arbitrary and discriminatory searches on the street. The Act, however, expanded the potential for such searches. It added major categories to the list of items for which searches can be carried out (on the basis of an officer's reasonable suspicion) including stolen goods, offensive weapons and articles to be used in connection with theft or burglary. These expanded powers were enhanced by the provision which allows police officers to use reasonable force (see below).

It was anticipated that these increased powers would result in far more people (or the same people more frequently) being stopped and searched. The purported safeguard is the requirement for detailed record keeping. As this applies only to compulsory searches it is generally accepted that the numbers of stops and searches recorded since the Act significantly underestimates the numbers of people subjected to this form of interference or harassment. A second safeguard is an attempt, in Annex B of the Code of Practice, to define 'reasonable suspicion' and to direct that it cannot be supported on the basis of skin colour, clothing or hairstyle; the writer is not aware of any research to measure the impact of this provision.

Women are far less likely to be stopped than men but, if they are, they should know that a refusal to open their bags or empty their pockets could result in the police using physical force to search them. In relation both to crime and to protest actions there is a risk that the police will stop and search women and girls as a means of gathering information; with their new, wider powers the police are less likely to be resisted in doing so.

Personal Search – Just for the Record

Before the 1984 Act there was no statutory power for the police to search someone they were holding in custody. It was a procedure which was generally accepted, although the manner in which it was done frequently gave rise to complaints. The courts had confined the police to removing only such items of clothing as they had good reason to remove and required them to give a reason for doing so to the person before the search was carried out.[4] The Act now authorizes routine searching removing jackets, coats, emptying pockets, and so on of all detained persons to enable a record to be made of all of their property. Force can be used, and there is nothing in the Act which requires the search to be commensurate with the offence or for the searcher to take into account the person's age or state of health. Women can only be searched by women police officers, but this could be in a room full of wisecracking men. The police can seize anything which is evidence of any offence and anything which they believe will be used to cause injury, interfere with evidence, damage property or aid escape.

Strip-searching, involving the removal of more than outer clothing, is not mentioned in the Act but is referred to in one of the Codes of Practice issued under the Act, which do not have the legal status of the Act itself. Strip-searching can include the removal of all undergarments and such further humiliation as requiring a woman to bend over so a WPC can look up her anus. Code C provides that a woman should only be made to remove more than her outer clothing if the custody officer thinks this is necessary in order to remove something she 'would not be allowed to keep'. There is no obligation for this view to be based on reasonable suspicion or to be confirmed by a more senior officer. Although only women can be present when a woman is strip-searched, in practice this affords little protection against either gross indignity or sadistic treatment. Before the Act was in force, three young women in police custody for the first time after being arrested for obstructing the police reported that they were woken up in the middle of the night so that a strip-search could be carried out. The fact that this was done by a WPC did little to lessen the indignity or to satisfy them that there was any reason other than sadistic harassment. The remedies available after the fact are inadequate as a deterrent and there is every reason to believe that incidents like this will proliferate under the Act.

One of the most controversial police processes which the government sought to regulate in the Act was the *intimate search*, described in section 118 as 'physical examination of a person's body orifices'. In its first bill, the government proposed intimate search of suspects to look both for evidence and for concealed weapons. The British Medical Association strongly opposed the idea of any of its members carrying out an intimate search without consent in order to look for evidence of an offence. Doctors and many others also objected to an intimate search being carried out by anyone except a qualified doctor. In its second bill, the government responded to public repugnance by proposing intimate search only in relation to a weapon which was thought likely to be used whilst in custody. The House of Lords amended the bill to restore intimate searching to look for a Class A drug (heroin, cocaine, but not cannabis) intended to be supplied to another. An intimate drugs search must be carried out by a registered doctor or nurse and only at a hospital or surgery. An intimate search for a weapon can be carried out by a police officer of the same sex, at the police station, if a doctor cannot or will not do it. An intimate search requires authorization by a senior police officer, who is supposed to authorize only if he has reasonable grounds for believing that such items are concealed and can only be found by an intimate search.

It is probable that intimate searches of women for weapons are most likely to be carried out when women are suspected of involvement in terrorism or political protest which includes some form of violence or when they are associated with violent offences. The courts have not yet considered what evidence a superintendent would need to submit a woman to so humiliating a process. At the time of giving approval, he will be within the totally closed system of the police station with no one of equivalent status to argue against doing so. Any protestations by the woman could be regarded by the police as reinforcing their suspicion. There thus remains the prospect that a woman could find herself in a police station subjected to search of her vagina or anus by an untrained WPC with all the attendant risk of injury or infection to herself or an unborn child.

Use of Force Legitimated

Police powers are substantially strengthened by section 117 of the Act, which authorizes them to use 'reasonable force, if necessary' to carry out such processes as personal search, taking fingerprints or samples of hair. Anything which the Act says they may do without a person's consent they can do by force. Before the Act the police were allowed to use reasonable force only to prevent a crime or to make an arrest.

The only constraints on the police are that force must be 'reasonable' (appropriate in the particular circumstances) and 'necessary' (other non-violent methods having been tried first). There is nothing in recent experience of police conduct to suggest that these constraints have been effective in moderating the force used by the police. The Act has not reduced the number of women who report physical injuries caused by the police.

If a woman is under the influence of drugs or alcohol when approached by the police, or if she is doing something she believes she is entitled to do, she may not appreciate swiftly enough the risk she faces and, failing to respond as directed, may find herself subjected to excessive and inappropriate force meted out by one or more male police officers. By authorizing the use of force by the police in the exercise of their new powers, the government has in effect acknowledged that consensual policing is a thing of the past. Co-operation is no longer an essential element as the police may now rely on force to stop vehicles or pedestrians and search them, to enter premises to search for evidence, and so on. The converse must also be true (and ultimately more significant in policing terms); aware of the likelihood of force being used, women (or men) will rarely resist police intervention, even when they believe it to be unjustified.

Towards Compulsory Self-Incrimination

Most of the processes of intervention and the sweeping powers of detention will produce self-incriminating evidence. They can also be used as exercises to gather wider information. Because of their vulnerability generally in confrontation with the police, women may be more likely to incriminate themselves and to succumb to pressures to tell the police about people known to them.

For example, in a stop-and-search operation, for which there is little recourse for complaint or compensation, police officers can ask wide-ranging questions and benefit from the intimidation felt by the woman stopped who may feel impelled to reply in order to gain her freedom as soon as possible.

A woman who is arrested faces the prospect of loss of liberty for hours or days. Since the House of Lords' decision in *Holgate-Mohammed v Duke*[5] while the Act was still before Parliament, the police can lawfully arrest a woman in order to question her and thereby obtain a confession. Although it defines powers of arrest under different headings, the Act effectively enables the police to arrest a woman on suspicion of having committed any offence. It is for the police to decide whether to exercise this power or to use the summons procedure instead to bring the woman to court. By enhancing arrest powers the government has made clear its preferred procedure.

The likelihood of the police getting the answers they want is reinforced by the nature of detention following arrest. Police detention is, in effect, imprisonment without a conviction, often without clear reasons and always of uncertain duration. Police cells are normally dank and smelly, without clocks or sunlight to measure the passage of time. For a woman, the distress of detention is compounded by the overt machismo which prevails and the coarse sexism of many police officers. If she is black or Irish, she is also likely to be affected by racism, which exists in most police forces.

As it is usually women who care for young children and/or sick or elderly relatives, detention for any period will include mounting anxiety about the well-being of those for whom a woman cares. In a letter to the NCCL, a woman described her arrest when she was accompanied by three children, two of whom were under five. Whilst she was locked in a cell she could hear her frightened children crying in another part of the police station. It is not surprising that she did not wait for a solicitor to be present before she was questioned nor that she made as many admissions as she believed the police required so that she could be released.

The government was not unaware of the effects of police detention when they enacted provisions which authorize detention *for questioning*, and in the face of statistical confirmation that most suspects made admissions within the first six hours of detention, they gave the police power to detain anyone for twenty-four hours on suspicion of having committed any offence. With magistrates' court approval, detention can be extended for up to four days for a 'serious arrestable offence'. The need to obtain evidence by questioning is one ground for prolonging detention.

There is little doubt that the best protection for a suspected person is early consultation with a lawyer, and having a lawyer present while she is questioned. Under the Act the right to consult a lawyer can be delayed for up to thirty-six hours if a woman is arrested for a serious arrestable offence. Women are often interviewed on their own either because in the chaos of their first minutes at the police station they are not properly advised of their rights or because the police will, as in the past, suggest that release will be sooner if time is not 'wasted' trying to find a solicitor (despite the existence of the twenty-four-hour duty solicitor scheme).

The process of personal search can be humiliating and can force a woman into offering self-incriminating evidence to avoid being further searched. In this Act, parliament has taken unequivocal steps towards obligatory self-incrimination by granting the police power to take fingerprints and non-intimate body samples (e.g. hair, fingernails, footprints) as part of their investigation before charge, without the suspect's consent and by use of force if necessary.

Intimate samples (e.g. blood, saliva, pubic hairs) can only be taken with the woman's consent but she will be warned that if she refuses consent the jury at her trial will be told so they can draw whatever inference they wish from her refusal. Faced with such a scenario, performed by a mostly male cast, very few women will find themselves able to respond to the prescribed caution 'you are not obliged to say anything . . .' by saying nothing.

It is difficult to imagine the intensity of police pressure on the government to go beyond the Act and to remove by statute the right of silence, which in practice truly protects very few from self-incrimination in some way. But that pressure was successful, despite opposition from the legal profession, and in May 1988 the Home Secretary announced that this basic right was to be taken away. In November 1988 an Order in Council abolished the right of silence in Northern Ireland, and in any trial the jury may now be invited to regard as evidence against the defendant the fact that s/he did not answer questions in the police station or did not give evidence in court. For England and Wales a bill along similar lines is expected.

Tape Recording – Illusory Protection

Tape-recorded interviews are referred to in the Act and will be required in all or certain cases when the Home Secretary makes the appropriate order. At the time of going to press (January 1989) tape recording is only in operation in a few police stations. The use of tape recorders was recommended as a step towards the eradication of abuses in police interviews. But experience of taped interviews suggests that without a lawyer present the suspect has only minimum protection. In a taped interview it is easier for the interviewing officer to draw upon his interrogation skills and training to create a seemingly 'friendly' relationship and then, having relaxed his subject, to probe for the information he wants.

A woman on her own with two police officers and a tape recorder in a sealed room is unlikely to feel sufficiently protected. And as in any interview there remains hanging over her the possibility of an extended period in custody, with the attendant japes and comments, which will not be part of the taped interview, which outweighs any reassurance the tape recorder might give her.

New Rules of Evidence

There are changes in the law of evidence which affect women as witnesses or defendants. Before the Act came into force, a married woman could only exceptionally be asked and never compelled to give evidence against or for her husband, although an unmarried woman could be compelled to give evidence against or for a boyfriend. Now, under section 80, a married woman can be *called* to give evidence *against* her husband, unless she is charged with him. She can be *compelled* to give evidence *for* her husband in all cases unless she is jointly charged and *against* her husband if the offence relates to assault or injury to herself or a child or a sexual offence against a child.

These changes were sought by the police to ensure that domestic violence prosecutions would not fail because a wife (pressurized or frightened by her husband) later declined to give evidence in court and have been generally welcomed by women's groups on the basis that the law should treat married and unmarried women equally. But a married woman who is both economically dependent and in fear of a violent husband may be deterred from calling in the police by the prospect of having to give evidence against him.

A second change, in section 81,[6] requires advance disclosure in all cases to be tried by a jury of any expert evidence intended to be used by the defence, as well as by the prosecution – as a first step towards removing the tradition of 'surprise' evidence from the defendant's armoury. Often, for a woman defendant under stress, expert evidence will be evidence of a doctor or psychiatrist. If this is seen by the prosecution in advance, they will be equipped not only to challenge the expert but also to attack the woman more aggressively and destructively when cross-examining her at her trial.

Section 78 potentially provides the most important change in the rules of evidence. It enables a Court to *exclude* any prosecution evidence if the Court considers that to admit it would have a seriously adverse effect on the *fairness* of the trial. Whilst there is not automatic exclusion if the police exceed powers, the circumstances in which the evidence was obtained is a central factor which the Court considers. Recent cases suggest that if the police act with impropriety or bad faith, or breach important provisions in the Act or the Codes, the evidence thus obtained will be excluded. When a suspect was denied access to legal advice [7] or when no contemporaneous note was made of police interview [8] then confessions have been excluded. The section applies to evidence of any sort. It remains to be seen how far the Courts will go, but already the police have had to take note of the possible effects at trial of their improper actions.

A 'Reasonable' Policeman

Central to the implementation of the Act is the notion of 'reasonableness' and the judgement of the police in particular situations. Reasonable grounds for suspicion are required for stop and search and for arrest; reasonable grounds for belief are needed to seek a search warrant; force must be reasonable, and reasonable grounds for belief concerning a suspect's intended behaviour forms the basis of decisions on detention and access to family and solicitor. The courts have added 'reasonableness' when a police superintendent decides whether an offence is a 'serious arrestable offence' with all the attendant disadvantages that can mean for the suspect. [9]

In view of the research evidence which illustrates the institutional sexism of the overwhelmingly male police force, serious questions must be asked as to how police officers communicate with women suspects and whether they are capable of forming objective judgements about them. How does a court measure the 'reasonableness' of a male police officer's decision? One conclusion must be that Parliament's repeated insistence on 'reasonableness' may be far less effective a safeguard for women than for men.

It is of course true that in many respects women are affected by the Police and Criminal Evidence Act in the same way as men. The differences and special implications emerge from the combining of coercive police powers with a body of police officers who are overwhelmingly male and sexist. The Act provides opportunities for abuse; the attitudes of officers towards women ensures that those abuses will occur.

Notes

1. Royal Commission on Criminal Procedure Report, Cmnd 8092, January 1981.

2. Report of an Inquiry by the Hon. Sir Henry Fisher, HC 90, HMSO, London, 1977.

3. Lord Scarman, The Scarman Report: The Brixton Disorders 10–12 April 1981, Cmnd 8427, HMSO, London, 1981; also published by Penguin, London, 1982.

4. *Brazil v Chief Constable of Surrey* (1983) 3AWER 537. After arrest for breach of the peace, a woman was told that everyone had to be searched 'for their own safety'. Then, because she was suspected of possessing drugs, she was forcibly searched down to her underwear. The Court held that a search could not be justified on the basis of a general rule; in each case a constable had to consider whether a search was necessary. Further, because of the affront to a person's dignity a constable could not carry out a search without first telling the person why it was necessary.

5. *Holgate-Mohammed v Duke* (1984) 1AWER 1054. A constable suspected a woman of theft, but lacked sufficient evidence. He believed that she was more likely to confess if she were questioned under arrest than at her home. The House of Lords held that this was a proper factor for the constable to take into account when he made his decision to arrest her and that he was acting within his lawful powers when he arrested her to question her.

6. Crown Court (Advance Notice of Expert Evidence) Rules 1987 (S.I. 1987 No. 716) bring this section into operation.

7. *Samuel* (1988) 2 WLR 920 and *Mason* (1988) 1 WLR 139.

8. *Foster* (1987) Crim. L.R. 821.

9. *Re Walters* (1987) Crim. L.R. 577. The defendant alleged that he had wrongly been denied access to a solicitor, but the Court was not prepared to exclude the evidence of his interview, since the Court found the police superintendent's decision to delay access to a solicitor was reasonable on the facts known to him at the time.

25. Under Surveillance

Nadine Finch

Few women would deny that society has a collective responsibility to protect its members from physical attack, fraud, theft or other threat to their livelihood. And that, in the course of their investigations, the police or security services (MI5 and Special Branch) may put individuals under surveillance.

However, we would want to assume that these agencies would either have some real evidence against their suspect and be trying to build up a case, or that they have reasonable grounds to think the suspect guilty of the actual crime being investigated.

Unfortunately, in a disturbing and ever-increasing number of cases, this is not true. The British state now has under surveillance millions of individuals who have become suspects merely because they belong to broad social groupings of race, nationality, belief – or even merely because they live on a housing estate thought to have a high risk of public disorder.

Those targeted for surveillance are seen by the police or security services as posing one of two broad threats to society. One group, the more 'political', is thought to seek to subvert society's beliefs. The other, which is perceived to be both criminal and 'political' in the widest sense of the term, is believed to pose a threat to public order.

The two categories are inter-related and are increasingly viewed as synonymous in police and security circles. Methods and strategies which were originally developed to deal with subversion in a colonial or cold-war situation, have now been introduced to deal with public disorder or the so-called 'enemy within'.[1]

In recent years, we have seen a shift in state definitions of 'subversion'. In his report on the Profumo Affair in 1963, Lord Denning defined a 'subversive' as someone who would contemplate the overthrow of government by unlawful means.[2] However, by the time the Home Office guidelines on the work of the Special Branch were issued in December 1984, the definition had been significantly extended to include 'activities which threaten the safety or well-being of the state, and which are intended to undermine or overthrow parliamentary democracy by political, industrial or violent means'.[3] Recent legal judgements (although not adhered to by the jury in the Clive Ponting case) have further defined this 'state' as the government of the day, who is to be seen as the judge and arbiter of what is or is not 'in the national interest'.

We are now in a situation where, if we do not subscribe to the political and social beliefs of the government of the day and say so publicly, or if we exercise our right to take industrial action, or join a political campaign, we can expect to be investigated. Recent revelations about the extent of MI5's surveillance of the Wilson government and attempts to discredit it have revived a very necessary demand for the security services to be made publicly accountable; on the other hand, they have also tended to perpetuate the myth that it is merely prominent politicians who are subjected to surveillance. But as Tony Benn, MP, said during the second reading of the Interceptions of Communications Bill, drawing on his experience as a Cabinet minister:

> I feel an obligation to tell those who do not know it that if they are communists, reading the *Morning Star*, *Militant* or *Socialist Worker*, or if they are active in strikes, or are perhaps members of Friends of the Earth, hunt saboteurs, or are engaged in, say, the activities of the Animal Liberation Front, they will be watched, intercepted and listened to.[4]

The case of Madelaine Haigh is one of many where individuals, believing they were exercising their legal right to voice a political opinion, have found that doing so qualified them for surveillance by MI5, the most senior of the 'watching' services. In 1981, Madelaine Haigh, a member of the Sutton Coldfield Peace Group, with no previous history of political involvement, wrote to her local paper, the *Sutton Coldfield News*, to protest at the siting of Cruise missiles in Britain. Shortly afterwards, she was visited by two men, who claimed to be investigating a mail order fraud and who obtained a range of personal information about her life and family. Concerned at the mistake that had obviously been made, she rang the firm concerned and discovered that there was no such enquiry. She complained to the local police and to her MP. At first, the police disclaimed any knowledge of the incident, but eighteen months later it emerged that the two men had, in fact, been Special Branch officers. The Chief Constable of the West Midlands, Sir Philip Knight, admitted that on account of the letter she had written, it was the view of the police and security services that 'she might be a person prepared to support or get involved in public protests of a nature likely to become violent'.[5]

There are signs that some women within the system itself are becoming concerned about the extent of surveillance and its threat to civil liberties, but as yet these cases are the exception not the rule. One of the most publicized cases was that of Cathy Massiter, an MI5 officer with twelve years' service. She resigned and agreed to appear on a programme in the Twenty/Twenty Vision series in March 1985 after she had been asked to catalogue and filter information on the Campaign for Nuclear Disarmament (CND) between January and December 1983 and, in particular, to request a tap to be placed on the phone of the Vice Chair, Dr John Cox. The fact that this was the result of a request from Michael Heseltine, then Defence Secretary, and that information on CND policies was used to smear the opposition campaign in the general election that year persuaded her that surveillance was being used by the state for reasons that had more to do with political gain than national security.

Mounting criticism of MI5 activities led in 1988 to proposals to amend the Official Secrets Act. Unfortunately, far from opening up security operations to public scrutiny these are likely further to criminalize dissent.

In the National Interest?

The situation is complicated further by the tendency on the part of successive governments, and in particular of Mrs Thatcher's administration, to equate national interest with national security and impose a blanket ban on information clearly outside the terms of the Official Secrets Act. The seizure of all material relating to the BBC2 series 'Secret Society' by Special Branch in 1987 is a good example of this. One programme on the Zircon Project[6] was banned despite having received some official co-operation previously. A further programme looking at the work of Cabinet committees was also banned temporarily. The former did deal with defence issues, but the latter was looking at functions of an elected government which should have been open to public scrutiny. The ban led to an emergency debate in parliament. During this, Duncan Campbell, a journalist for the *New Statesman* and the producer of the series, was singled out as an example of those 'conducting a campaign of political warfare against our organs of state'.[7] This phrase could be said to represent the views of many MI5, Special Branch and police officers.

A television programme on the factors behind the Birmingham Six Appeal and a radio programme on the security services, 'My Country Right or Wrong', were also withdrawn later in a year notorious for the government's judicial intervention to prevent British publication of *Spycatcher* by Peter Wright, former Assistant Director of MI5.

More recently, in 1988, all representatives of Sinn Fein, even democratically elected councillors, have been banned from radio and television broadcasts, in the national interest.

The Influence of the Conflict in Northern Ireland

The experience of eighteen years of combat in Northern Ireland, together with nine years of industrial strife and urban uprisings in Britain, has militarized both the perceptions and activities of all those involved in surveillance.

MI5, in particular, have played a key role in Northern Ireland, enabling the British army to overhaul the antiquated manual records kept by the RUC and replace them with the powerful 'Vengeful' computer records. This followed the recommendations of a British army officer, Sir Frank Kitson, serving in Northern Ireland in the 1974–5 period, who had experience of counter-insurgency campaigns in Malaya, Cyprus and Kenya. He distinguished three phases of such campaigns as the Preparatory Period, the Non-Violent Phase and Open Insurgency. Within the Preparatory Period, Kitson recommended unifying military and civil resources and forces and establishing an effective system of intelligence designed to obtain a large volume of low-grade information.[8]

In Northern Ireland, intensive surveillance of every vehicle, its movements, passengers and owners, 'fishing' raids on homes, and detentions without charge under the Emergency Provisions Act and the Prevention of Terrorism Acts, has enabled a large amount of information to be gleaned, cross-referenced and filed for future use. In the process, surveillance equipment and techniques have been developed and refined. Night-sight cameras, helicopters fitted with stabilized video cameras, techniques for gathering useful low-level intelligence (Multi-Agency Policing); all were developed as a response to the Northern Ireland conflict and are now available to the police and security services in Britain.

The Watchers

The Government Communications Headquarters (GCHQ) at Cheltenham is the largest British security agency, with 11,500 staff and a £600 million budget. It intercepts and monitors all international calls, cables and radio and radar messages, and its employees are forbidden to join a trade union on the grounds that this would be incompatible with their national security role. However, most internal surveillance is the responsibility of MI5 and its public face, Special Branch. MI5 keeps more than 500,000 files on possible subversives. Different departments have operatives responsible for monitoring, infiltrating and bugging a range of groups and individuals. Russian Embassy employees, trade unionists, feminists, members of CND, teachers, journalists and left-wing groups are all of interest. However, as MI5 officers have no legal powers of arrest and prefer to remain anonymous, Special Branch officers are used to arrest suspects and initiate any court procedures. Special Branch also has a number of specific duties in relation to the registration of aliens, the Prevention of Terrorism Act and the enforcement of deportation orders, which are clearly related to a role described by Merlyn Rees when he was Home Secretary in 1978. He stated that 'Special Branch collects information on those whom I think cause problems for the state'.[9]

Special Branch also has particular responsibility for maintaining public order, working with the support of local police forces, assessing possible sources of disorder and acquainting itself with all potentially subversive groups and individuals on behalf of the Home Secretary.

To fulfil its dual role of maintaining public order and keeping a watch on subversives, Special Branch has learnt much from the experiences of Northern Ireland and from the Army Land Operations Manual, Volume III, *Counter-Revolutionary Operations*. This is shown by the value it attributes to collecting low-level intelligence that can be pieced together to reveal patterns of association or project the likely development of a campaign 'long before an emergency has arisen'.[10] Special Branch monitors a wide range of newspapers, magazines and public meetings to develop profiles on different groups and communities in an exercise which is intensive and well coordinated.

Information gathering is also now a primary function of all police officers. In the case of the Lothian and Borders force, this role is written into their job description and they are instructed to 'secure the services of at least one observer in every street, not a paid professional informant, but someone who knows the inhabitants and is inquisitive enough to find out what is going on and is willing to pass it on'.[11] In the Metropolitan Police, beat constables and Neighbourhood Watch schemes provide similar information and intelligence.

Locally gathered data will be a dangerous mixture of information (i.e. hard factual data) and intelligence (i.e. speculation, supposition, hearsay and unverified notes about places frequented, known associates and suspected activities), but it will nevertheless be recorded and passed on to the local collator who will then pass it up to intelligence and surveillance units. It may then be placed on computers used by Special Branch. In this way, rumour and innuendo can become recorded fact and retrievable data.

Many within the police force are aware of the possible repercussions of blanket surveillance. Questioned on Newsnight in 1984, John Alderson, former Chief Constable of Devon and Cornwall, said that he found that a lot of the records in this force were 'totally out of date, irrelevant, petty, and 50 per cent were either useless, unnecessary or shouldn't have been collected'.[12] Others have expressed concern at the harm caused by intelligence that is subjective and suppositional.

An independent inquiry into the events at Broadwater Farm in 1985 was established by Haringey Council. One of the conclusions it drew was that the police response, which had also relied on rumours and prejudiced opinion was aggressive and intimidatory and contributed to the subsequent events.[13]

The Influence of Kenneth Newman

What happened at Broadwater Farm was a graphic and tragic example of allowing intelligence gathering to precipitate a crisis. It is one that is likely to be repeated if the Metropolitan police and other forces adopt the strategies developed by Newman, Commissioner of the Met from 1982 to 1987. He built on experience gained as Commissioner in Northern Ireland between 1976 and 1979. In a speech to the European Atlantic Group in 1983, he emphasized two key strategies: 'the efficient collation and exploitation of intelligence and an imaginative community relations and crime prevention pro-gramme'.[14] During his five years with the Met, he developed a complex strategy to target and scrutinize communities who were deemed to pose a threat to public order, or who lived in areas where burglary or street crime were high. Police officers were encouraged to visit local community groups to pick up local information or to join committees to look at local pro-blems alongside local government representatives. The Multi-Agency approach to policing also, in some instances, gives the police access to local government files.

In London, Newman created Divisional Information Officer posts with the task of assessing local communities in relation to a number of 'tension indicators' and reporting this information to the Central Information Unit within A8, the Met's Public Order Branch. Communities with a high density of population and/or ethnic mix, who showed hostility towards the police, or adopted a high political profile were deemed to have a potential for disorder. A 'hit list' of housing estates where unrest was expected was produced.[15] This marked not only an extension of surveillance in practical terms, but also signalled a further 'militarization' of policing; the police now perceived them-selves as being in permanent conflict with certain communities. For example, not only did the criteria list ethnic mix as one of the determinants of tension, but all except one of the locations identified had large black populations.

This shift in strategy came at a time when the Met was achieving a mere 16 per cent clear-up rate on crime and when their capacity to deploy sufficient officers to investigate crime was severely constrained by the diversion of resources in order to police first the miners' dispute of 1984–5 and then the Wapping dispute of 1985–6. Newman's strategy was to offer a 'political' solution to the rising crime rate and falling clear-up rate. To appear to achieve results, he targeted crimes that caused most public concern (street crime, rape, burglary) and concentrated resources on communities that he hoped could be held responsible for them, such as unemployed youth or the black community. This led to increased surveillance of individ-uals within those communities and a shift in emphasis from the individual crime and factual evidence relating to it, to creating files on those likely, in the eyes of the police, to commit such a crime.

However, the last six years have been proof of the inability of such a strategy to reduce crime. What Newman has succeeded in doing is to increase racial tension, fuel calls for police accountability and introduce a massive system of surveillance which has no place in a democratic society.

The power of the Association of Chief Police Officers and the National Reporting Centre brought into use in the miners' dispute has unfortunately ensured that this system of targeting and surveillance has spread nationwide. Just one look at the categories on the Police National Computer used by Special Branch ('of long term interest to the police', 'seen and checked in noteworthy circumstances', 'insufficient evidence to charge immediately') indicates that the state is preparing to defend the 'national interest' against any number of hypothetical future events, basing their judgement on class and racial prejudice.

Surveillance Techniques and Technology

Both MI5 and Special Branch have developed a range of methods to watch suspects. Some are highly labour intensive and cannot be sustained for long, or used except in exceptional circumstances. Tailing individuals or having a constant tap on their telephones fall into this category.

Infiltration is still used by MI5 for political surveillance. Special Branch were busy disguising themselves as pickets during the miners' dispute of 1984–5. For example, one miner remembered,

> the boys used the Station Café at Margan when on picket duty to have a warm and get a cup of tea. The lady behind the counter told us of a 'picket' who came in and sat down at a table. Suddenly, a short wave radio came on from inside his coat. He got up, embarrassed, and went out immediately.[16]

In fact, Special Branch has a long history of such practices dating back to before the First World War, when they infiltrated the suffragette movement and a group campaigning for full rights for illegitimate children.

Mail interception, which has been legal since the 1711 Post Office Act, is also widely used. MI5 and Special Branch both use a special investigation unit, which 'creams off' targeted mail, copies it and returns it the same day into the regular post office system. Despite advances in letter opening, or the treatment of envelopes in order to scrutinize the contents, human error still results in the contents being replaced in the wrong envelope. For example, in 1973, mail for the Communist Party regularly included letters addressed to a left-wing bookshop, Rising Free.[17]

Telephone taps are also used widely. Between 1980 and 1984, 2,774 taps were agreed by the Home Secretary. But due to the fact that some of the authorizations cover a complete organization or trade union head office, and that illegal taps are not unknown, this figure does not give a whole picture. At the moment, police and security services are constrained by limited technology. Taps have to be attached manually at the exchange by telephone engineers specially employed for the purpose. And at times they can be recognized by the subscriber. Joan Ruddock, when Chair of the Campaign for Nuclear Disarmament, discovered that by gently tapping the bar of her phone, she could set off a recording of her last call.[18] And, most telling of all, hours of tape have to be logged, analysed and stored.

However, advances in computerization are about to revolutionize the eavesdroppers' job. System X, due to be installed throughout British Telecom, will enable taps to be programmed into the system centrally without any manual taps or interference with circuits. It will also be able to provide instant print-outs of all calls made and received by a subscriber. Like a diary, this will provide the eavesdropper with a complete profile of association and contact. This system will be on line for domestic users within the next couple of years.

MI5 uses bugs as a short-term measure because they can monitor and record conversations at a distance. However, bugs are inconvenient as they require covert entry to premises to install and their batteries need replacing.

Techniques of visual surveillance have improved rapidly over the past few years thanks to research for military use. Both police and the security services now rely heavily on still photography and video film to build up 'rogues galleries' for future identification purposes. Video cameras attached to helicopters can pick out details and faces up to a distance of 2km. The police also use specially adapted cars and vans to film suspects; cameras are adapted to be sensitive in all lighting conditions. In London, the police can also take advantage of being able to 'tune into' any one of the six permanent closed circuit televisions erected by A8 Division on public buildings in Central London.

Two further technological developments are now being perfected that will vastly increase the police force's ability to analyse information collected, which is the most time-consuming and skilled part of the process. A WISARD system is being developed at the cybernetics department of Brunel and Imperial Colleges which will be able to match photographic facial characteristics to those in the data files. And at the same time, the Home Office is conducting a pilot scheme called Photographic Retrieval from Optical Disc (PROD) which can take stills from video film and store them as computer data.[19]

Developments in computer capabilities are similarly revolutionizing data storage and retrieval. The Special Branch computer, for instance, has a free text retrieval facility which can find any information stored across the system under the word entered or its synonym. Even local station computers are capable of producing an analysis of crime patterns locally and their 'command and control' systems can locate a suspect's usual pattern of movement on a grid system of the local area. And most of Britain's fifty-one police forces can now interface directly with the vast amounts of information held on the Police National Computer.

When these capabilities are considered alongside the sheer amount of information and intelligence being collected, the extent of the potential threat to individual liberty can be recognized. In addition to the amount of data gathered by the police and security services themselves, there is now a proliferation of computerized information on us all held by other government departments and private firms, which can be used for surveillance purposes. The police and security services have carte blanche to dip into any other data banks: DHSS, Inland Revenue, Customs & Excise, immigration and so on, without any record of this being made. They also have access, for example, to the information held by the Economic League. The League is an anti-socialist organization, first established in 1919. It has sixty full-time officers who keep files on some 250,000 individuals with left-wing views who may be deemed by the employers who are their customers to be unsuitable for employment. They work closely with the police, as revealed in a World in Action programme in 1987.[20] In a secretly filmed interview, Alan Harvey, League representative in North Yorkshire, admitted that the League hands over all its information to the police and receives help in kind.

The first danger posed by this proliferation of information is that, in the majority of cases, the subject of the computer files has no means of access to information held on him or her. MI5 and Special Branch files are completely inaccessible under the Data Protection Act 1984. Police computer files are inaccessible in any case where the police can argue that to produce them would prejudice the prevention or detection of crime or the apprehension or prosecution of offenders, which may be an effective impediment to any right of disclosure. A second, and crucial, danger (as explained above) is that there is no guarantee that this data is even accurate. Quite apart from the known human error factor in entering data, the Lindop Committee on Data Protection[21] drew attention to the fact that the police and security records are a mixture of information and intelligence and that therefore the likelihood of innocent civilians being criminalized must be high.

In January 1987, the government announced plans to establish a Government Data Network to bring together information held by a number of ministries. Joint registers linking the Inland Revenue and the DHSS systems already exist using the NINO (the national insurance number) as the identifier, and this is in the process of being computerized.[22] A DHSS Central Index is being developed at the same time, for all Britain's 54 million inhabitants. We are moving toward the establishment of national identity numbers based on the national insurance number. The young unemployed have already been given cards with their number. Some housing departments ask for the number in case tenants need housing benefit. The MI5 and Special Branch computers already use it as the file identifier.

At the same time, National Health Service records are being computerized. A computerized version of the Suspect Index used by immigration officers was being tried out at Dover Car Ferry Terminal in 1987. (The old index carries 20,000 names; journalists like Duncan Campbell and well-known political activists like Vanessa Redgrave and Tariq Ali are listed beside drug traffickers and terrorists.) Computerization coincides with the introduction in Britain in 1987 of machine-readable passports. Internal Home Office papers express one of the major benefits of this as 'the potential for performing automatic Suspect Index checks'.[23] Computerization will make it possible for any information encoded on the lamination of the passport (which is invisible to the human eye) to be machine-read. As reported in *New Scientist*, this will 'assist the immigration officer in obtaining very fast and effective checks against a much larger suspect index'.[24] As immigration and the Prevention of Terrorism Act fall under the remit of Special Branch, it is possible that port officers will have some access to Special Branch computer data as well.

Conclusions

The most law-abiding among us have little chance of disappearing into anonymity. Our life histories are too well documented on governmental or commercial files. But if our activities have involved any form of industrial or political activity, this will also have been recorded on the massive Special Branch 'C' Computer at Scotland Yard, amongst the two million MI5 computer files, or increasingly, in the intelligence sections of local police command and control or crime report computers.

This information network ties those under suspicion because of their beliefs, associations, or even their race, into what is essentially a criminal record system. And it does so on criteria of 'national interest' or 'public order' which have been redefined to such an extent that few of us could identify with them. In the divided Britain of today, as more and more people, including a disproportionate number of women, are pushed out of a share of the wealth and opportunities of the society they live in, they may be seen to pose a threat to the state by virtue of their mere existence.

Governments have always sought to control dissent and prevent disorder, but targeting and surveillance on the scale made possible by the developments described in this article, which are based on such broad definitions of subversion, seems to belong in a thought-police nightmare rather than in a society which professes to protect and defend its members.

Notes

1. Phrase used in the popular media during the miners' dispute 1984–5, to describe those challenging the state's decisions.

2. *Report on the Profumo Affair*, Cmnd 2152, 1963.

3. *Home Office Guidelines on the Work of a Special Branch*, Home Office, 1984.

4. *Hansard*, 12 March 1985.

5. Report of the Chief Constable – Ms Haigh Inquiry, County Council of the West Midlands Police Committee, 16 November 1983.

6. Zircon was the secret code name for a signals intelligence satellite being developed by the British government. The launch was originally planned in 1988 as an electronic listening post in space, able to eavesdrop on Soviet, European and Middle Eastern communications and beam them back to GCHQ, the government monitoring centre at Cheltenham. Duncan Campbell exposed the fact that the government had not accounted to parliament for this expenditure.

7. Ray Whitney, MP, *Hansard*, 3 February 1987.

8. F. Kitson, *Law Intensity Operations*, Faber, London, 1971.

9. *Hansard*, 2 March 1987.

10. *Technocop*, BSSRS Technology of Political Control Group, Free Association Books, London, 1985.

11. *Police Powers and Politics*, R. Kinsey and D. Baldwin, Quartet, 1982.

12. BBC2, *Newsnight*, 2 March 1984.

13. *The Broadwater Farm Inquiry*, Karia Press, London, 1986.

14. Newman's speech to European Atlantic Group, 24 October 1983.

15. *Policing London*, Nov/Dec 1986.

16. *Striking Back*, Welsh Campaign for Civil and Political Liberties and NUM (South Wales Area), 1985.

17. *Technocop*, BSSRS Technology of Political Control Group, Free Association Books, 1985.

18. *Guardian*, 19 April 1984.

19. *Policing London*, Jan/Feb 1987.

20. *World in Action*, Granada Television, 16 February 1987.

21. *Lindop Committee on Data Protection Report*, 1978.

22. *New Statesman*, 24 April 1987.

23. op. cit.

24. *New Scientist*, 5 January 1987.

26. Police Accountability

Teresa Thornhill

The fact that the British police are answerable to the law, that we act on behalf of the community and not under the mantle of government, makes us the least powerful, the most accountable and therefore the most acceptable force in the world.

Sir Robert Mark, ex-commissioner of Metropolitan Police, 1977

The history of policy accountability in Britain is closely tied to the history of local government. Once upon a time, local law enforcement was in the hands of the Justice of the Peace (JP), many of whose functions were handed over to local government in the nineteenth century. Today, as central government encroaches further and further on the powers of local government, we have a nationally-controlled police force in all but name.

From the Middle Ages until the end of the eighteenth century, law enforcement was seen as something which all citizens should participate in. Unpaid watchmen walked the streets at night. Like all citizens, they had the power of arrest, and would hand over suspected criminals to the local constable in the morning. The constable, also unpaid, was the right-hand man of the local court and the JP who presided over it. In the sixteenth century, this system began to break down. Wealthy families employed private security people; government did nothing.

With the Industrial Revolution came a massive movement of population from the countryside into the towns and cities. The new urban working class lived and worked in appalling conditions, did not have the vote, and were obliged to resort to civil disobedience to air their grievances. In the absence of an organized police force, the government put down uprisings by sending in the troops, for example against the Luddites[1] in 1811 and against a crowd of 60,000 listening to Henry Hunt speak on universal suffrage outside Manchester in 1819. On the latter occasion 11 people were killed and 400 wounded.

It was in response to this perceived threat to public order that the first police force in the land was formed, ten years later, by Home Secretary Sir Robert Peel, who had previously been Chief Secretary for Ireland. (The Dublin government had created a police force in 1786, to suppress anti-British dissent.)

The Police Act of 1829 created a police force for London only. In the next ten years, as the government came to see that it was politically preferable to use police rather than troops to combat the emerging labour movement, legislation was passed enabling the creation of forces by the towns, cities and counties outside London. For example, the County Police Act 1839 was rushed through parliament in an attempt to put down the Chartists.[2]

The early police forces were created at the same time as the modern system of local government, and they were put largely under its control. However, London in 1829 had no local government, and so the Metropolitan police were placed under the sole control of the Home Secretary. When the London County Council (LCC) was formed in 1888, it demanded to be given control of the Metropolitan police force, but this was refused, partly on the pretext that the Met police area was much larger than that of the LCC. Thus demands for police accountability in London go back over one hundred years.

Outside London, under the Local Government Act of 1888, county forces were controlled by joint standing committees; made up half of magistrates, half of councillors. Urban forces were controlled by 'watch committees' which had greater powers of control over their forces than did their rural counterparts. They did not have magistrates among their members, and were thus more independent of the judicial system. (The inclusion of magistrates in the county 'joint standing committees' had been hotly debated, with the landed aristocracy supporting their inclusion.) By 1857 there were 239 police forces up and down the country.

Over the next hundred years, the process of centralization took place gradually. The Police Act 1919 introduced the concept of a centrally guided and largely uniform system of local police forces. The Home Secretary was given power to pass regulations on pay and conditions for the police. The introduction of standard police training also began to undermine local autonomy. Strong links began to be forged between the Home Office and local chief constables, with the result that the real power of the latter grew in comparison to the power of the local committees. The Chief Constables had begun to form their own organizations as early as 1858: precursors to the highly influential Association of Chief Police Officers (ACPO), formed in 1948, whose modern role is discussed below.

In the later years of the nineteenth century, policemen came increasingly to behave as a national body of workers. They were the first in the public sector to organize a union. London police went on strike in 1872 and 1890 for better pay and conditions and towards the end of the First World War there was a nationwide police strike. The authorities reacted swiftly. All the supporters of a second strike were summarily sacked, the wages of non-strikers were doubled, and the government banned the further organizing of a police trade union. The formation of the Police Federation was recommended, with an express ban on its affiliating to the TUC.

The Current Constitutional Position of the Police

The present provisions for police accountability are laid down in the Police Act 1964. In theory the police remain organized as local, autonomous forces. The country is divided into forty-three areas, each having its own constabulary. In London the Met, as previously, is accountable solely to the Home Secretary. The City of London police, the force which polices the square mile at the heart of London, continues to be controlled by a committee of elected councillors, an anomaly which has existed since its inception in 1839.

Outside London, the joint standing committees and watch committees were replaced by 'police authorities' composed of one-third magistrates and two-thirds councillors. They are responsible only for finance, equipment, accommodation and staffing. So-called 'operational' and 'policy' matters are the exclusive responsibility of the Chief Constable (CC).

The police authority has the power to appoint and dismiss the Chief Constable, but this is subject to the approval of the Home Secretary. In practice, it is almost impossible for a police authority to dismiss its Chief Constable, and no authority has yet succeeded in doing so. Attempts to dismiss James Anderton, CC of Manchester, have only resulted in the Home Office ordering him to clear contentious public statements with them.

Funding

Police forces outside London are funded 51 per cent by central government and 49 per cent by local government, through a levy on the rates. In London a larger percentage of the cost of the Met is paid by central government because the Met is responsible for many 'national' police services as well as for policing London.[3] In 1984–5 approximately a quarter of total Met expenditure was paid for by the boroughs, again through a levy on the rates.

Who is Really in Charge?

The dual roles for CC and police authority are not clearly defined under the Act. The police committee can only exercise a limited measure of control through its control of the funds. If it attempts to criticize policing methods or priorities, the CC can choose to ignore this on the basis that operational and policy matters are for him alone to determine. He may appeal to the Home Secretary to back him. The police authority can call for written reports on policing matters but again, if the CC so chooses, he may seek the Home Secretary's backing for a claim that the required information should not be released 'in the public interest', or that the police authority does not need it to carry out its functions. It is thought to be rare for a police authority to obtain a report.

Outside the big cities, the majority of police authorities take a laissez-faire attitude to the activities of their CC. Those of Manchester and Merseyside, on the other hand, prior to their abolition,[4] tried hard to exercise over their CCs the maximum control allowed for by the Police Act 1964. The public rows that resulted demonstrated how untenable the statutory relationship is.

In 1983 James Anderton decided, without consulting his police authority, to arm patrolling officers. When they questioned him, he told the authority that, 'the policies were mine, the responsibility mine and not yours' – yet he went on to blame *them* for the public outcry which followed his decision. Rows have also broken out between several police authorities and their CCs over the latters' unilateral decision to stockpile plastic bullets. The police authorities of Merseyside, West Yorkshire and Derbyshire all discovered plastic bullet purchases by their forces when it was too late to prevent them. West Yorkshire and Derbyshire managed to obtain assurances that the stocks would only be used for training and would not be replaced. But the value of these assurances was negated when, in May 1986, Home Secretary Douglas Hurd announced that where police authorities objected to the purchase of plastic bullets, he would provide them from the central store of equipment at Home Office expense. This decision was challenged by Northumbria Police Authority by means of judicial review but, in 1987, the Court of Appeal upheld the Home Office position.

Thus, although under the Police Act 1964 the police authority is responsible for both finance and equipment, in practice many CCs hold their duty to take instructions from their authority in utter contempt, and are supported in doing so by the Home Secretary.

It should also be noticed that, with the decline in local control of the police, the modern chief constable, especially in inner city areas, has increasingly taken on an overtly political role. In recent years spokesmen for the Police Federation and for ACPO have made a habit of speaking out on issues of crime and public order. James Anderton, the CC of Greater Manchester, following a series of highly offensive public pronouncements on homosexuality and AIDS, declared that he saw himself as a divinely inspired guardian of public morals.

The National Riot Police

According to the statute book, Britain, unlike most European countries, has no national police force. This is the official picture, but for some years now this has been used to hide the fact that in addition to our local forces, we have a nationally organized 'third force' ('third' because its role is between those of the army and police). This force is trained for paramilitary operations and can be mobilized very quickly. It is sent to suppress strikes, political actions and demonstrations under the guise of maintaining public order.

The ACPO has taken it upon itself to organize this force, which is not provided for in any statute. At times when it is thought necessary, the current president of ACPO takes charge of the National Reporting Centre (NRC) at Scotland Yard. The NRC was set up in 1972 in the wake of the Saltley Coke Depot pickets during the miners' strike. It has been used on at least four occasions since, including during the prison officers' dispute in 1980, the 1981 uprisings in Brixton and Toxteth and the 1984/85 miners' strike. In a situation such as the miners' strike, the NRC received information from the police forces in the areas affected as to the movements of picketers and the situation on the picket lines. It then requisitioned men from forces outside those areas and arranged for their deployment. The requisitioned men were members of each force who had already received training in riot control. The equipment issued to them is standard throughout the country, and although in London, riot-trained officers are now known as 'Territorial Support Groups' and in Derbyshire as 'Special Operations Units', once brought together to police a dispute, they operate as a single force. Clearly it is nonsense to talk about a locally accountable police force, in these situations.

It is now over 160 years since the first British police force was established. The system which began as a series of small local forces under local (albeit ruling-class) control has gradually evolved into what is effectively a national body with a loud public voice and a large measure of autonomy in its operations and policy-making. .

In the social and economic crisis of the late 1980s, the police are inevitably being asked to play a key role in suppressing social unrest. The need for a return to a strengthened form of local accountability is paramount. The Labour Party has developed a set of proposals for local accountability in London.

A local accountability structure could answer many of the complaints that are currently being voiced against the police: changes in personnel (in terms of gender and race), changes in training and a reduction in police powers are all equally badly needed. However, with the progressive dismantling of local government by the present Conservative administration, the likelihood of such changes seems alarmingly remote. Nevertheless a framework of local accountability would at least provide the opportunity for such changes.

Notes

1. The Luddites were opponents of mechanized industry.
2. Chartism was a movement demanding universal suffrage.
3. These 'national' duties include the protection of royalty and visiting dignitaries, the security of the Houses of Parliament and government buildings, the Special Branch, the Diplomatic Protection Squad, central criminal records and the Central Drugs and Illegal Immigration Unit.
4. Since the abolition of the Metropolitan County Councils in 1985, police authorities in the former Metropolitan areas have been replaced by 'joint boards'. Member councillors are appointed by constituent metropolitan district councils, strictly in proportion to party strengths within each council. In the other 'joint boards',

no clear majority exists for any one party, with the result that the magistrates, who tend to vote en bloc, have much more influence than before.

27. The Criminal Justice System

Teresa Thornhill

Who Prosecutes?

The two parties in criminal prosecutions are usually the Crown and the individual(s) accused (except in private prosecutions where the victim prosecutes the accused directly). The prosecution is brought in the name of the Crown (the state) because the state has the duty to enforce the criminal law.

In most countries which have legal systems comparable to our own, there is a state body responsible for initiating and conducting all criminal prosecutions, which is (in theory at least) independent of the police. In England and Wales, however, until 1986, the conduct of prosecutions was the responsibility of the police (with the Director of Public Prosecutions (DPP) taking over prosecutions on the most serious charges). Thus the police both investigated criminal matters *and* presented the prosecution case in court – either through police officers or through their own lawyers.

This system was ended with the introduction of the Crown Prosecution Service (CPS) in October 1986. Under the new system, the police's role is limited to preparing the prosecution evidence and initiating the criminal proceedings. The CPS, which is headed by the DPP, is responsible for deciding whether to continue with or drop proceedings and for conducting prosecutions in court. In theory the CPS could decide to take over a private prosecution or to initiate a prosecution themselves. This could prove useful to people who have been subjected to racial or sexual attack and found the police unwilling to initiate proceedings. There seems to be nothing to stop you from approaching the CPS directly and asking them to initiate a prosecution, or to take over a private prosecution if you have started one yourself.

The arguments used to promote the idea of an independent prosecution service were that prosecutors should be seen to be independent of the police; that a separate service would ensure a consistent national prosecutions policy; and that this kind of service would be able to weed out weak cases, thus saving costs. This idea was presented as a libertarian measure which would counterbalance the extension of police powers in the Police and Criminal Evidence Act. However, the original proposal was for local prosecution services, accountable to a local police and prosecution authority, and headed by local chief prosecutors. Instead the CPS is a centralized, national service and is accountable only (through the DPP) to the Home Office.

The service we have ended up with has been widely criticized. It is doubtful whether it is genuinely independent from the police, since the majority of its 1,550 staff are lawyers who previously prosecuted for the police. They are also of course, dependent on the information supplied by the police when they make the decision to proceed with or drop a prosecution. Moreover, the police continue to exercise a strong influence over prosecution policy, for it is they who make the decision to charge and arrest a person in the first instance, thereby bringing them to the attention of the CPS.

So far, the CPS has been seriously understaffed and very disorganized, often creating chaos in the daily operation of the courts.

The Criminal Courts

Criminal justice is administered in the Magistrates' Courts and the Crown Courts, with appeals to the High Court and the Court of Appeal Criminal Division. There are over 1,000 Magistrates' Courts in England and Wales. All criminal proceedings begin in the Magistrates' Court. If you are arrested, the police are obliged to bring you before a magistrate within a short time of charging you; alternatively, for instance for minor road traffic offences, a police officer 'lays an information' before a magistrate and the magistrate then issues a summons requiring you to attend court.

Certain minor offences may only be tried 'summarily', that is, before a magistrate. These include common assault, threatening behaviour, being drunk and disorderly, and minor road traffic offences. Obstructing a police officer in the execution of his duty is triable summarily only, more for policy reasons than because it is regarded as a minor offence – because magistrates tend to accept police evidence more readily than juries. Various offences under the new Public Order Act are 'summary only' for the same reason. Very serious offences are triable only 'on indictment', that is, before a jury at a Crown Court. Other offences are 'triable either way', and the defendant may choose between summary or jury trial. When a case is to be tried by jury, it is transferred from the Magistrates' Court to the Crown Court by way of 'committal' proceedings. These may involve the hearing of live evidence and legal argument.

Magistrates have maximum powers of sentence of six months in prison, or a fine of £2,000, for one offence. If the defendant has substantial previous convictions and the magistrates want to see a stiffer sentence imposed than their limits allow, they will send him or her to the Crown Court to be sentenced there. Magistrates also issue warrants for arrest and search and, when sentencing, can make recommendations for deportation.

The Crown Court sits in about ninety different centres throughout England and Wales. The best known of these is the Old Bailey, or Central Criminal Court in London. Besides hearing trials, the Crown Court hears some appeals from the Magistrates' Courts and sentences those people convicted by the magistrates who have been sent to the Crown Court for sentence.

The Judiciary

It is a fundamental tenet of the theory of democratic government that the judiciary must be above political influence. In the English system, full-time judges (that is, all judges apart from Recorders who, when not sitting, can practise privately as solicitors or barristers) are disqualified from being MPs. The law lords must also abstain from politically controversial debate. However, the Lord Chancellor, who is head of the judiciary, is himself a political appointee. Senior judges (i.e. High Court Judges or presiding judges, of any court) are appointed by the prime minister on his or her advice. The Lord Chancellor is responsible for other appointments and for the behaviour of judges. He is a member of the cabinet and has his own civil service department.

Magistrates

Most magistrates are lay justices of the peace (JPs). There are only about fifty-two legally qualified 'stipendiary' magistrates, who are paid for their work, nearly all in London. The system for appointing lay JPs was reformed in 1965. Political parties now have less influence in the selection process; anyone wanting to become a JP can now apply. The Lord Chancellor makes the final decision, using the advice of local committees.

Ninety per cent of criminal cases are dealt with in magistrates' courts, the vast majority by lay magistrates. It is therefore essential that the magistracy should be representative of the community.

However, the social background of JPs has remained homogenous and strongly establishment. The work is unpaid and most lay magistrates are suburban middle-class people who tend to be middle aged or elderly. Approximately 40 per cent are women, partly as the result of a drive to recruit more women, but also because more middle-class women than men are in a position to work unpaid. Nationally, there are between 250 and 300 magistrates of black and other ethnic minority origins, a much lower percentage than in the population at large. A Cobden Trust report in 1985 alleged racial discrimination in the selection of JPs.

JPs receive some initial training, and then receive information circulars from the Home Office. They are encouraged to attend refresher courses and conferences. There is no testing of their knowledge or competence, although if serious imcompetence comes to light, a JP can be prevented from sitting. In practice, lay JPs rely heavily on the court clerk, who is almost always legally qualified, for their understanding of the law. As a result, the clerk often exercises an alarming degree of influence over their decisions.

In the Magistrates' Courts, probably even more than in the Crown Court, the type of justice a defendant can expect to receive depends very much on the particular bench (JPs sit in groups of three) sitting on the day in question. As a result, some lawyers find out who the bench is composed of before advising their client on how to plead and whether to opt for summary trial or trial by jury.

Judges

Although solicitors as well as barristers can be appointed as judges to sit on the less serious trials, most judges must be appointed from among senior barristers. Senior judges are almost always selected from among those barristers who have been appointed Queen's Counsel (an honour which depends on having the right connections and politics, as much as on skills and abilities). Many are, or have been, members of parliament though they must resign from the House of Commons if they accept. MPs who have been law officers when their party was in government (for example, Attorney General, Solicitor General) can usually expect to be rewarded by being made a judge. (They will then not be able to stand for parliament again without relinquishing the judicial post.)

The vast majority of all judges are still white men from upper middle-class backgrounds. The high percentage who were educated at public school and Oxbridge has not changed much over the past hundred years. Senior judges must retire at seventy-five, circuit judges at seventy-two. High Court judges (who hear the most serious criminal cases and are the most senior judges outside of the Court of Appeal and the House of Lords), and those senior to them, can only be removed for misbehaviour (by the Queen) but this has never occurred. Judges who sit on the less serious cases may be removed from office by the Lord Chancellor for incapacity or misbehaviour, but this rarely happens. In 1977, a Scottish judge was removed for the 'misbehaviour' of publishing a political pamphlet advocating a plebiscite on Scottish home rule. The rare judge, such as Judge Pickles, who dares to publicly criticize the Lord Chancellor is at risk of being disciplined or ultimately removed from office.

Senior judges cannot be sued for anything they say or do in the course of their work. However, they may sue for statements made about them. In 1980, a Northern Ireland County Court judge successfully sued *The Economist* for an article which suggested that his appointment had been based on the fact that he was a Catholic rather than on his personal ability.

Judges are not supposedly allowed to make political statements in public. But certain judges do frequently make statements in the course of their judicial work which have right-wing political overtones.

Trial by Magistrate or Trial by Jury: Current Issues and Changes

A person charged only with a summary offence has no option but to stand trial before magistrates. A person charged with an indictable only offence is obliged to stand trial before a jury in the Crown Court. Many fairly serious offences, however, are 'triable either way', which means that the person charged can choose whether to have a summary trial or jury trial. Assaults occasioning actual bodily harm, indecent assault, many offences of dishonesty, criminal damage where the damage exceeds £2,000 and possession of controlled drugs are all offences triable either way.

A defendant chooses which court to be tried in when he or

she first appears at the Magistrates' Court. If the defendant intends to plead 'not guilty', it is usually preferable to opt for trial by jury. With a jury trial, the prosecution are obliged to provide the defendant with copies of the prosecution statements in advance. There is a better chance of a fair trial because, while magistrates tend to be prosecution-minded and case-hardened, juries come to cases fresh from the real world and tend to be more open minded. However, choosing trial by jury can mean waiting longer before the case is heard and people often choose a Magistrates' Court simply because they want to get the case over and done with.

The Criminal Justice Act 1988 removed the right to jury trial for the offences of common assault, driving while disqualified and taking a motor vehicle without consent – all of which were previously triable either way. This move has been presented as 'the redistribution of business between the Crown Court and the Magistrates' Court', that is, as a purely administrative move. In fact, it denies the right to jury trial to about 12,000 defendants a year, and is yet another in the long series of small but significant erosions in the rights of people facing criminal prosecution which have occurred in the last ten years.

In Northern Ireland, the right to jury trial for many offences of violence was removed in 1973 with the introduction of non-jury Diplock Courts. It has long been feared that this may one day be extended to Britain.

The Jury System

Trial by jury is one of the most remarkable features of the English legal system. In a jury trial, the jurors decide whose version of the *facts* is the true one, and their decision cannot be challenged unless new evidence is unearthed after the trial. The judge directs them on the *law*, but, while they must accept this as he or she explains it, any mistake on the judge's part may result in the conviction being overturned. (In the Magistrates' Court, the decision both about the facts of the case and how to apply the law is left to the magistrates.) The criminal law is complicated and it is doubtful whether most jurors understand most of the law which the judge is obliged to explain to them. It seems that juries decide cases to a large extent by weighing up the facts of the case and using their common sense, and by forming an opinion as to whether or not individual witnesses and defendants are telling the truth. This rooting of the jury system in the lay judgement of the defendant's peers is the English judicial system's most valuable aspect, though of course its benefits are limited if those who sit on juries do not share similar backgrounds to those whom the system brings before the courts.

Eligibility

The theory of jury trial is that jurors are a randomly selected cross-section of the population. Until 1974, however, only householders could sit on juries. The Juries Act of 1974 provided that everyone aged eighteen to sixty-five who is on the electoral register and who has been resident in the UK for five years since the age of thirteen, is eligible for jury service unless they come within one of the excluded categories. The judiciary and the legal profession are excluded, as are police, probation and prison officers, the clergy, the mentally ill and many ex-offenders. Until 1984, the exclusion of people with criminal records was limited to those who had served a prison sentence of a minimum of three months in the previous ten years, which effectively excluded about 250,000 people. The Juries (Disqualification) Act 1984, passed by the Thatcher government without much public debate, extended the exclusion to those who have received a suspended sentence, community service order or probation order within the last five years – a further 500,000 people. The assumption underlying this exclusion – that a person who has been through the criminal justice system would inevitably approach jury service determined to acquit regardless of the evidence – is highly questionable, and if it is true it surely reflects very badly on the system itself!

Thus, although jury service is open to many more working-class and young people than previously, juries can still not be said to be randomly selected. The fact that many black people are not registered to vote means that they continue to be under-represented on juries. If people cease to register as voters because they are unable to pay the poll tax, this will remove their eligibility for jury service.

Jury Vetting

The practice of jury vetting first came to public light in 1978 when it was revealed that the jury for the 'ABC' trial had been vetted. (The ABC trial was a 'secrets' trial involving two ex-soldiers who had served in Northern Ireland and Duncan Campbell to whom they had allegedly revealed the secrets.) Under the guidelines in existence since 1974, the Attorney General had sanctioned jury vetting in twenty-nine cases. In 1980, he issued new guidelines which said that jury vetting was acceptable in 'terrorist' cases and in cases involving evidence which for reasons of 'national security' would have to be heard in camera. Where vetting takes place, the Special Branch are asked to check their files for information on members of the prospective jury panel. They pass this to the DPP, who decides how much of it to divulge to the prosecution. For the trial of Michael Bettaney in 1984 (an MI5 officer accused of passing information to the Russians), 700 prospective jurors were vetted. It is difficult to know exactly how many trials involve jury vetting at present.

Challenges to Jurors

Many aspects of the jury system which benefited the defendant have been gradually eroded in recent years, a trend which has culminated in the Criminal Justice Act 1988. For example, in 1967 majority verdicts were introduced (of 11:1 or 10:2). Previously a jury could only convict on a unanimous verdict. In 1977, the number of jurors who could be challenged by the defence was reduced from seven to three. Before the Criminal Justice Act was passed, each defendant had the right to 'perem-ptorily' challenge up to three of the group of jurors called into court, without giving a reason, before they were sworn in, and have them replaced by other jurors. The prosecution could also 'stand by' (reject) a juror without giving a reason. (There is no limit, apart from the size of the panel of the potential jurors, to the number of selected jurors the prosecution can stand by. Before trial, the prosecution often has the names of the entire panel run through the police computer, thus enabling them to stand by jurors who have convictions they have not declared. The onus is on people called for jury service to declare their ineligibility, if appropriate.) The defence has no such access to information on potential jurors and has to challenge purely on the basis of dress and facial expression. However, such challenges could make all the difference both to whether defendants got a fair trial and whether they felt they were getting one.

The Criminal Justice Act abolishes the defence's right to peremptory challenges, while retaining the prosecution's right to stand a juror by. This change has been condemned by members of the legal profession of all political persuasions, and by the Criminal Bar Association. In support of the measure, the government repeatedly cited the Cyprus secrets trial, in which a young jury acquitted a group of young soldiers of passing secrets. They claimed that the defence lawyers co-ordinated their use of challenges (three per defendant) to achieve this result. Since the principle behind jury trial is that people should be tried by their peers, there could be no objection to this use of challenges. Furthermore, the right to peremptory challenge was centuries old, and there was no reason to suppose it was leading to any more acquittals of the guilty than it had done in the past.

Following the uproar provoked by this provision in the Criminal Justice Bill, the Home Office undertook research into the use of challenges. The preliminary results in January 1987 showed a mere 1 per cent difference in conviction rate in cases where challenges had been used from cases where they had not. The real reason behind the abolition of peremptory challenges is the government's realization that British juries – now drawn from a wider cross-section of the community than previously – cannot always be trusted to lend their support to its policy of criminalizing those sections of the community whose voices it most wishes to silence.

Crown Court Trial

There are other aspects of Crown Court procedure where defendants' rights have been eroded. At trial, the prosecution traditionally present their case before the defence. When the prosecution witnesses have given their evidence, defence counsel cross-examines them. The purpose of cross-examination is to discredit witnesses, whether by showing that they are lying, or that their evidence is unreliable for other reasons. At present, all prosecution witnesses have to give evidence in person unless the defence consents to a written statement being read in court, which would only happen if the defence does not wish to challenge that particular witness's evidence. The Criminal Justice Act, however, provides for a great extension of the use of written prosecution statements at trial, regardless of whether or not the defence consents. This is a very worrying aspect of the Act, for if defence counsel cannot seek to discredit prosecution witnesses by cross-examination, there is very little else that they can do to defend the defendant.

Other worrying provisions in the Act extend the powers of the Court of Appeal. Previously the Court of Appeal could only reduce a sentence on appeal. The Act enables it to increase a sentence where it considers the Crown Court to have given too lenient a sentence. This part of the Criminal Justice Act is due to come into force in summer 1989.

If the defendant does not wish to give evidence, the judge must tell the jury that they are to attach no significance to his or her silence. Traditionally, the defendant who refused to give evidence (thus shielding him- or herself from cross-examination by the prosecution) had the right to make a statement from the dock. This right was removed in 1982, in order to prevent defendants in political trials from making political statements.

Attempts to insert a clause into the Criminal Justice Act to abolish the defendant's right to silence while in police custody were unsuccessful, partly due to vehement opposition from the civil liberties lobby and the Criminal Bar Association. But, at the time of writing the government has announced that they intend to bring in new legislation to end the 'right to silence'.

This right has been fundamental to the criminal justice system for centuries. It means that the fact that an accused person refuses to answer questions put to him or her by the police (or anyone else investigating an offence) cannot be presented to a jury as evidence of their guilt. It is a crucial right and its abolition will be a very serious erosion of a defendant's rights. The police have pushed for its abolition because their job will be infinitely easier if, in a case where there is little or no independent evidence, they can point to the fact that the defendant has refused to answer questions as evidence against him or her.

The particular importance of the right to silence has to do with the fact that people held in police custody are often refused access to a solicitor or do not know they have the right to ask to see one. In these circumstances, the police may use their powers to 'lean' on suspects to persuade them to make incriminating statements (see also chapter 24). The decision to abolish the right to silence is an indication of how far British justice has travelled in recent years down the road to dispensing with the concept of a fair trial.

28. Sheffield Policewatch

Taking Action

Janet McDermott, Jenny Owen, Cath Whitty

How We Started

'With every day that passes in this dispute, evidence is accumulating of police activity that . . . should be considered quite outrageous in a democratic society' (*Guardian*, 3 April 1984). Responsible members of the public should make themselves available as 'legal observers' to observe, record and report on police activity during the dispute. Your help, and the help of your friends, is now requested in an exercise of public monitoring.

So ran a leaflet issued by Sheffield Trades Council soon after the miners' strike began in March 1984. It quoted examples of restrictions on movement in and out of Nottinghamshire and invited people to a public meeting on 6 April. Over two hundred people attended the meeting and the decision was taken to set up 'Operation Policewatch'. Groups of volunteer observers met over the weekend to organize rotas and by Monday, 9 April the first observers were going out. Two-thirds of us were women.

We wanted to publicize as widely as possible an accurate picture of police activity and to make ourselves available as witnesses in court, where appropriate, in cases where miners had experienced violence, intimidation or arbitrary arrest at the hands of the police. Equipped with notebooks, sometimes cameras and eventually, small tape recorders, we set out to record the exact details of individual incidents, and to describe the broader sequence of events within which incidents or confrontations could be understood.

Observations were written up into daily reports by each team of observers, as soon as possible after getting back from a picket line: these were summarized into weekly reports and sent out to a mailing list of MPs, reporters and others, which soon totalled over 150.

We also formed links with local NUM strike centres. An evening phone call to the NUM contact person established what time the miners would be meeting at the strike centre next morning – any time between midnight and 6 a.m. The Police-watch team of two or three observers would drive to the strike centre in time to let the miners know of our presence, and then follow them as they set off to a pit. Unlike press or TV reporters, we aimed to monitor police activity from the miners' departure from a strike centre right through to their return hours later.

In the early weeks of the dispute, this process was often interrupted by the police at one of the many local roadblocks: like the miners, we would be stopped and told to turn back, police officers stating that 'there are too many people in the area, we consider that your presence might contribute to a breach of the peace'. At first we were unwilling to challenge these statements, as a refusal to turn back could result in arrest for obstruction. Gradually we grew more confident, and argued, sometimes successfully, for our right to travel freely. When we finally reached picket lines – whether after getting through a roadblock, or after finding our way around it – we often found that 'too many people in the area' had actually meant dozens, not hundreds.

We established a weekly Sunday evening meeting in a member's house. Here we dealt with rotas, fund-raising and other tasks; in discussion we also acknowledged the fears and uncertainties we all felt at different times, and released some of the tensions that arose from each week's experiences. We rotated chairing and taking minutes and also tried to share opportunities to speak to the press or other organizations.

For many of us, this was an approach rooted in the women's movement, emphasizing mutual trust and support and discussing personal experience as well as policy. As individuals, our starting points varied. Some of us wanted to publicize policing developments we knew were already familiar to black communities and in Northern Ireland. Local black organizations had been documenting their experiences of policing for years, although this work was largely ignored or marginalized by labour movement organizations and local government. Some were most disturbed by police roadblocks as an infringement of civil liberties; others wanted to support the collective rights of trades unionists to picket and demonstrate. For women, monitoring and publicizing police activity was a way to intervene in a male-dominated and sometimes violent situation, without being marginalized or overwhelmed. For parents of small children, a weekly place on the rota seemed a manageable commitment.

There were tensions, differences and uncertainties. But the urgency of the shared practical work, along with the attempt to create an informal and supportive atmosphere, helped us to live with those that we couldn't resolve. Meetings remained lively and well attended throughout the dispute.

We received regular donations from individuals, unions and other organizations. We never requested, nor received, funds from the NUM.

Police Tactics

We observed over 300 picket lines at 57 different locations, between April 1984 and March 1985. These were mainly in Nottinghamshire, Derbyshire and South Yorkshire. We saw at least 39 different constabularies deployed. We witnessed the use of the whole spectrum of police tactics: saturation roadblocking in Nottinghamshire; 'traditional' policing in Derbyshire, albeit using vast numbers of officers; and the new style of 'public order policing' in South Yorkshire, involving the use of horses, dogs, armoured police vehicles and riot-clad policemen. Roughly one quarter of our reports record violent incidents, largely in South Yorkshire and between August and early November 1984, in the phase of 'public order policing' for which the precedent was set at Orgreave in May and June.

Almost all the reports illustrate the way in which the police set the agenda for their encounters with the miners, determining the atmosphere in which tensions would either be inflamed or defused.

Nottinghamshire

'It's not a police state; we're just saying you can't go any further.'

(Police officer at a Nottinghamshire roadblock, April 1984.)

We had three major concerns in Nottinghamshire, during April and May 1984:

- the lack of any basis in law for police use of roadblocks: through the nationally co-ordinated deployment of police officers from all over England, parts of the county were effectively sealed off;
- the high levels of arrests and the stringent bail conditions then imposed, according to which miners could be prevented from re-entering the county pending court hearings;
- the frequent occasions on which people unconnected with the dispute were also stopped, to be questioned about their movements, sometimes prevented from travelling on and also having their details checked on the police computer.

Women observers sometimes got through roadblocks on the strength of police officers' sexist assumptions, being waved through with a grin and the comment that 'you nice young ladies won't be going picketing, will you?'

A short extract from an observer's report made at Edwinstone on 18 April 1984 illustrates the then routine operation of roadblocks:

We were stopped along with the miners' van which we were following. When we asked why, we were told 'You know very well'. The van driver said he had no intention of turning back, because he and his passengers wanted 'to get to our destination and be peaceful'. He was arrested. As the driver was being escorted to a police minibus, the seven passengers made it clear that they would continue on foot; they were all arrested. All were charged with obstruction. (In February 1985, 308 days later, the driver was convicted but the seven passengers were all acquitted.)

The Chief Constable of Nottinghamshire estimated that a total of 164,508 'presumed pickets' were turned back at the county boundaries during the first six months of the strike. Twelve per cent of all miners arrested during the dispute were arrested at roadblocks; the bail conditions then imposed on them, as they awaited trials that could take up to a year to come to court, effectively prevented many from taking part in further picketing.

Derbyshire

'We have not been aggressive. There is no point, because if you become aggressive they become aggressive, nobody wins do they?'

(Senior police officer at a Derbyshire picket line, May 1984.)

Derbyshire Constabulary owns no horses and we saw shields brought out only once. Here the police controlled picket lines by the careful use of intelligence and the deployment of extremely high numbers of men. Having observed pickets' movements in the early hours, the police would be in position before a mass picket assembled at Shirebrook, Bolsover or Cresswell; on average, we observed a ratio of two police officers to one picket in Derbyshire.

The rules were rigid: miners were divided into a maximum of six 'official' pickets, positioned near the pit gates, and 'demonstrators' (everybody else) who were kept at some distance from the gate within a tight police cordon. A very large picket might also be split into several smaller 'demonstrations'. Given the restrictions on movement, we frequently commented on the miners' self-restraint; their most common protest was a sarcastic 'baa' as they were herded along their own street or pit lane.

Further control was exercised by the threat of arrest. Anyone was liable for arrest who did not do exactly as they were told, and the orders were inconsistent. Some officers – but not all – forbade the use of the word 'scab' and this could sometimes be an excuse for arrest. A person could be arrested for standing somewhere that different police officers had not objected to. Consequently large numbers of miners were arrested, often arbitrarily. The police cordon would be reinforced at any sign of tension, in particular as working miners drove into the pit in cars or darkened minibuses. There was rarely any opportunity for the official pickets to talk to the working miners. With these restrictions on their action, the main direct response of the pickets was the 'push', in which they pushed against police lines as working miners arrived. Early in the dispute a senior police officer commented to our observers that this was often the occasion for unnecessary trouble, 'caused by hotheads *on either side*'. Later, both sides learnt the rules of the game. In some senses the push became part of a ritual macho exchange, and gave both sides a sense of purpose. In contrast to the sensational scenes chosen for TV news bulletins, both police and pickets could sometimes be heard to comment 'that was a good push', and to applaud.

A pattern of tight control in Derbyshire was sustained throughout the dispute. In contrast with police responses to our presence in Nottinghamshire earlier, or in South Yorkshire later on in the dispute, here senior officers generally recognized our right to an independent vantage point. We had a good opportunity to observe the different styles adopted by different outside constabularies, and how senior officers took advantage of these. For example, Devon and Cornwall, and other largely rural constabularies, were often deployed to form the basic cordon; their approach was low key and rarely raised levels of tension. The Metropolitan Police, on the other hand, were commonly brought in as reinforcements. Their reputation for toughness and violence grew as the months passed, and they were indeed associated with many damaging incidents.

In Derbyshire, our concerns may be summarized as follows:

- the very high ratio of police officers to picketing miners, and the restrictions they placed on movements and on contact between official pickets and working miners;

- the variations in approaches adopted by different constabularies, sometimes resulting in large-scale and arbitrary arrests.

The miners paid a high price for sustaining large and frequent pickets.

The Derbyshire example does prove that senior officers *could* choose to police large crowds without· much overt aggression. In stark contrast, the police tactics adopted in South Yorkshire soon came to obscure this fact entirely.

South Yorkshire

Suddenly, the police at the roundabout charged and hundreds of riot police ran past us into the village. We ran after them. A miner tried to hide in his car. He was told to get out. As he did, the windscreen was smashed by a truncheon and he got his face cut with glass.

We heard the police officer in charge shouting through his megaphone for his men to come back. I saw one riot policeman being dragged back by a sergeant. This policeman wanted to carry on. He was waving his truncheon and struggling with the sergeant to 'go and get those bastards'.

(Policewatch report 19 October 1984, Brodsworth.)

Outside forces were deployed in South Yorkshire for the first time at a picket on 16 March 1984, just two days after the National Reporting Centre was established (see chapters 23 and 26). The widespread use of officers from all over the country remained noticeable in South Yorkshire over the ensuing months.

No miners returned to work in South Yorkshire until August 1984. Apart from the demonstrations in Sheffield and elsewhere, Yorkshire miners encountered the police first at road-blocks and picket lines in Nottinghamshire and Derbyshire; then came the three weeks of confrontations at Orgreave Coking Plant, just two miles from Sheffield, in May and June 1984. Events at Orgreave set the scene for what was to come later in South Yorkshire, and so it is worth looking at what happened there before describing police tactics in the county after August 1984.

On Bank Holiday Monday, 28 May, there was a massive peaceful gathering of miners and other trades unionists outside the coking plant. It was closed, and the police were barely in evidence. The next day, another large and good-humoured crowd gathered. But this time, police from twelve different constabularies came, equipped with horses, dogs and riot gear:

> At 7.35 a.m. a group of mounted police officers rode into the crowd . . . at 7.40 there was a further charge . . . These moves failed to clear the road, but considerably increased tension and restlessness among the pickets. At 8.20 a.m. another group of mounted police rode straight into the crowd in wedge formation, for no apparent reason . . . panic had ensued, and people ran up the road and into the fields . . . there was confusion amongst the police themselves; we heard one officer comment 'that was a silly order'.
>
> At 9.05 a.m. just before the coke lorries arived, someone at the front of the crowd let off a small smoke bomb; this caused no physical threat to anyone, but marked the beginning of a series of charges by mounted police and officers in riot gear. Chaos and violence reached a peak.
>
> (Policewatch report, Orgreave, 29 May 1984.)

If the unprovoked charges with horses and riot gear took the miners by surprise, they did not deter them from returning to Orgreave for mass pickets which continued for three weeks. The situation culminated in a pitched battle on June 18. The stones thrown by a small proportion of the crowd (perhaps five per cent) came as a response to charges by mounted police and officers using truncheons, short shields and long shields; often the stones fell among the miners trapped in the front lines. Police charges did not end with dispersing the crowd:

> The horse and riot squad charges continued into the area of the road where there are houses on one side and factories on the other . . . I found myself pinned into a private garden. Four or five pickets were with me and the riot police entered the garden and attacked the pickets. I was pushed against a wall by a riot shield. I shouted who I was, and was let free to move back onto the road. During the retreat, I did observe closely one attack by two riot police on one picket; he was hit with a truncheon by one officer while the other was holding him.
>
> (Policewatch report, Orgreave, 18 June 1984.)

During the day 93 pickets were arrested, some to be charged subsequently with riot and unlawful assembly; 50 police horses and 58 police dogs had been used; 181 Police Support Units (PSUs, riot police) had been deployed, making a total of 4,163 officers. During the period from 25 May to 18 June, police estimated that approximately 32,500 'demonstrators' had attended at Orgreave. 1,349 PSUs were deployed: 31,027 officers. There were 273 arrests; 232 police officers and 107 pickets were recorded as injured. Hundreds more injuries among the miners went unrecorded. (Figures from the South Yorkshire police report on the dispute.) The men eventually charged with riot or unlawful assembly in connection with events at Orgreave on 18 June awaited trial for months. They knew that conviction could have resulted in a life sentence. In May 1985 the trials began. The prosecution withdrew its case after forty-eight days. Inconsistencies in police evidence were a significant factor and police video film of the day, produced at the insistence of miners' defence lawyers, itself undermined police evidence.

During cross-examination of police officers, the existence of the Association of Chief Police Officers' Tactical Manual was revealed. This details the manoeuvres to be used – by shield units or mounted police 'in a controlled manner', in order to disperse crowds, 'sweep' streets and 'incapacitate' missile throwers. Yet at Orgreave, the adoption of these tactics resulted above all in a loss of control over events, for the police and for the miners. Charges by mounted police and officers in riot gear made the conventional large demonstration, culminating in a short 'push', impossible. Some miners eventually reacted by throwing stones, and putting up barricades; these were never a match for the military-style tactics and equipment deployed by the police. Orgreave was the first sustained public demonstration of a style of policing which was again adopted in South Yorkshire after August 1984, and which has been used since against the 'hippy convoy', at Broadwater Farm and at Wapping.

South Yorkshire After August 1984

On 28 August 1984 we witnessed a single van carrying working miners being driven into Brookehouse pit escorted by fifty-four police vehicles. Between mid-August and mid-November the National Coal Board undertook a determined campaign to get some miners back to work in South Yorkshire. The policing that accompanied this campaign produced some of the most disturbing scenes of the whole dispute. After mid-November, small numbers of men were going into enough different pits to ensure that many strikers only picketed at their own place of work. Picket lines became smaller; horses were not used at all after 12 November, and although riot equipment was often visible, it remained more often in reserve. Nevertheless, the atmosphere was still tense at many picket lines, and in view of everything we observed between August and November, we were not surprised. Our concerns included the following:

- a massive police presence in many communities, including the complete sealing-off of Armthorpe village for several hours on one occasion;
- a tendency for police officers to chase and beat pickets indiscriminately, rather than making arrests (which would have had to result in definite charges);
- where there were arrests, refusals by police officers to allow the arrested man to state his identity to an observer who had witnessed the arrest;
- the presence of police officers wearing no visible number (documented sixteen times in our South Yorkshire reports);
- many occasions on which we were denied a separate vantage point from which to observe by the police, and some on which we experienced physical or verbal abuse.

All these were different aspects of an aggressive pattern of policing about which two general comments can be made. Firstly, it often failed to conform to the legal requirement that the police should use 'minimum force' in pursuit of their duties; secondly, it produced a vicious circle of violence and retaliation from which it was hard for either miners or police to withdraw.

During October and November 1984, only 32 per cent of the picket lines we observed in Yorkshire were entirely incident-free; in Derbyshire the figure was 67 per cent.

Watching and Being Watched: The Media

We knew we would need media coverage for our work to have much effect. Early on in the dispute, at least some of us expected that, since we were telling the truth and could back it up with photographs and eyewitness accounts, our reports would be seen as newsworthy. We had some limited success in the early weeks of the dispute, for instance by getting reports into the local press about the widespread use of police road-blocks. But it proved hard to get consistent coverage, for at least two reasons.

Firstly, we were trying to put across a picture that conflicted with the mass media presentation both in style and content. Press and TV reports emphasized sensational events in general, and violent behaviour from the miners in particular. Our reports documented a context of provocative and sometimes violent action by the police, within which particular incidents often occurred. At picket lines or demonstrations, we made our observations from vantage points physically separate from both police and pickets (unless prevented from doing so by the police); on the other hand, it was common for reporters and camera crews to remain behind police lines and rely uncritically on police statements, both for comments on events and for suggestions of where to go 'to see the action'. Not surprisingly, the resulting articles and broadcasts often differed radically from what we had observed (a contrast which miners experienced even more frequently).

Secondly, the police themselves left little to chance where relations with news reporters were concerned. The report on the coal dispute produced by South Yorkshire police describes in detail how liaison with the press was organized, including early morning press conferences and the issue of regular press releases. It cites miners' hostility towards the press as a reason *for* press reliance on the police, rather than as a consequence of it. The Campaign for Press and Broadcasting Freedom, on the other hand, commented that 'to go behind the pickets' lines' was to make oneself a 'legitimate target for police actions'. Bearing in mind the many examples quoted above of common police tactics, and their consequences, this is by far the more convincing view.

The political effects of the way the police were deployed during the coal dispute may be judged from the examples quoted in this chapter, and from the many other accounts which have been published since the dispute ended. But images in the press, and particularly on television, were a crucial influence on the attitudes of viewers who had no direct experience of the dispute themselves. These images were constructed according to decisions made by cameramen, journalists, editors and senior staff in newspapers, the BBC or ITN. A brief example is provided by the difference between the early evening news bulletins from ITN and from the BBC on 18 June, concerning Orgreave. Both showed film of fighting between miners and the police; but while the ITN version included shots of a policeman repeatedly truncheoning a miner over the head as the miner lay on the ground, the same sequence was cut just before this scene in the BBC version. When the scene became the subject of heated discussion, following the ITN broadcast, the BBC showed it too. (This and other examples are documented in the Campaign for Press and Broadcasting Freedom pamphlet, *Media Hits the Pits*.)

In July 1984 we finally had the opportunity to get substantial media coverage when we met a team for the BBC's 'community access' series, Open Space. They listened to our accounts of what we had seen, they spent time at our meetings and in local mining communities, and over the following weeks we were able to agree a framework for a forty-five minute programme under our own editorial control. The Open Space team's sensitivity and technical skill helped to ensure that the resulting film, *Taking Liberties*, recorded both our concerns about threats to civil liberties, and accounts of personal experiences from people in local mining communities.

However, the BBC refused to broadcast the film on the date originally intended. We made contingency plans for a showing for MPs. Eventually, it went out on 8 November 1984, followed immediately by a live discussion from which we (but not the police!) had been excluded. Later, minutes leaked from the weekly meeting of the BBC heads of news and current affairs confirmed how strong opposition to the programme had been within the BBC. The programme had been referred to within the BBC as 'deeply biased and fundamentally damaging to the BBC's interests'. At the time, Open Space was billed publicly as 'the series where the public sets the agenda'. We were fortunate that, by the autumn of 1984, we had a wide network of contacts through which we could obtain support and publicity. We probably have that network, and the determination of the Open Space team itself, to thank for keeping the issues raised in *Taking Liberties* briefly on the BBC agenda.

The showing of the programme gave us opportunities to publicize our work above and beyond the broadcast itself. We published a short pamphlet at the same time. Favourable reviews of both in the national press considerably increased the numbers of requests we received to circulate our reports and speak at meetings. Videos of *Taking Liberties* are still in demand as a source of discussion material for groups concerned with policing and civil liberties issues.

Conclusion

Some of the powers assumed by the police during the miners' strike, which we tried to publicize as threats to civil liberties, now have the force of law. The Police and Criminal Evidence Act, for instance, makes provision for police use of roadblocks. The right to assemble and demonstrate is undermined by the constraints embodied in the Public Order Act. The well-established capacity of the police to mobilize in enormous numbers, and to impose severe restrictions on movement in a given area, has been illustrated again during the printworkers' dispute in Wapping and at Broadwater Farm in 1985.

Whether police monitoring takes place at mass demonstrations, or day-to-day in communities, it will not be sufficient on its own to reverse these developments. But monitoring does provide a way of documenting police activities in detail, and this is important – both in order to publicize what is happening and to gather information which individuals and communities can use in their own defence.

Finally, small individual acts – taking photographs, noting police movements – come together in a process which becomes public and collective: the construction of a basis of knowledge, confidence and mutual support, on which we can challenge increases in police violence, abuse and intimidation.

29. Complaints and Legal Action

Teresa Thornhill

Procedure and Background – the New Complaints Authority

The Police and Criminal Evidence Act 1984, was supposed to reform the system for investigating complaints against the police. The existing system had been widely criticized for various reasons, in particular because investigations were carried out by the police themselves. This had long given rise to demand for an independent system. It was felt that the Police Complaints Board merely rubber-stamped decisions made by Chief Constables as to the conclusions to be drawn from investigations.

For example, in 1981, out of 15,000 complaints against the police, nationwide, in which Deputy Chief Constables had recommended that no disciplinary action should be taken, the Police Complaints Board differed (by recommending the bringing of disciplinary charges) in only twenty-six cases. The double jeopardy rule was also widely criticized. This provided that where the Director of Public Prosecutions (DPP) had decided that no criminal proceedings should be taken in respect of a given complaint, or where they had been brought but the police officer was acquitted, he or she could not then be subject to disciplinary proceedings as an alternative. The system resulted in the overall percentage of complaints upheld being remarkably low. In the four years from 1983–6, it fluctuated between three and four per cent.

In the debates on the Police and Criminal Evidence Bill, a proposed new system was presented as a palliative to critics of other measures in the Bill. It was said that the extension of police powers would be balanced against the establishment of a 'truly independent' complaints investigation system.

The new system came into operation in April 1985. The Police Complaints Board (PCB) has been replaced by a Police Complaints Authority (PCA). The PCA is headed by a Chairperson appointed by the Crown, and has a minimum of eight members appointed by the Home Office. All appointees are paid and they cannot be former police officers. They serve for a maximum of three years, with a back-up staff of over fifty. It is already clear that the PCA has a greater caseload than it can adequately cope with. The difference between the two is that whereas the Board *reviewed the results* of a complaint investigation carried out exclusively by the police, the Authority has the power to supervise the actual investigation of certain complaints. However, in practice, relatively few investigations are supervised by the PCA and the most problematic features of the old system remain unchanged. The police still carry out the investigative work and it is still for the Chief Constable, in the first instance, to decide whether criminal or disciplinary proceedings should be instituted against officers. The PCA can overturn his decision, but it has no more constitutional powers to do so than the old PCB had.

If the Chief Constable decides that criminal proceedings are appropriate, as previously, he refers the case to the DPP, who takes the decision whether or not to prosecute. Needless to say, the DPP's reluctance to prosecute policemen has not altered. In 1981, out of 1,471 cases referred, the DPP decided to prosecute in only twenty-one cases. In 1985, out of 1,268 cases, the decision to prosecute was made in only three.[1]

The new system works as follows. The complainant sends the complaint to the Chief Constable of the relevant force (the Commissioner if the complaint is against the Met). If the complaint is against a senior officer, the PCA must handle it. If not, the Chief Constable may try to persuade the complainant to settle for 'informal resolution', such as an apology. In this case, no action will be taken, or even recorded, against the officer concerned (who may well deny the substance of the complaint) and the complaint is not recorded as such by the PCA.

But if the complainant refuses, or if it is clear that criminal or disciplinary proceedings are warranted, the Chief Constable has to refer the complaint to his senior officer in charge of complaints to assess. Then it has to be referred to the PCA to decide whether or not they wish to supervise the investigation. They must supervise complaints of assault, corruption or dishonesty, and can decide whether to supervise other complaints. In 1985, the PCA took on 24 per cent of cases referred to them.

Whether or not the PCA supervises an investigation, it will be carried out in much the same manner, usually by a police officer from the 'area complaints branch' of the force complained about. But if the PCA are involved, they have the power to approve the investigating officer, to say how the investigation should be run and ensure that it is given sufficient resources. In both cases, the Area Complaints Officer (ACO) interviews the complainant, the officers concerned and any witnesses. In London in 1985, 44 per cent of all complaints were withdrawn or not proceeded with at this stage.

If the PCA is supervising, they then send a statement to the Chief Constable, saying whether or not the investigation was conducted to their satisfaction. It is then up to the Chief Constable to decide how to proceed. If he considers that the evidence suggests a criminal offence has been committed, he may send the papers to the DPP, who decides whether or not to institute a prosecution. However, he may decide, despite the fact that a criminal offence appears to have been committed, that disciplinary proceedings are more 'appropriate' than criminal ones; or indeed, that even disciplinary charges should not be preferred.

The Chief Constable must inform the PCA of the action or inaction he has decided upon, whether or not the complaint was one investigated under their supervision. If the PCA disagrees with his decision, they may overturn it, for example, by ordering him to send the papers to the DPP, or to prefer disciplinary charges. In 1986, the PCA disagreed with the Chief Constable in a mere 0.4 per cent of cases.[2]

Disciplinary proceedings involve a hearing before a tribunal consisting of a Chief Constable plus two members of the PCA. Penalties range from demotion and suspension without pay to dismissal. Out of 150 complaints upheld in London in 1985 (the year in which the PCA came into operation), a mere 28 disciplinary charges resulted, in addition to the three criminal charges mentioned above. In some of the remaining 119 cases, it may be that sanctions less serious than disciplinary charges were applied, such as cautions.

In the vast majority of cases, the PCA accepts the Chief Constable's finding that the investigation has thrown up no evidence or insufficient evidence that the conduct complained of occurred. It is frequently claimed that it has proved impossible to identify the officers complained of. The complainant receives a letter saying that the matter has been investigated and has been found not to be substantiated by the evidence, and that is the end of it. This is hardly surprising when one considers that most complaints arise out of situations where there are no non-police witnesses; and that for a complaint to be upheld, it must be proved on the criminal standard of proof – 'beyond all reasonable doubt'. For obvious reasons, evidence obtained through an internal inquiry will rarely reach this standard.

Cases

A few cases illustrate the complaints system operating in relation to serious complaints.

After the shooting of Mrs Cherry Groce by DC Lovelock in the course of a house raid in Brixton in September 1985, a complaint was lodged. As a result, DC Lovelock actually stood trial at the Old Bailey, on a charge of unlawful wounding. He was acquitted. Following his acquittal, it was not possible to bring disciplinary action against him due to the double jeopardy rule (explained above) which is preserved by the new complaints system.

A complaint made against DC Randall, the officer who pushed Mrs Cynthia Jarrett in the course of a house raid, leading to her death, in October 1985, resulted in no prosecution being brought and no disciplinary action being taken, even though in the opinion of Lord Gifford QC and the Broadwater Farm Inquiry team, the coroner's inquest into Mrs Jarrett's death revealed serious misconduct which could have formed the basis of disciplinary action (see chapter 10).

In August 1983, five youths were assaulted by police officers in the notorious Holloway case. The police jumped out of their van and spontaneously set about the youths with truncheons. The youths complained but the inquiry failed to penetrate the cover-up. After two and half years of internal investigation, Scotland Yard announced that the assailants had not been identified. Twenty-two officers were reprimanded.

This case was widely reported and fuelled arguments for a more rigorous and independent investigation system. The new system for the investigation of complaints (which had been in operation for the second year of the inquiry) was proved to be no better than its predecessor at breaking down networks of mutual protection within forces. An editorial entitled 'Beyond the Law' in the *Guardian* wrote:

> The sad, usually unspoken reality today, as yesterday, is that if any police officers commit an act of violence against a member of the public (particularly if they are black or left wing) they will get away with it. Their own colleagues won't split on them. Their superior officers won't dare discipline them. Their union, the Police Federation, will support them. The Police Complaints Authority will not identify them. The Director of Public Prosecutions won't prosecute. The Home Office will apologize for them. And, to cap it all, the Prime Minister will denounce anyone who even suggests that there is anything wrong with the police. What has happened in the Holloway case isn't a freak. It isn't a shocking exception. It is what happens whenever any police officer does anything against the law to anyone whom the police regard as fair game. It is, for example, exactly what happened in the case of the murder of Blair Peach in 1979 when – never let it be forgotten – a police officer killed a protester in full view of his SPG colleagues and got away with it because nobody would identify him.[3]

An embarrassed Kenneth Newman, then Metropolitan Police Commissioner, set up a special phone line and guaranteed anonymity and freedom from prosecution provided the informant did not take part in the assault. Within two days four officers were charged after an anonymous phone call. In July 1987, five officers were gaoled for offences including assault, and conspiracy to pervert the course of justice.

The case of the Stoke Newington PC who persuaded a Nigerian woman to have sex with him shows the new Complaints Authority in a more positive light. The officer had told the woman (wrongly) that her immigration status was irregular and that he could have her deported, but that if she complied with his demand, he would 'ensure' her continued stay in England. Following investigation of her complaint, the police recommended that the officer should not be disciplined (let alone prosecuted). The PCA overruled this recommendation; he appeared before a disciplinary tribunal and was dismissed. In 1987, he appealed against the dismissal but lost. Four years earlier, when it was alleged that the same officer had attempted a similar bribery with a Turkish couple, the DPP had refused to prosecute.

Alternatives to the Complaints System

In practice, many people who feel aggrieved by police conduct towards themselves or their families decide not to make a complaint. Many have no confidence in the system of investigation and its shockingly low rate of upholding complaints. Some fear further harassment from the police if they show that they are prepared to stand up for their rights. (See for example chapters 1, 4, 6, and 13.)

If you have had one unpleasant experience with the police, you may well feel you do not wish to court further contact with them in the course of an investigation. But if you do decide to make a complaint, it is advisable to get legal help. Legal Aid is available for this purpose. It is particularly important not to disclose the *substance* of your complaint until you have had confirmation from the police that an investigation is underway, because, if the complaint is not upheld, an initial letter of complaint setting out detailed allegations can be used against the complainant in an action for defamation by the officer concerned. The Police Federation gives financial backing to officers who wish to sue to clear their names, whereas members of the public cannot get legal aid to defend themselves in this situation.

Recently, it has become increasingly common for people who feel they have been seriously mistreated by the police to sue them in the civil courts. Legal aid is available. If you have a strong case and are willing to go to these lengths, a civil action against the police is undoubtedly a more satisfactory method of getting redress than a police complaint. The essential difference is that, with a complaint, it is basically the police who judge the evidence (subject to the approval of the PCA), whereas in a civil action, a judge does so. The two methods of seeking redress are not mutually exclusive and people often pursue both options.

For a civil action, it is still important to have non-police witnesses, but the evidence of police witnesses will carry less weight before a County Court or High Court judge than before an investigating police officer and Chief Constable. Medical evidence and/or photos are necessary if you are alleging assault.

A civil action is judged on the civil standard of proof, the 'balance of probabilities', which is easier to attain than the criminal standard. For you to succeed, the judge must decide that on the balance of probabilities the officer *did* commit the alleged act of misconduct, whereas with a complaint, the Chief Constable must be sure beyond all reasonable doubt that he or she did so.

The consequence of winning a civil action is compensation in money whereas if a complaint is upheld, you receive nothing beyond the satisfaction of knowing there is a chance that the officer(s) in question will be disciplined, or, just possibly, prosecuted. It is extremely rare for an officer to be disciplined as a result of a member of the public succeeding in a civil claim in respect of his or her conduct.

In practice, many civil actions are settled by the police out of court. The following figures include cases against the Metropolitan Police that went to trial, as well as out-of-court settlements. Even allowing for inflation, they show a dramatic increase in the use and success rates of civil actions over the past fourteen years.

Survey of Metropolitan Police damage claims 1973–1986

Year	No. of cases concluded	Total paid in damages (£)
1973	27	200
1979	7	1,991
1982	33	87,325
1984	107	178,603*
1985	68	193,588
1986	126	373,168

* Includes £120,000 settlement of Stephen Waldorf's claim

Source: *Policing London*, no. 19, August 1985 and no. 27, May 1987.

Outside London, the number of claims against the police is rising too, although the total sums paid out in damages do not compare with those paid out by the Met.

Survey of police authority damage claims 1980–1984

Police authority	No. of cases received	Years	Total paid in damages (£)
Merseyside	368	1982–84	n/a
Lancashire	123	1983–84	9,638
Greater Manchester	245	1983–84	13,000
Derbyshire	13	1980–84	4,900
West Yorkshire	435	1980–84	29,042
Northumbria	192	1980–85	6,702
Sussex	23	1983	6,000
Total	1,399		69,282

Source: *Policing London*, no. 19, August 1985.

Broadly speaking, your case must fit one of certain recognized 'causes of action': assault, wrongful arrest, false imprisonment, malicious prosecution, trespass to land, wrongful interference with goods and malicious abuse of power. For example, if you are strip-searched in a situation where the police are not entitled to do this, you may be able to bring an action for assault. If you are detained in police custody in circumstances where the police had no reasonable grounds for detaining you, you may have a claim for false imprisonment. Wrongful interference with goods would be the appropriate claim if for example the police groundlessly seized and kept an item of your property. Malicious abuse of power, despite its appropriate-sounding name, is a course of action which has rarely been used against the police to date. It would be suitable for instance where a police officer had procured the issue of a search warrant without reasonable cause.

If you are charged with a criminal offence in connection with the incident in respect of which you want to sue, it will usually only be worth doing so if you are acquitted. In actions for assault and trespass taken against people other than police, for example by women against violent boyfriends or husbands, it is usual to consider applying for an injunction ordering the defendant to stop molesting the woman. In the same way, it is theoretically possible to obtain an injunction against a police officer who is harassing you, although most judges would be loathe to grant it. An unsuccessful attempt to obtain such an injunction was made by a member of the Peace Convoy after the police invasion of Stonehenge in June 1985. There are, however, examples of civil actions against the police brought successfully by women plaintiffs.

In the case of *George v Commissioner of Police for the Metropolis* (1984)[4] a black South London woman was awarded £8,000 damages for trespass and assault. Several police officers forcibly entered her home and searched it for her son, whom they claimed to suspect of involvement in a stabbing. Mrs George told the officers that he was not in, and in any event the judge held that the police lacked reasonable cause to suspect the son of the offence. They therefore had no right to attempt to arrest him nor to enter his mother's home, let alone to use force against her. At the civil trial, Mrs George said that one or more of the officers had hit her with his fists, kicked her, and ransacked the house for half an hour. The officers denied touching her, saying that she had become hysterical during the 'two or three minutes' they were there. The judge believed Mrs George's account in preference to that of the officers, whose behaviour he described as 'outrageous'. He included £2,000 exemplary damages in the award, 'to mark the court's disapproval of the officers' actions and to stop their repetition by others'.

The first reported case where damages were awarded against the police for injuring demonstrators was that of *Ballard, Stewart-Park and Findlay v The Commissioner of Police for the Metropolis*.[5] The three women plaintiffs were on a Reclaim the Night march in Soho in 1978. Trouble broke out between the police and the demonstrators, and nineteen demonstrators were arrested, including the third plaintiff. All three plaintiffs sued for assault, the first two claiming they had been hit over the head with truncheons. The second woman also said she had been carried spread-eagled for some distance and dumped on the ground from a height of four feet. The third alleged that a particular police officer had straddled her, poked her in the stomach as she lay on the ground, and hit her over the eye with the result that she had subsequently suffered migraines. The judge accepted the women's evidence and held that there had been no justification for the use of truncheons. The women were awarded £400, £600 and £3,000 respectively, each award containing a sum for aggravated damages.

A middle-aged black Sunday School teacher and mother of three, Mrs Lorna Lucas, won £26,000 damages in the High Court in February 1986. She was left bruised and bleeding when police arrested her after an incident in a builder's office where she had gone to complain about shoddy repair work to her house. As she was carried, protesting, from the police station to begin her journey to the magistrates' court, a policeman had looked up her skirt and made an offensive remark.

Mrs Lucas was awarded £10,000 for assault (she was kicked

and punched by the police during her arrest), £1,000 for false imprisonment (she had been held overnight in a police cell), and £15,000 exemplary damages after the court found that the police had lied to Camberwell magistrates when they unsuccessfully prosecuted Mrs Lucas for assaulting them.

In 1983, the Police Complaints Board had accepted a police recommendation that no proceedings should be brought against the officers who assaulted and insulted her.[6]

If you decide to sue the police, it is, as mentioned, open to you to make an official complaint as well. However, it may not be advisable to do so. It is undesirable to let the police know the details of your case against them earlier than you have to for the civil action, and if in giving them a statement for the complaint you accidentally make an error or admission, they could use it against you in conducting their defence.

Private Prosecutions

In a case where the DPP refuses to bring a criminal prosecution against an officer whose conduct has amounted to criminal offence (such as assault or grievous bodily harm), the victim of the conduct has the right to bring the prosecution herself. Legal aid is not available for this purpose; thus prosecution is very expensive. However, it is an avenue of redress that should be considered, especially following an incident where a campaign can mobilize to raise the necessary funds.

Whether you are considering suing the police, making a complaint, or bringing a private prosecution, it is essential to obtain sound legal advice before you begin. There are still not very many lawyers who are willing to sue the police or who are experienced at doing so. It is no good going to a lawyer who has never done this before and feels nervous about the possible consequences for her or his firm's relationship with the local force (through whom they may get most of their criminal work). It is advisable to contact your law centre or the NCCL and ask them to recommend a suitable lawyer.

The examples quoted above show that it is possible, in some

cases, to get a satisfactory result from a civil action against the police. The amounts of damages now being paid out by the Met must be causing the Home Office some alarm, and a result such as that obtained by Mrs Lucas is encouraging for everyone who has experienced police harassment and felt powerless to do anything about it.

Notes

1. *Policing London*, nos 5 (January 1983), 22 (July 1986).
2. *Policing London*, no. 28, July 1987.
3. *Guardian*, 5 February 1986.
4. *The Times*, 30 March 1986.
5. *Legal Action*, no 10, 1984.
6. *Guardian*, 6 February 1986.

Notes on Contributors

Surinder Bains has been a worker in and served on the management committees of various women's refuges, including the Leeds Asian Women's Refuge. She was a research worker for the Manchester City Council Police Monitoring Unit where she carried out the research on crimes against women described in her article. The Unit was wound up on 16 December 1987, because of council cuts. She is now Community Safety Officer with Manchester City Council, working on women's issues.

The Broadwater Farm Defence Campaign was formed in the aftermath of the disturbances in mid-October 1985 to give support to families and to publicize issues arising from the policing of the estate. Most of the workers were volunteers but by the end of November there were two paid workers. The Campaign gave legal support to families (providing basic legal advice, referring them to solicitors and monitoring court cases), and practical support to families suffering hardship, and they visited prisoners. On the publicity side, they have circulated notices and articles to the press and have co-operated with television programmes such as Brass Tacks, World in Action and Diverse Reports, all of which have shown programmes relating either to the uprising, the subsequent policing of the estate or the convictions.

The Campaign still meets every Monday, concentrating largely on prison visits to the three men convicted of murder (those sentenced for lesser offences have now been released), and on commemorative events. At the 1988 anniversary of the uprising they laid wreaths for both PC Blakelock and Mrs Jarrett, and protested about the convictions which were also the subject of substantial criticism in an Amnesty report.

Barbara Cohen is a solicitor in private practice. She was formerly legal officer for the National Council for Civil Liberties in which capacity she was involved in lobbying and briefing Parliament on the Police and Criminal Evidence Bill, and in drafting amendments to it.

Alison Dickens grew up in Somerset, moved to Manchester in 1979 and (gradually) became a radical feminist. She has been involved in a number of feminist groups and campaigns – including Manchester Rape Crisis Line, as a counsellor and trainer – and is currently a rather tired worker in a voluntary sector project. **Sara Scott** has been active in the women's liberation movement since 1980. She is a member of Manchester Rape Crisis, and is on the editorial collective of the radical feminist magazine, *Trouble and Strife*.

Susan Edwards is currently senior lecturer in sociology at the Polytechnic of Central London. Since 1975, she has been researching into the treatment of women offenders and the victimization of women by the criminal justice system and male offenders. She is committed to using research as a tool for exposing inequalities and discrimination in the criminal justice system both in respect of 'punishment', including the use of police powers and the sentencing of women offenders by the judiciary, and 'protection'. Her work involves campaigning to improve police protection for victims of rape and domestic violence. Her publications include: *Female Sex Offenders and the Law* (Martin Robertson, 1981), *Women on Trial* (Manchester University Press, 1984), *Gender, Sex and the Law* (Croom Helm, 1985) and *Police Response to Domestic Violence* (Polytechnic of Central London, 1986). Her latest book on policing and domestic violence will be published by Sage in 1989, and she is currently working on an evaluation of the new Metropolitan Police policy on domestic violence.

Jill Evans lives in the Rhondda. She worked with miners' support groups during the coal dispute, and was on the picket lines. She is one of the group which produced *Striking Back*, about the dispute in Wales. She is involved with the peace movement and various women's groups and is now a Plaid Cymru candidate for the European elections. The network of the Wales Congress in Support of Mining Communities – churches, unions, women's groups and peace groups – has recently come together again to campaign against the poll tax.

Alison Faulkner trained as a psychologist. At the time of writing her article, she was working for MIND, the National Association for Mental Health, as a member of a research team looking at the workings of section 136 of the Mental Health Act. She is currently working as a qualitative social researcher for Social and Community Planning Research.

Nadine Finch was a lay member of a local police monitoring organiza-tion who joined the GLC police monitoring unit as research officer, continuing under the London Strategic Policies Unit. She now works as women's co-ordinator for Ealing Council. She is doing a post-graduate diploma in socio-legal studies and is active in the Labour Party on the National Labour Women's Committee.

For various reasons, the **Gurdip Kaur Campaign** was unable to proceed with a private prosecution. Instead, it is in the process of setting up the Gurdip Kaur Trust Fund to provide financial assistance to similar campaigns involving Asian women. For more information, the Campaign can be contacted through the Women's Information Centre, 6 Silver Street, Reading, RG1 2ST.

Olga Heaven is a development worker. Since 1986 she has worked specifically with black women who have come into contact with the criminal justice system. Through her experience, she has found that black women prisoners and ex-prisoners have, on the whole, suffered from physical, sexual and racist abuse from the police. **Maria Mars** is a psychologist and counsellor who has worked with black women who have come into contact with the criminal justice system.

Rebecca Johnson: 'The most important influences in my life have been feminism and revolutionary nonviolence. They took me to Greenham Common, where I lived and worked at the Women's Peace Camp for five years. This article was originally written in 1986 while I was still living there. I now live in London and carry on working for justice, peace and freedom in as many ways as I can. I still seem to keep falling foul of Britain's legal system and will, I suppose, continue to do so as long as it perpetuates the violence and injustice of patriarchal society.'

Cathie Lloyd taught in further education for eleven years and left to work with the Public Order Research Group (a trade union based group started by Westminster Trades Council) in 1983. From 1985 she worked as information officer for the Police Committee Support Unit at the Greater London Council, and subsequently, from 1986, at the London Strategic Policies Unit. She has continued to work voluntarily for the Public Order Research Group since 1985, and in 1986 worked with the NCCL on their campaign against the Public Order law. Her current job is research officer at the Campaign for Racial Equality. She is also editing a book for Lawrence and Wishart on police monitoring.

Chris McAuley was catapulted into political awareness when she was nineteen by the events of 1969 in the Lower Falls area of West Belfast where she lived. She became active in street resistance and received a four-year prison sentence. Subsequently she became active in Sinn Fein and was one of the women responsible for the Sinn Fein women's policy document and the formation of the Sinn Fein Women's Department. She has been on several Sinn Fein delegations and speaking tours to Britain and has been an active opponent of strip-searching – to the extent that she was barred by the Northern Ireland Office from visiting Armagh prison. She works as a full time voluntary reporter for *An Phlobacht* (*Republican News*), the Northern political weekly newspaper, and has three young children.

Caroline Natzler is a solicitor and writer living in London. She was involved in the Law Centres Federation lobbying against Clause 28 in the Lords. Her short stories have appeared in *The Reach* (Onlywomen Press), *Everyday Matters* (Sheba Feminist Publishers), and *Girls Next Door* (The Women's Press).

Maire O'Shea is a radical psychiatrist. She has worked since 1953 as a psychotherapist and in psychotherapeutic communities since 1960, both within the National Health Service. She is a member of the Network for Alternative Psychiatry, the Transcultural Psychiatry Society and the Irish Mental Health Forum. She was one of the organizers of the Irish in Britain Representation Group conference on mental health out of which the Irish Mental Health Forum developed. She has worked with Asian clients in an Asian area in Birmingham. She does independent psychiatric reports for the Mental Health Tribunal, working towards the release of long-term compulsorily detained mental health patients in special hospitals.

She is a member of most British groups campaigning for a united Ireland, and is now president of the Irish in Britain Representation Group, an Irish community organization campaigning for equal opportunities for the Irish, fighting anti-Irish racism and claiming an input into Irish politics. She has set up an inquiry involving senior psychiatrists into the psychiatric effects of strip-searching.

Janet McDermott teaches English as a second language and does community liaison work from a large secondary school in Sheffield. She has been active in the Labour Party, the women's peace movement and a black workers' group in education. She is currently deeply involved in a number of Asian women's projects.

Jenny Owen is a teacher and community worker now doing a research degree at Sheffield Polytechnic. She has two children and is active in the women's movement.

Cath Whitty has worked as a teacher. She is active in the Labour Party and is part of a network of carers for people with Alzheimer's disease. She has two young children.

Kalsoom Sarwar has a law degree and worked as advice worker with an Asian Women's Centre in South London, dealing with cases relating to immigration, domestic violence, welfare rights and housing. She is now equal opportunities officer for Wakefield Metropolitan District Council.

Sue Shutter works for the Joint Council for the Welfare of Immigrants, an independent voluntary organization which advises and represents people with immigration and nationality law problems, and campaigns against the injustice and racism of these laws. JCWI has argued publicly since 1978 that infringements of the immigration law should be civil, not criminal, offences and that the police should have no role in its enforcement.

Southall Black Sisters is an autonomous black women's group. It has been in existence since 1979 and consists of Asian and Afro-Caribbean women who first came together soon after the 1979 uprisings in Southall. The aim was to highlight and articulate the experiences and needs of black women, to fight racism and to challenge the systematic degradation and oppression of women both outside of and within the black community.

SBS has organized locally, initiating campaigns and activities around issues such as domestic violence, arranged marriages, policing and homelessness; some of these issues had not previously been raised outside of the black women's movement. On a day-to-day level, they provide advice, support and information to women on a wide range of issues from violence to welfare rights. SBS are grant aided by Ealing Council although, for political and financial reasons, obtaining funds is a constant struggle. Over the years, the composition and perspectives of the group have changed, but the central aims remain: to organize as black women and to continue to develop the work undertaken since 1979.

Chris Tchaikovsky is an ex-prisoner. She read philosophy and government at Essex University. In March 1983 she founded Women in Prison, an ex-prisoner pressure group set up to campaign specifically for women prisoners. She speaks on television and radio on issues concerning WIP, such as the prison medical service, self-mutilation by women prisoners, male prison officers and lifting crown immunity (which prevents fire and health inspections at prisons). She has contributed to the *New Statesman* and the *Guardian* and to *Criminal Women* (Basil Blackwell, 1986).

Teresa Thornhill is a practising barrister working in the fields of criminal defence and family law. She was formerly a campaign worker at Haringey Independent Police Committee (a GLC funded group campaigning for police accountability). She has been a member of the London Armagh Group (campaigning against the strip-searching of women in Armagh prison) and the Broadwater Farm Defence Campaign, and is currently active in Jews against the Clause (against section 28). She is also a freelance writer.

The Women's Aid article was put together by the **Women's Aid Federation for England and Wales, Northern Ireland Women's Aid Federation** and **Scottish Women's Aid.** Women's Aid provide advice, support and safe refuge for women who have experienced physical, mental or sexual violence from their partners, and for their children. Their work is as crucial now as it was when it started in 1973. There is still only one third of the refuge provision recommended by the 1975 Select Committee on Violence in Marriage, and this is in some jeopardy because of government policies.

A major setback to the work of Women's Aid remains the absence of an overall government strategy. Women's Aid survives by networking nationally because women need to be moved from an area where they are at risk to another; however, lack of provision often makes this impossible.

It is crucial that Women's Aid remains a campaigning organization, addressing the roots of violence against women in society and educating the agencies – general practitioners, the social services and the police – to whom women who have experienced violence turn for help, protection and information. Police response is still a matter of considerable concern because it is hindering the operation of the relevant legislation in protecting women and children. It is increasingly difficult for Women's Aid to campaign and provide education (such as the much needed training of police officers) when financial pressures are compelling them to concentrate on trying to provide an even remotely adequate refuge service. Much of their work is only able to continue because of the commitment of women, often working unpaid.

ALSO OF INTEREST

INSIDERS

Women's Experience of Prison

Una Padel and Prue Stevenson

Women's prisons are secret places, hidden from public view, the stuff of myth and occasional scandal. The eleven women whose stories are here told in their own words offer a view of prison life very different from the stereotype – and far more shocking. White or black, lesbian or heterosexual, with or without children, serving short or long sentences, they share a common experience of humiliation, anger and alienation, the effects of which remain long after their release. They speak movingly of their lives before prison, of the circumstances leading to their arrest, of their first depersonalising encounter with the prison system when strip searches are mandatory and all outward traces of individuality denied, of the months and years of boredom, petty rules and loneliness. And they speak angrily of the twin systems of arbitrary punishment and systematic cruelty all too common in most institutions. Cut off from family, children, friends, each finds her own means of survival – be it rebellion, withdrawal, new friendships or a sense of humour. Set within the broad context of Britain's criminal justice system, these personal, candid accounts are both a revelation and a stunning indictment.